DESI HOOP DREAMS

Desi Hoop Dreams

Pickup Basketball and the Making of
Asian American Masculinity

Stanley I. Thangaraj

NEW YORK UNIVERSITY PRESS

New York and London

NEW YORK UNIVERSITY PRESS
New York and London
www.nyupress.org

References to Internet websites (URLs) were accurate at the time of writing. Neither the author nor New York University Press is responsible for URLs that may have expired or changed since the manuscript was prepared.

ISBN: 978-0-8147-7035-1 (hardback)
ISBN: 978-0-8147-6093-2 (paperback)

For Library of Congress Cataloging-in-Publication data, please contact the Library of Congress.

New York University Press books are printed on acid-free paper, and their binding materials are chosen for strength and durability. We strive to use environmentally responsible suppliers and materials to the greatest extent possible in publishing our books.

Manufactured in the United States of America

10 9 8 7 6 5 4 3 2 1

Also available as an ebook

To

Alena and Jeya

You are my golden sun

CONTENTS

ACKNOWLEDGMENTS

This book is a product of years of hard work and support from many wonderful people. I want to acknowledge all of those who have played a part in making this manuscript a reality. I want to apologize in advance to those whom I may have forgotten, the error is solely mine.

A book of this sort would not be possible without the time, energy, and kindness of the members of the community I studied. They were gracious enough to let me into their lives and to share their stories with me. I want to thank the team members of Maryland Five Pillars for inviting me into their basketball spaces and for their hospitality. The information on the Chicago Indo-Pak National Basketball Tournament (IPN) would have lacked any depth without the extended time Rathi and Max spent in detailing their experiences for me. Their generosity is infinite, and I feel honored to be part of their community. They welcomed me into their home and shared their lives and wonderful children with me.

I want to thank my main interlocutors in Atlanta: Mustafa, Ali, Sanjeet, Daniel, Harpreet, Mohammed, Imran, Riad, Amir, Dr. Said, Sultan, Sharif, Ahmed, Mahmoud, Mustafa and Ali's parents, Susan, and Madeleine. I especially want to thank Mustafa and Ali for making so much time for me. I can never express in words my gratitude to them for their friendship, our histories, their humor, and their compassion. They are my brothers. I hope I have done justice to their experiences.

Sanjeet was engaged in my work and was very open in talking through my questions. I am also grateful to Daniel, Harpreet, and the Monday/Thursday night basketball crew in Atlanta. Daniel has been a willing reader of my work, and his words have encouraged me. I would not have been able to add complexity to this project without my interactions with Sharif. Sharif opened up a whole new world of Muslim America that I had not previously known. I am lucky to be in his presence, and he has become a very important part of my life.

I thank John Kuprevich, Sr., Carol Kuprevich, Andrea and Denny Merz, Uncle Bill and Aunt Barb, Uncle Jack and Aunt Colleen, Aunt Linda and Uncle Chris, Pap, Nan, Grandma, John Adams, Theresa, Hannah, Jack, William, Tascha, Eric, Emma, Jonathon, and Ben "Bear" Kuprevich for the love they give me. My in-laws always find ways to make me laugh; I appreciate and love them all. DadK, MomK, Andy, and Uncle Bill were sources of strength and wisdom during a compli-cated time. The generosity of my fantastic neighbors on Hampton Av-enue made this book a possibility: Mrs. Bright, the Wests, the Stroups, the Dunkerleys, the Tates, the Cristofersens, the Bologhs, the Shells, the Custers, the Robbins, the Shulmans, the Levy and Stalma family, the Nixons, and the Duvalls. I offer my deepest gratitude to Mauro, Kate, Hope, Tess, and little Mauro Mastrapasqua; Amy, Steve, Daniel, Isa-bella, Abigail, and Alexandria Manoukian; Judy, Tommy, T. J., Robert, and Mathew Lewis; Bruce and Susan Spaulding; and Judy and Kelly Wright. And I offer many thanks for the friendship of Jan Shipp, Jen Zaja, David Jester and Altaf Tadkod, Marcie Smeck and Steve Bryant, Dick and Brigitte Porter, Josephine and John Darwin, the Parikhs, the Nashville International Center for Empowerment, the Tennessee Immi-grant and Refugee Rights Coalition, and fellow members of Mayor Karl Dean's New American's Advisory Council in Nashville.

I am grateful to Matthew Wright. He believed in my work and was a supportive friend from the very beginning in Nashville. Matthew, Verna, Maya, Camille, and Margo Wright brighten my world; they made Nash-ville home for my family. I look forward to each encounter with them; they are infinite sources of compassion and support. Matthew helped me secure a post-doctoral fellowship in sociology at Vanderbilt University, which made possible the time to write this book and to do it with care.

This book first took shape through the skeleton/framework given to me by Shaul Kelner and Laura Carpenter. Andre Christie-Mizell is a wonderful friend who read portions of chapters 1 and 2. Andre, Patrick, Katherine, Caroline, Truman, and William are amazing. Tyson Brown always made me feel comfortable in my own skin; he provided strength and wisdom. Trica Keaton found ways to invigorate my soul and walk the difficult path with me. She encouraged me to share my work and always found ways to make me smile. Rich Milner made sure I was al-ways true to myself. I am grateful to Sandy Stahl, Dan Cornfield, Pallavi

Banerjee, Ellen Armour, Linda Willingham, Gary Gerstle, Paul Kramer, Samira Sheik, Julia Cohen, Ruth Rogaski, Ben Tran, Tracy Miller, and Ifeoma Nwankwo. Pam Tichenor and Deanne Casanova were pillars of strength and kindness during tough times. Anne Wall made me feel at home. David Rubin's efforts at opening spaces for "sexuality studies" immediately facilitated rich conversations; he is incredible, and I admire him. Charlotte Pierce-Baker and Houston Baker have been beacons of inspiration, honesty, and humility. They are family, and I cherish each moment with them. Thank you Tommy Crowe for the wonderful conversations at Reno's for Hair; I appreciate you and Reno. Joanne Zach and Angel Sims-Wright are shining stars who brought us home.

I am grateful to the following graduate students and teaching assistants: Marka Anderson, Alice Bae, Samantha Perez, Taryn Foshee, Rebecca Keng, and Ebony Duncan. Ebony is an intellectual force. The sports medicine team played an instrumental role in my recovery from back surgery: Thank you Andrew Gregory, Clint Devin, and Jenn Fletcher.

Through the course of my fieldwork, there were many people who lent their homes, energy, and support. I want to thank Tom Frank and Gail O'Day, the Gulley family, Mat and Darlene (Joseph) Matthews, the Flores Family (Anton, Charlotte, Jairo, and Eli), the Lipmans, Bobbi Taxali, Young Nam, Nash Tehrani, Sung, Catherine Zidow, and the Kim family. Nash's physical training expertise secured my body for the demands of basketball. Catherine let me stay at her place for a month; she is wonderful. James and Jenn have been there from the very beginning and have given me compassion, love, and shelter. I got into basketball shape by working out with James. He always found ways to keep me grounded and laughing. Jenn made me think deeply about my project, and baby Dylan and baby Ryan awed me. I always loved playing basketball with Dan Dressler. He, Irina, Joshua, and Rachel made me smile.

Many faculty, graduate students, undergraduate students, and staff at the University of Illinois played an important role in the development of this research topic: Brenda Farnell, Alejandro Lugo, Arlene Torres, Nancy Abelmann, Helaine Silverman, Alma Gottlieb, Andy Orta, Matti Bunzl, Liz Spears, Karla Harmon, Lisa Cacho, Yutian Wong, Soo Ah Kwon, Mimi Nguyen, Fiona Ngo, Matthew Gilbert, Viveka Kudaligama, Mary Ellerbe, Adrian Burgos, Jennifer Guiliano, Batamaka Some, Jennifer Hardin, Teresa Ramos, Jilian Baez, Aisha Durham, Celiany Rivera-Velazquez, Dan Wong, Viraj Patel, Alison Goebel, Grenita Hall, Nathan Todd and the volleyball gang, and Brian Montes. I thank Hasan Shahid for his help with the census data. Kevin Lam was instrumental in both talking about my research and for playing basketball weekly. Carolyn Randolf's incredible scholarship and friendship enrich my world more than words can describe. Constancio Arnaldo, Jr., and Christina Chin made collaborating so invigorating and affirming; I adore them. Constancio and Norma Marrun are family.

Beth Tarasawa gave me links to various resources and has been such a great reader. She is great, and I treasure our friendship. I thank Desmond Lewis for his wisdom and generosity. John Blake gave time and brilliance. The Atlanta Regional Commission and Geoffrey Walker provided the map of Atlanta that I use in the book. Ahmed Afzal, Kemi Balogun, and Kimberly Hoang have been excellent readers whose suggestions have polished my work in so many ways; it is my good fortune to know them. The reading circle with Kimberly and Kemi has pushed me in ways I never before imagined, and I admire them greatly. They deserve credit for the sharp insights in the book. Surbhi Malik has given me positive motivation to write. Luther Smith and Helen Pearson continue to give me strength and love for which I am forever grateful; they offer peace and love during storms and sunny days. Helen and Luther embody social justice in the most compassionate and profound ways.

Various sport scholars have been supportive of my work: Daryl Adair, David Rowe, Thomas Carter, Toni Bruce, Samaya Farooq Samie, Richard Pringle, Rachael Joo, C. Richard King, David Andrews, Scott Brooks, and Ben Carrington. Daniel Burdsey's scholarship has provided an important template that I have tried to emulate. His generosity, patience, commitment to social justice, and compassion is unmatched. I appreciate him as a brother.

Many scholars at various universities, conferences, and talks have helped me along the way. I thank Benny Hary, Robert Brown, Namita Manohar, Linta Varghese, Pawan Dhingra, Jack Halberstam, Rajinder Dudrah, Courtney Berger, Kathryn Koziatis, Ryan Reft, Alex Cummings, Daryl Maeda, Shilpa Davé, Shalini Shankar, Seema Sohi, Louisa Schein, Sunaina Maira, Thomas Holt, Rod Ferguson, Kale Fajardo, Mike Wilson, and Chia Vang. Jennifer Doyle, Erica Rand, and Degane Sougal lent much-needed compassionate hands during a difficult stretch in my life. Linda Espana-Maram provided compassionate examples of life in the academy. Rachel Buff has quickly become a dear friend. What an honor to know her; I respect her and cherish her. I am grateful to the College of Charleston and the University of Wisconsin–Milwaukee for inviting me to discuss this book.

I would like to acknowledge three scholars who have influenced me profoundly on both personal and professional levels when I began my research and continue to do so: Martin Manalansan, Junaid Rana, and David Roediger. I cherish them and love them dearly. My greatest professional accomplishment would be to mentor young scholars as they have mentored me. The ongoing conversations with Martin, Junaid, and Dave have been excellent and inspiring. They continue to read my work, offer brilliant suggestions, and provide support. I am enriched through every encounter with them.

Jon Hale has become a brother through the years, and I love him. He has read my work and provided rich feedback. Jon has been a rock through some difficult times. I am so glad we never have to play badminton again.

I am fortunate to work with such supportive, intellectually sophisticated, creative, and honest scholars like Arthur Spears, Diana Wall, Lotti Silber, and Asha Samad-Matias at the City College of New York. They have made professional life rewarding, safe, refreshing, and affirming. I am honored to share space with them. Herbert Seignoret livens up my experience of Harlem. The Colin Powell School for Civic and Global Leadership and its staff have supported me in many ways. Many thanks to Vince, Ginny, Kamilah, Wanda, Charlene, Dee Dee, Brooke, Leslie, Nkem, Amanda, Asshur, Chinomso, Aaron, Natalie, Michael, and Tiffany.

I have enjoyed working with NYU Press from the onset of this project. The reviews, comments, and suggestions from the anonymous reviewers were most constructive and instructive. Constance Grady was patient and helped me work through my technological challenges. I cannot stop raving about Jennifer Hammer. I am very fortunate to have worked with her. She has an incredible balance of compassion, editorial focus, stern hand, and gentle suggestions. Jennifer made writing this book such a thing of pleasure. Her keen eye to detail made possible a narrative arc that was polished, accessible, and articulate. She helped me bring out the poetics of social life. How lucky I am to have worked with her! All the beautiful points in this book come through my discussions with her and Gary Jaeger. The places where the book is not clear were solely my fault.

Gary Jaeger has seen this manuscript from the early stages when it was jargon filled, generalizing, and disjointed. He played an instrumental role in transforming it into this much more lucid, analytical narrative. He was able to pick up the minute errors and major thematic shortcomings in my work; he pushed me to think deeper. It became a biweekly ritual to meet with him. Gary has affected my scholarship and my teaching. He is a dear friend, and I treasure my time with him.

My appa, my amma, and Naveen (Thomas, Cecilia, and Grace Thangaraj) have given and continue to give so much to me. The gratitude I owe to my family is something that cannot be measured. Naveen (Grace Thangaraj) has supported me even though she was not the least bit interested in what I do. A whooping from her in tennis has always humbled me. I thank her partner, George Brooks, for his support. Appa and Amma refused to ever let me sulk or feel isolated. I have never had to walk alone as I knew they were always there. I love them; no words could express to them how lucky I know I am to have them as parents.

The love of my life, Alena Thangaraj, gives in unbelievable, unexpected, and heartwarming ways. She stabilizes the shaky ground in my life and dispels my worries. Alena's strength, her determination, and her drive are sources of envy. I respect Alena as the great professional she is. I admire her as the most incredible mother to our child. She is the greatest love of my life. I thank her for her patience through this project. How grateful I am for the infinite ways she has motivated me, guided me, and loved me. She inspires me! Alena sacrificed a lot to help me attain my professional dreams, and I am most grateful for all she does for me. I learn about her and love her more each day.

Jeya is a dream that continually becomes reality. There is no way that I could have prepared myself or forewarned myself for the emotions and relationships that I would experience when Jeya Evelyn was born. Jeya kutty's smile extends into all areas of my life. I love every moment with her; my tears are always those of joy. She amazes me, every little thing she does surprises me. I love her and nothing I ever write could ever fully capture how much I love her. Jeya is the poetry of my life.

***

I am grateful to the following journals for allowing me to use portions of published articles for this book. Parts of chapters 1, 2, and 3 originally appeared in smaller scale in the following journals but this book offers new analysis and different ethnographic supplements.

Thangaraj, Stanley I. 2013. "Competing Masculinities: South Asian American Identity Formation in Asian American Basketball Leagues." *South Asian Popular Culture* 11(3): 243–255.

———. 2012. "Playing through Difference: The Black-White Racial Logic and Interrogating South Asian American Identity." *Ethnic and Racial Studies* 35(6): 988–1006.

———. 2010a. "Ballin' Indo-Pak Style: Pleasures, Desires, and Expressive Practices of 'South Asian American' Masculinity." *International Review for the Sociology of Sport* 45(3): 372–389.

———. 2010b. "Liting It Up: Popular Culture, Indo-Pak Basketball, and South Asian American Institutions." *Cosmopolitan Civil Societies: An Interdisciplinary Journal* 2(2): 71–91.

Introduction

On a warm Sunday afternoon in May 2009, I played with a mostly Muslim Pakistani American basketball team called the Atlanta Rat Pack in the Asian American basketball league known as the Asian Ballers League. We played in a gym adjoining an orthodox Greek church in DeKalb County, Georgia. The gym was entrenched in the immediate vicinity of staunchly middle-class families, but lower-middle class and working-class communities existed on the other side of the first traffic light to the west of the gym. The members of Atlanta Rat Pack—Mustafa, Mohammed, Imran, Amir, Khan, Saleh, Sultan, and I—arrived separately from different parts of Metro Atlanta. We met at the front of the gym to exchange greetings and then walked into the gym where we changed from our casual footwear to our basketball shoes.

Halfway into this competition, 34-year-old Mustafa and 21-year-old Imran got into a shooting groove and made the majority of their shots. With only a few minutes left in the game, Mustafa and 28-year-old Mohammed looked at each other and summoned the starters to the bench. In their place, an energetic wave of substitutions ran onto the court, including Khan, a 19-year old, 6'3" slender basketball novice and Sultan, Imran's 29-year-old brother. Unlike Sultan, who played regularly and had years of tournament playing experience, Khan rarely played at this high level of competition. Today, he entered with shaky knees that made his lanky discomfort mixed with enthusiasm obvious to veterans on the court. This was his opportunity to shine. With his long frame and slender muscularity, Khan's athletic ability was immediately on display. On a missed shot, Khan soared high in the air to get the defensive rebound over the outreached hands of his opponents. This athletic feat caught the eye of the occupants of the gym. It was clearly a sign of physical excellence. Khan clearly out-jumped his peers. Kdol (a Cambodian American organizer of the Asian Ballers League), who was working the scorers' table, looked at me with astonishment. "That kid's got potential," he said. "You guys need to work with him."

But that feat in itself did not provide him the respect and praise of his peers. Khan's inexperience showed despite his physical gifts. He frequently lost control of the ball or had it stolen away by the opposing team. After one such fumble, Mustafa called a time-out and drew everyone into a huddle with the goal of providing advice to young Khan. Mustafa looked firmly into Khan's eyes and flexed his muscles in the manner in which he thought Khan should hold a basketball. Mustafa raised his hands over his head to show Khan the way to secure the basketball off a rebound. He then brought the imaginary ball to his chest and pushed his hands inward, squeezing it, thereby showing the force it would take for an opponent to pry the ball away. The forceful move of the ball inward caused Mustafa's chest and biceps to flair. He demanded of Khan, "You got to play strong, man up!" This display was the model for Khan to emulate. Mohammed nodded his head in agreement and chimed in, "Be a beast!"

Asian Americans in general and South Asian Americans in particular are not commonly associated with mainstream American sports such as basketball. Although there are a few figures such as Jeremy Lin, Taiwanese American basketball player for the National Basketball Association (NBA) team the Los Angeles Lakers, Lin's rise in professional basketball is seen as exceptional, an anomaly. There are few other male Asian American players who have received such fame in mainstream U.S. sports (see Yep 2009). When looking specifically at the South Asian American presence in U.S. sports, the absence is that much more revealing. In fact, no South Asian Americans register on the rosters of any of the four major U.S. professional sports organizations in basketball, baseball, football, and ice hockey. The exception includes a mixed-race white–South Asian player, Brandon Chillar, who played for the Green Bay Packers in the National Football League. The most frequent studies of South Asian Americans and sport stereotypically focus on the relationship between South Asian Americans and the game of cricket.[1] The frequent association with cricket, as opposed to U.S. sports, helps to frame South Asian Americans as "forever foreign."[2] The affiliation with cricket does little to show how South Asian Americans men such as those in this book engage with American[3] popular culture and its respective sporting cultures.[4] Their participation in realms of American sport is under-researched and appears almost non-existent. Yet South

Asian Americans do participate in basketball and other mainstream U.S. sporting cultures to express their sporting desires and perform identities as certain types of racialized athletes.

Along with the problematic affiliation with cricket as the perceived quintessential South Asian sporting form, common stereotypes of South Asian Americans fluctuate between two representations that portray them as non-normative—as either nerdy or as possibly terroristic—but always foreign.[5] They are seen as incapable of fully enculturating into an American-ness commonly embodied by the white, middle-class, heterosexual male. The presence of South Asian American men in the Asian Ballers League is not accidental or irrelevant. Instead of conceptualizing basketball as simply a whimsical hobby, they devote significant time to the sport, transforming it into an important means by which South Asian American men socialize, navigate, and express their identities in 21st-century America. Mustafa and his peers choose to play in the Asian Ballers League as a way to reconfigure the racializations they encounter in American sport in particular and in American society in general. The many experiences of exclusion in U.S. society with which they have contended are embodied and negotiated on the basketball court. Their process of crafting identities in sport is part of a larger attempt to claim their versions of racialized masculinity and American citizenship as convergent themes, rather than polar opposites.

With each win and loss on the basketball court, the members of Atlanta Rat Pack adjudicate their place within the basketball hierarchy in the Asian Ballers League while negotiating their place in diasporic and national spaces. Making South Asian American masculinity involves performing athletic ability and creativity in relation to many other subjects at the intersections of gender, race, sexuality, class, and ethnicity. The social interactions and pleasures of homosocial competition on the basketball court that we will encounter in the book are not alien to the South Asian diasporic communities in Atlanta or in larger U.S. society. These young men express a deep love for basketball, demonstrating an ongoing engagement with American popular cultural forms as one means to express their identity.

Their love for the game provides a window into how certain South Asian American men fashion themselves in U.S. society and within their own South Asian American community. Their participation in basketball is one platform, among many, for performing South Asian American identity. The young men, as practitioners of sport, find meaning in their athletic capabilities on the court while carving out a space for subsequent social interactions with co-ethnic peers and racialized Others. Leagues such as the Asian Ballers League offer respite from racialized marginalization in mainstream, multiracial basketball circuits. The Asian Ballers League and other places where South Asian American basketball is played, then, become spaces in which to negotiate the relationships among masculinity, race, and nation.[6] When stereotypes of South Asian American men portray them as effeminate, the young men perform sporting feats on the court to represent themselves differently. Although the stereotype of the nerd spreads across racial communities, it has a particular essentialized grounding in depictions of Asian American and South Asian American communities. Accordingly, it flattens the diversity, "heterogeneity," and "multiplicity" (Lowe 1996) within these communities while failing to acknowledge how these communities are in differential relationships to citizenship, sport, capitalism, and race. Even as the nerd stereotype levels heterogeneity, stereotypes of South Asian American men as "terrorists" further limit the honest representation of differences within South Asian America.[7]

In the game described in the opening vignette, Mustafa and Imran showed deft shooting touch by making 3-point shots and out-dribbling their opponents for easy points. Mohammed, at 6'2" and over 200 pounds, overpowered some of his opponents on the team Practice Squad for some easy baskets. South Asian American athletes like these showcase their athletic abilities in ways that have the possibility to reshape the mainstream imagination of the South Asian American body. Through a variety of skilled basketball maneuvers and with their muscular bodies, they represent themselves as strong, able-bodied, aggressive, respectable, and heterosexual men. Each successful execution of a skill set on the court allows players, within basketball time, to deem each other as manly or make demands of each other to perform their considerations of normative masculinity by "manning up." Although the players take for granted the act of playing basketball as masculine, I contend that the plethora of acts, signs, and gestures that South Asian American men foreground as "by men" and "for men" are part of a larger process of becoming a certain type of racialized national subject.[8] However, for some of these young men, that act of reshaping racializations to enter within the realm of normative "belonging," contradictorily, involves participation in ethnically exclusive and bounded sites.

The active participation of some South Asian American men in U.S. sporting cultures does not take place in social venues sealed from greater political concerns. Sporting cultures do not exist in a vacuum; rather, they provide instrumental information on larger social phenomena within sport and the larger society.[9] In the C. L. R. Jamesian intellectual tradition of linking leisure activities to macro-level social phenomena, sporting cultures offer sites of hope that challenge the status quo, but they also have their own forms of social stratification.[10] Unlike James and his contemporaries, who focused primarily on West Indian cricket and its respective racial and class stratifications, in this book I interrogate gender hierarchies within sport. Instead of separating categories of masculinity, race, sexuality, class, and ethnicity, I underscore the critical role that gender plays not only in structuring racializations of South Asian American communities but also their responses to them. Khan, in the vignette above, offers the hope of a strong, dominating South Asian American athlete. When Mustafa and Mohammed exhort him to "man up" and "be a beast," they seek to align their racialized bodies within the fabric of normative American sporting identity. This book offers a study of South Asian American involvement in basketball cultures to illuminate the structure of U.S. society, forces of racialization, and practices of "cultural citizenship" (Rosaldo 1994; Maira 2009) that are facilitated through the category of gender but that are always at the intersections of race, sexuality, class, ability, and ethnicity.[11] It draws on four years of ethnographic research, including interviews, oral histories, and participant observation within an Indo-Pak (Indian Pakistani) South Asian basketball league, to argue that, through their efforts to "man up" on the court, South Asian American men fashion their own versions of American masculinity. Within South Asian–only venues, players inscribe meanings to their brown bodies that are not available in other realms of society. At the same time, the limits of these meanings provide useful information about other types of exclusions present in masculinity formations.

The boundaries of political and cultural citizenship are not new to sport. Sport is often the site for representing and training the proper national subject with regard to race, gender, class, and sexuality.[12] Therefore, the different diasporic locations and histories of South Asians produce a variety of affiliations to sport and nation.[13] For example, the anthropologist Thomas Walle, the literary scholar Sameer Pandya, and the sociologists Daniel Burdsey and Samaya Farooq Samie highlight how South Asian diasporas in Norway, Fiji, and the United Kingdom, respectively, utilize cricket, golf, boxing, soccer, and basketball as both the methods of inclusion and exclusion from the national fabric.[14] Moving across the Atlantic back to the United States, some sports, such as cricket and soccer, do not carry the same resonance in the American context. Instead, marginalized communities in the United States turn to sports, like basketball, to perform cultural citizenship.[15]

The historians Andrea Bachin and Linda Espana-Maram contend that early in U.S. history sports were understood as a two-part project to train the proper (white heterosexual male) citizen and to civilize Others through U.S. imperialism.[16] Like the Filipino boxers in España-Maram's monograph, *Creating Masculinity in Los Angelos's Little Manila*, the peer group of South Asian Americans sets the stage for identity formation, constructs new desires and pleasures in an ethnic sporting body, and inverts the stereotypical relationship between "race and ability" (España-Maram 2006: 92). Sport is a realm where one publically displays one's body and produces various social meanings through simultaneously quotidian practices yet spectacular displays.[17] The anthropologist Susan Brownell contends that "sports can be mundane and they can be dramatic; it is this versatility that makes them socially significant and theoretically interesting" (1995: 29). Even though the South Asian American men we meet in this book are playing in ethnically closed circuits, the experience is not just about simply playing the sport. It is part of a larger process of demonstrating athletic swagger through which they negotiate, manage, and challenge their place on the court, in their communities, and in the national fabric. Their choice to play in the Asian Ballers League is an expression of a national belonging and an expression of self—a stylistic, cool, athletic self. The court, like España-Maram's boxing ring, becomes a safe space in which to test out multiple expressions of masculinity while facing the ideological and subjective force, as Mustafa implies, to "man up." In the process of developing and refining a repertoire of masculine practices, these young South Asian American men manage the gendered regimes of an American belonging.

What Mustafa and Mohammed ask of Khan is to perform an accept-able comportment of sporting masculinity. They suggest a version that is readable, palatable, and normative within their sporting space and the larger U.S. public. The body, as emblematic of the state, presents an important gendered and sexualized forum in which to tease out the par-ticularities of citizenship and national representations. Khan's inability to hold the ball properly and express muscular strength negates the re-lationship between "biological sex," gender, and claims to national mas-culinity.[18] "The social definition of men as holders of power is translated not only into mental body-images and fantasies, but into muscle ten-sions, posture, the feel and texture of the body. This is one of the main ways in which the power of men becomes naturalized" (Connell 1987: 85). Khan's muscularity and athleticism affirms his potential for possible inclusion within sporting spaces and the nation as a man. Khan has not yet lived up to his full ability to be a "man," but he has shown promise. His biological expression as male does not necessarily guarantee entrée into the esteemed realm of masculinity or within American-ness; mas-culinity is determined through social practice (Halberstam 1998). Khan may have been born and assigned a biological designation as "male," but the process of racialization depicts South Asian American men as outside the parameters of a normative masculinity. He is generally seen as not man enough in relation to white, middle-class, heterosexual nor-mativity and black hyper-masculinity or in relation to men with "swag" (a vernacular term for swagger) like Mustafa. Thus, Mustafa and his peers, through their encouragement for him to "man up," ask Khan to display some confidence and "basketball cool" through his swagger. A perception that they are not man enough to play basketball, a common stereotype of South Asian American men, informs how young men on the court challenge the stereotype of their bodies as unfit for claiming American-ness in full.

Embodied Memories and South Asian America

When South Asian American men fashion their bodies on the court to demonstrate toughness they challenge mainstream racializations while staying attuned to the historical ways in which their bodies, their par-ents' bodies, and bodies of other South Asians in the United States have been read. Their bodies are repositories of memories.[19] The anthropologist Brenda Farnell's assertion that the body must be centered as a site for agency rather than an existential site is useful in understanding how Indo-Pak Basketball players actively commit to embodied actions of complicated, multiply-inflected identities.[20] Most of the young basketball players and their friends whom we will meet in this book were either born in the United States or grew up here. They are U.S. citizens, though imagined by mainstream society as "always foreign." When they play, they engage with much longer histories of the racialization of South Asians in the Americas. But not all players have the same resources to perform sporting American masculinities or to dismantle mainstream stereotypes. The South Asian American players I met during my fieldwork came from a variety of social locations determined by the professional status of their parents, the immigration wave through which their family arrived in U.S. history, their class resources, and their own individual educational-professional status. Even within the Atlanta Rat Pack there exist "heterogeneity" and "multiplicity" (Lowe 1996) that highlight how the parents of athletes arrived at different moments of U.S. imperialism and capitalism.

The communities of South Asian American basketball players do not have one single relation to citizenship or basketball. These relationships are always multiple, complicated, and sometimes contradictory. However, South Asian American bodies have generally been read historically as outsiders to American-ness. These histories are imprinted in their skins and their community's memories. Early South Asians arrived on North American shores on merchant ships in the late 1700s, but the first substantial wave took place in the late 1800s and early 1900s.[21] One early wave consisted of Sikh, Hindu, and Muslim agrarian workers migrating from the sub-continental region of Punjab to Canada. With increasing white nativist hostility in Canada, the Punjabi men eventually migrated south to the United States, where many of these young men ended up in California's agricultural fields.[22] The agrarian workers endured the racialization as "Hindoos," which was simultaneously a census category and a daily experience of abjection. The census category of "Hindoo" represented Punjabi farmers as ethno-religiously, racially, and sexually different from American-ness.[23] Similarly, for the Bengali peddlers traveling through the southern cities of Atlanta, New Orleans, and Charleston in early 1900s, the category of "Hindoo" emphasized a difference from white normativity and black masculinity (Bald 2013). The cultural representations of "Hindoos" were naturalized as a racial difference and imprinted upon their bodies. Although considered "Caucasian" by "racial science," these workers did not have any rights afforded to white men such as owning land, marrying white women, or garnering naturalized citizenship (see Koshy 2007). Anti-immigrant policies, vagrancy codes, and anti-miscegenation laws colluded in constructing an image of South Asians as possessing an abnormal, licentious, and un-American masculinity.[24]

Increasing xenophobia from the early 1900s till the 1924 Johnson-Reed Act stymied immigration from Asia and other areas listed as the "Barred Zone."[25] The U.S. government delineated regions of the world into zones through which certain zones could continue to send people, based on certain quotas, to U.S. shores while others, such as majority of the East Asian and South Asian countries, were stigmatized as "Barred Zones" and restricted from entry within American borders. The majority of South Asian American teams in Atlanta's Asian Ballers League as well as the larger Chicago Indo-Pak National Basketball Tournament (IPN) have little to no sanguine ties to these earlier communities of "Hindoos" in the Americas. Rather, the young players' families came to the United States through two contemporary immigration waves. Their parents arrived with either the passage of the 1965 Hart-Cellar Act or the 1980 Family Preference Acts.[26]

Doctors, nurses, scientists, and engineers from South Asia came after 1965 as part of the U.S. imperial strategy to compete against the Soviet Union at the height of the Cold War in all scientific and technological fields.[27] One major segment of Indo-Pak players, including many members of the Atlanta Rat Pack, are children of this wave of professionals (see Bhatia 2007; Dhingra 2007). Accordingly, these children are themselves primarily professionals in fields such as finance or medicine, with considerable social mobility. Imran's and Sultan's father is a medical doctor while Mohammed's parents are scientists. Sultan attended a prestigious private university in Atlanta while Mohammed and Imran attended a highly recognized public university in the city. These professional young men are often commonly labeled as the "model minority," a stereotype that portrays them as having the brains, cultural traits, work ethic, and drive for success due to their ethnicity. It is most often the case that the children of the post-1965 wave of professionals have the resources to structure the large Indo-Pak Basketball tournaments that take place across the United States in Chicago, Dallas, Washington, DC, and San Francisco. These same men also have the capital affluence to attend most, if not all, of these North American tournaments, including a prestigious tournament in Vancouver, Canada.

There are, however, various populations within South Asian America who lack the same social mobility as the professionals detailed above. The sociologist Pawan Dhingra and the religious studies scholar Kyati Joshi show that, proportionally, more South Asian Americans live in poverty than their white counterparts.[28] The parents of Mustafa, whom we met earlier, entered the United States through the 1980 Family Preference Acts.[29] His father, Amin uncle (I use "uncle" as a term of respect for elders in South Asian America, and not as an indication of filial relationship), followed his older brother, an engineer, who relocated to the United States. Amin uncle, although also an engineer, arrived in the 1980s—a much different and tumultuous economic time. He and his family did not have the same resources, or the equity based on residence, or the social mobility as his brother. Many of the post-1980 immigrants and their children are not high-level professionals. Players like Mustafa did not have access to highly rated high schools and do not pursue or have the opportunity to pursue a four-year college/university degree. The post-1980 young men are mostly lower middle class and working class. Their patterns of employment are precarious, and they face the wrath of economic downturns, such as that of 2007–2009, much more intimately. Their lives do not resemble those of the players deemed the "model minority" even though they feel the ideological pressure of that category. Unable to find the luxury of time to regularly play basketball, some of young men work long hours, as their families are dependent on their income (Thangaraj 2012).

On the basketball court, men like Mustafa garner status based on their strong basketball acumen. Their athletic social clout does not fully translate into other aspects of social life. Mustafa and many of the other children of the post-1980 wave are seen as embodying failed masculinities in relation to the financial professionals—the "model minority." On the basketball court, these types of class differences are interwoven into the interactions and performances of sporting identities. As the queer theorist Roderick Ferguson contends, "The universality of the citizen exists in opposition to the intersecting particularities that account for material existence, particularities of race, gender, class, and sexuality" (2004: 12). With these differences in class, South Asian American basketball players have differential means with which to "man up" as athletes and differential claims to belonging, citizenship, and nation.

Politics of Masculinity

Mustafa and Mohammed's insistence that Khan "man up" and "be a beast" demonstrates the dynamic and performative realm of masculinity.[30] Membership within this sporting community and in the larger society involves a multiple, contradictory, complex, and relational rendering of masculinity.[31] In Khan's case, he does not play and practice in isolation. He plays in a larger social field with an extensive list of acceptable practices, its own disciplinary regimes, and many other racialized characters. When I asked Khan to define "masculinity" in his terms, he responded,

> Manhood is like strength. To be a man you can't be cocky, and you can't backbite. Gossiping is for women not men. Men take charge and get things done. They don't back down from challenges, and they use their heads as much as they use their strength. Basketball relates to being a man in that it builds bonds of brotherhood which is also important as a man. It gives you chances to take charge, and no one likes a cocky player. You can be good at bball [basketball] and still be a cool person.

Khan created the parameters of masculinity not in a vacuum but in relation to femininity and middle-class respectability. Within this conceptualization we see forces of regulation, delimiting those who belong and those who do not. Using a queer of color critique, as seen in the works of Chandan Reddy and Roderick Ferguson, we can see how diasporic and ethnic nationalist dictates of masculinity involve particular conditions for containing gender, sexual, and racial social formations.[32] Khan elaborates on practices of masculinity that relate to disassociation, counteridentification, and expulsion—in this case, cockiness and related class sensibilities, femininity, and "gossiping" like a woman.[33] At the Asian Ballers League, Khan must perform aggressiveness and toughness in relation to stereotypes of South Asians in the American imagination, in relation to his teammates on the Atlanta Rat Pack, in relation to his opponents on other teams, in relation to femininity, and in relation to the audience who will gauge and value his movements. There is no end point to masculinity as it is never finished or accomplished. His masculinity is always "in process" and "becoming";[34] it must be constantly performed, iterated, and reiterated to give it substance and construct the "parallel lines" (Ahmed 2006) of the failed gendered, raced, and sexualized Other.[35]

In Khan's case, "manning up" is the disciplinary regime that precedes masculinity; it provides insight into the acceptable and not acceptable comportments of identity on the court. The gender theorist Wendy Brown, in her interrogation of women's studies programs, notes: "There is not, as Judith Butler has remarked, first gender and then the apparatus that regulates it; gender does not exist prior to its regulation. Rather, the gendered subject emerges through a regulatory scheme of gender—we are literally brought into being as gendered subjects through gender regulation" (2008: 25).[36] Thus gender practices with regard to citizenship, belonging, and sport are invoked and structured through the continuous processes of managing, policing, and disciplining.[37] Acts of "manning up" require boundaries of acceptability through which to regulate who can and cannot be man enough. By asking Khan to "be a beast," the basketball players demand toughness in order to shed any worries of femininity or gay masculinity but in contrast to the "bestiality" of black masculinity.[38]

The relational dynamic of gender identities and its regulatory schema is constituted within a complex set of what the masculinities scholar Robert Connell (1995) refers to as the "gender politics" within masculinity. This book delves into the gender politics at various intersections of race, masculinity, sexuality, ethnicity, and class that both produce the racializations of South Asian Americans in U.S. society and subsequently ignite their responses to such stereotypes. This book is one of the few ethnographic texts to look at the construction of South Asian American masculinity rather than focusing solely on their means of emasculation. In line with the anthropologists Kale Fajardo (2011) and Alan

Klein (1993), it examines the processes of emasculation and documents attempts to recuperate and perform a tough, heterosexual masculinity. In that process, young men like Mustafa manufacture their own acceptable arrangements of masculinity within U.S. society and within their own South Asian American communities. As gender is constitutive of the experiences of daily life,[39] participation in sporting cultures constitutes one means by which young South Asian American men perform cultural citizenship.

The sporting practices we saw in the opening vignette stand in contrast to the nerd stereotype associated with the "model minority" moniker. The term "model minority" came about through journalistic depictions of Asian Americans in the 1960s, during the civil rights movement, and was quickly appropriated by the political system. Asian Americans were positioned as the "model minority," which supposedly had the proper cultural constitution and work ethic to succeed, in contrast to African American and Latina/o communities that were judged more negatively. But the moniker did not account for the professional skill set and resources with which the early Asian American professionals arrived on U.S. shores.[40] In time this term came to be used to describe South Asian Americans who fluctuated in and out of the category of Asian America.[41] Asian American and South Asian American men are stereotypically seen as nerds composed of all brains (Prashad 2000, 2001). In counterpoint, mostly African Americans and some Latinos, Prashad argues, are positioned as all brawn, with bodies that need domestication, while white men are the perfect mix of brain and brawn (Prashad 2000, 2001). The American Studies scholar Roderick Ferguson (2012), in his analysis of the formation of ethnic studies and women's studies, invokes June Jordan's activism at the City College of New York to demonstrate how she understood early on the particular matrix of racialization that involves race, gender, and class. He remarks that Jordan "was in fact obliquely referencing the social construction of African Americans and Puerto Ricans as culturally pathological subjects unfit for civic participation and educational advancement, a construction assisted by members of the academy, government, and media" (Ferguson 2012: 95).[42] The South Asian American man, in contrast, is seen as ideally suited for the realms of the academy and professional work. However, as we will see, such a fit does not promise full citizenship.

The "model minority" stereotype, although couched in positive terms, is a relational signifier with gender undertones that does not guarantee to South Asian American men all rights, benefits, and privileges accorded to white men. South Asian American men are seen to lack the ability to perform in any realm that requires strength and athletic aptitude. Strength and aptitude slip into the realms of sexuality, thereby positioning "all brain" subjects as failing bodies without the ability to penetrate the nation or female bodies through heterosexual intercourse. The emphasis on the brain renders the body, a key constituent used to talk about masculinity, as different and non-normative in relation to the middle-class, Christian, heterosexual white man.[43]

The call to "man up" and "be a beast" is meant to challenge this racialization in order to fit into the bodily standards of sporting masculinities and national subjectivity. "Manning up" is a process of engaging with mainstream dictates of masculinities mixed in with South Asian American experiences of emasculation. The term "man up" is common in U.S. society and has many meanings. It pops up frequently to cover a gamut of social activities such as work, family obligations, gendered expectations, and sport. In particular, the anxiety surrounding the need to "man up" arises out of a fear of the "increased feminization" of men, a "crisis of masculinity" (Connell 1995), and with the rise of the feminist movement and women's entry into previous male social realms.[44] Some pundits of gendered anxieties long for a "tough" masculinity they perceive to have been lost with the emergence of feminism. For example, *Newsweek* offered a feature on the state of American masculinity and its related anxieties (Romano and Dokoupil 2010).[45] The title of the article was "Man Up." On the cover, the editors make clear the anxiety by showing a white man (assumed to be heterosexual) with a muscular chest, bulging biceps, hairless body, cleanly shaven face, and well-trimmed hair holding an infant boy. The article asks how men maintain their masculinity and pass it on to the next generation while taking an increased role in parenting, which is gendered feminine. In this case, a modern masculine identity consists of incorporating caring and metrosexual aesthetics alongside toughness and hard, muscular heterosexual body. Such contradictory dictates comprise the larger U.S. social context through which South Asian American men navigate their identity formation.

Mainstream U.S. media outlets do not, however, monopolize the conversation about shifting realms of masculinity. South Asian American media sources, such as *Nirali Magazine*,[46] have featured articles on what they consider the South Asian American crisis of masculinity. In contrast to the *Newsweek* article, the South Asian American female authors of *Nirali Magazine* depict these anxieties based on the particular stereotypes and expectations of South Asian American men. The female authors question whether the "modern desi male" has evolved enough from the "sexist, boorish man" who is linked to South Asia instead of the western, enlightened space of the United States.[47] Here, they reference an abstract white man as the embodiment of the modern male that the desi man needs to emulate, while failing to address the multiple realms of modernity performed across international spaces that do not require a Western center. The authors call for South Asian American men to "man down" by expressing feminist sensibilities. They project traits for modern desi masculinity that consist of having gay friends, the willingness to date older women, and socialization by women.[48] *Nirali Magazine*'s depiction of South Asian American masculinity, however, is at odds with the gendered expectations to "man up" within South Asian American basketball circuits. If Khan and his peers were to "man down," they would be in danger of slipping into the racialized stereotype of the nerd and its subsequent exclusions. In sporting circuits around the United States, men are asked to perform a tough aggressive masculinity as normative.

Mustafa and Mohammed emphasized to Khan their conceptualizations of a normative sporting masculinity, one that is both the ideal and a model to live up to. Although masculinities scholar Robert Connell (1995) would call this athletic dictate an expression of "hegemonic masculinity" as it means dominating women and gay masculinities, the South Asian American basketball players perform it in a much more complex and contradictory field. The players on the Atlanta Rat Pack occupy positions of dominance, complicity, and marginality/subservience simultaneously. The cultural studies scholar Toby Miller, in *Sportsex*, contends that men occupy multiple locations on Connell's masculinities hierarchy.[49] He uses the case of a gay, aboriginal rugby player, Ian Roberts, who takes part in hegemonic practices of dominating men on the field, underscoring a muscular body, and making the presence of men in sport commonsense but also feels the brunt of sexualized and racial marginalization. Roberts's coming out does not change the patterns of social relations around masculinity and femininity. The system of power remains. It is also evident in practices of South Asian American identity on the basketball court. South Asian American athletes claim power to work through their agency—thereby instituting moments of regulation and exclusion in the process of expanding South Asian American identity.[50] The young men must enforce their own boundaries to consolidate what is and who can be "man enough."

Although I use the term "masculinity" in this book, there is never a singular category of masculinity in play. Rather, in agreement with Connell (1995), there are multiple *masculinities*. The social location of South Asian American athletes, which is heterogeneous and multiple even within the Atlanta Rat Pack, plays out in the multiple evaluations and renditions of masculinity. Notions of basketball masculinity are informed by their ethno-religious histories, their lived experiences of race, their consumption of popular culture, their socioeconomic status, and the joy they garner in co-ethnic sporting socialization. In contrast to the masculinities scholars Michael Kimmel (2005) and Michael Messner (1992, 2002), who do not attend enough to the role of race within masculinity, this book underscores the relationships between gender and race. More important, it contends that racialization is a gendered process through which to lay claims to spaces and places in the national fabric. To perform a strong, athletic, virile masculinity, some South Asian American basketball players feel the need to initially create exclusive ethnic basketball formats to escape the racist sentiments they experience in other multiracial arenas.

Browning Out Basketball at the Intersections of Race, Masculinity, and Class

The term "brown out," as I use it in this book, is a mix of common U.S. sporting vernacular and aesthetics alongside the shifting, ambiguous, ambivalent racial classifications of South Asians in U.S. society.[51] Although the term "brown out" may not be commonplace in U.S. society, the vernacular juxtaposing is found in sporting spaces and leisure spaces across the country. At various high school, college, and professional basketball venues, marketing campaigns and gimmicks called "black outs," "white outs," "red outs," and so on, are produced by organizers, corporations, institutions, and fans. Fans show team loyalty by coming to games dressed in their team's colors. For example, a team with black on their jerseys might ask for a "black out" where all the fans in the stadium arrive to the game sporting black outfits and form an "imagined community" (Anderson 1991). In this book, "brown out" highlights the choice by South Asian American players to create a racially exclusive space available to co-ethnic peers and Other vaguely "brown" racialized bodies. Production of exclusive spaces provides a way to construct communal identities through the exclusion of various Others. Additionally, I use "brown" to further demonstrate the racially liminal contours of brotherhood in the social context of the U.S. South, where racial legibility is founded and practiced through the black-white racial binary (Bow 2010). South Asian American athletes complicate the simplistic binary of both race and basketball in the United States, which is understood as black and white. Their performance of sporting masculinity extends the racial boundaries of citizenship and racial legibility beyond the black-white racial dichotomy by reconfiguring national belonging through brown bodies playing a quintessentially American sport.

South Asian Americans exist, especially in the U.S. South, outside the dominant logic of race and citizenship. The anthropologist Judith Goode, in *Western Welfare in Decline*, addresses the importance of race in determining citizenship in U.S. society. She states that, without racial legibility, one is thought not to exist.[52] The racial category "brown" is a reference to certain racial ambiguity that comes with flexible racial subjectivity and its subsequent shifting racial classifications. Such racial flexibility allows for certain levels of social mobility.[53] Yet this racial ambiguity results in a racial illegibility that produces gendered valences about what type of "brown" men they are and their subsequent social (im)mobility. The anthropologist Junaid Rana, in *Terrifying Muslims*, emphasizes the expansive nature of race and racializations when he addresses how the category of the "terrorist" and "dangerous Muslim" continuously extends to capture a variety of raced subjects. He provides the example of the U.S. response in the "global war on terror" that implicates Native Americans, Latinos, Arabs, Middle Eastern subjects, South Asians, and other Asian subjects as communities to be controlled with an escalation of violence, deportation, and detention.[54] In sport and in society, South Asian Americans are read through and against other "brown-skinned" subjects, such as Latinos, Southeast Asians, and Middle Easterners, who are lumped together as a result of their illegibility in the black-white racial logic.

The process of browning out a space is the intentional construction and delineation of social spaces with contours of membership that are open to certain co-ethnic peers as well as acceptable racialized Others. The South Asian American men in this book co-construct their South Asian American selves through the production of a brown-out basketball space.[55] My use of "brown" is also intentional in an effort to link race to the performances of masculinity. In this case, brown outs are not marketing campaigns but, rather, a social practice through which young South Asian American men incorporate their own lived experiences as racialized men to assert their identity with the creation of safe but exclusionary sporting spaces. When South Asian Americans play basketball in other public settings, they often feel marginalized. As Pukh, an ethnic Punjabi Sikh American from New Jersey who plays in North American Indo-Pak Basketball tournaments, reflects, "In other leagues [pause], there are racial comments." The racial comments in open basketball leagues are a symptom, on a microscopic scale, of marginalization in U.S. society in general. For example, on January 28, 2014, *Deadspin* covered a racial incident in which fans of Pittsford Sutherland (a New York state high school) started shouting "We want slurpees (an icy fruity drink)" at a Brighton (another New York state high school) player of Indian American heritage when he was shooting free throws after a foul.[56] The mention of "slurpees" is a classed, raced, and gendered projection of foreign-ness upon South Asian Americans who are stereotyped as convenience store owners who sell such drinks (Dave 2012). Incidents like this at a high school game are a common story for some of my informants. These young men experience deeply and subtly harbored racial sentiments that construct South Asian American players as not "American enough" or "man enough" for basketball. In order to invert such racial comments and stake a claim to belonging in the United States and in sport, South Asian American players create ethnically and racially contained spaces in order to "man up" to a viable U.S. sporting masculinity.

As we will see in the book, not all brown outs suffice as a basis for a desired basketball-centered South Asian American masculinity. There are hierarchies and differential values across the gamut of South Asian American basketball venues. Mustafa, one of the premier South Asian American players in Atlanta and a founder of the team Atlanta Outkasts, contrasts local Indo-Pak Basketball tournaments in the early 1990s with the prestigious Chicago Indo-Pak National Tournament, which he attended with the Outkasts in 1998: "[In Atlanta] we didn't play against, I am going to say, desi people. Whenever we did, we were always better than them. . . . I did not want to play against these local desi kids 'cause anywhere we went we dominated them—until we got invited to the Indo-Paks. This is a different level of basketball dude. These guys can play." On the local scene in the early 1990s, Mustafa felt like the exceptional desi player.[57] Dominating less-skilled desi players did not produce the same joys of competing against equally skilled players. By playing against the weak players, he and his peers were competing against young men who were the embodied representations of nerd stereotypes.

As noted, certain realms of brown-out basketball do not always suffice. Things changed for Mustafa when he played in the national Indo-Pak Basketball circuit. His linguistic coding of "guys" in opposition to "local desi kids" to describe the Indo-Pak players already represents them as athletic men and embodiments of a prized masculinity. Thus, Mustafa did not equivalently value the many desi basketball circuits. He placed the invitation-only Chicago IPN on a higher pedestal and likewise chose to play locally in the Asian Ballers League with the stronger South Asian American basketball players like Mohammed and Imran. The premier desi "guys" at the IPN tournament and in the Asian Ballers League constitute the people he wants as part of his South Asian American community. However, to attain these pleasures, young men like Mustafa and other desi players need to exclude certain other South Asian American players, certain racialized Others, women, and queer men in order to secure the pleasures of competitive, ethnic-only basketball. It is a space where inclusion is built through the forces of regulation and exclusion.

Playing and Studying Basketball

To understand the performance of masculinity in South Asian American co-ethnic basketball, I conducted extensive ethnographic research in Atlanta from the summer of 2006 until the fall of 2009. However, I first entered this scene in 1994 as a player with the team Atlanta Outkasts. I was a college student at Emory University when students Kumrain and Little Sheik (children of the professional waves that came after the 1965 immigration act) invited me to play with their Muslim Pakistani American peers. Thus, my first encounter with post-1980 immigration wave participants was when I met Mustafa, Ali, and their older brother Qamar in 1994. I played with these young men as a member of the Atlanta Outkasts from 1994 to 2002.

In 2006, I began my research project and got back in touch with them. Mustafa and his peers asked me to join their teams. Standing at 6'1" and weighing 180 pounds, my physical stature and athletic ability benefited the teams I would then play for in the following years. My years of playing basketball and coaching it at the high school and collegiate level endeared me to this community, although players still more frequently sought Mustafa's and Mohammed's advice on the court. As a Christian Tamil Indian American, my own ethnic status allowed me to enter the various Indo-Pak Basketball leagues and South Asian American basketball spaces to make sense of the racialized, gendered, and sexualized climate of these sporting spaces. Yet my religious and ethnic identity was a point of difference from many of the other South Asian Americans I encountered. I did not experience the frequent, explicit, subtle, and ongoing state surveillance that most of the young Pakistani Americans have encountered in U.S. society.[58]

I conducted an "experiential ethnography" (De Garis 1999, 2000; Sands 2002; and Wacquant 2006) in which I implicated my own body in the regulatory schema of "manning up" on the basketball court. I participated as a key member of the Atlanta Outkasts and Atlanta Rat Pack teams. Training with the teams, working out at gyms with them, and competing on the court allowed me to make sense of the value they put on bodies, bodily abilities, and particular basketball movements. An experiential ethnography of this sort made possible an understanding of how certain pains, pleasures, and desires were mapped onto bodily actions. I witnessed what actions counted as exceptional and how players got into "the zone." Finally, I channeled my own competitiveness to help teams and chart how I had to act, think, and play on the court. Thus, there were moments in which I could not be a researcher on the court as I had to stay attuned to the intricacies of the game in order to help my team succeed.

In the process of playing on these teams and in these leagues, I was also introduced to many people affiliated with South Asian American sporting cultures through the "snowball" sampling method. Players invited me to share in other aspects of their daily lives, such as dinners, religious events, weddings, and other forms of leisure. The majority of ethnographic data drawn upon in this book comes from the everyday experiences of South Asian American basketball cultures in Atlanta, even though descriptions of Chicago IPN in 2006 and 2008 stand out as touchstone moments. Atlanta is a key, large-scale destination city in the U.S. South. Metro Atlanta is the largest city in the U.S. state of Georgia and is the capital city. Atlanta's growing financial sector and large service industry make it a favorable city for low-wage and high-wage employment.[59] Metro Atlanta is composed of many counties. The historian Kevin Kruse, in *White Flight*, details how the original parameters of metro Atlanta in 1950 were Fulton, DeKalb, Gwinnett, Cobb, and Clayton Counties.[60] Other counties were incorporated in 1980 and 1990, including Barrow, Bartow, Butts, Cherokee, Coweta, Douglas, Fayette, Forsyth, Henry, Newton, Paulding, Pickens, Rockdale, Spalding, and Walton Counties. Although you can find small pockets of South Asians in numerous counties in Georgia, the largest communities reside in Gwinnett, DeKalb, Fulton, Cobb, and Clayton Counties. Atlanta, with Gwinnett County in particular, has one of the larger and faster-growing South Asian communities in the United States. According to the 2010 census, 86,042 Asian Indians live in Metro Atlanta.[61] The same census form declares that there are also 9,685 Pakistanis, 3,741 Bangladeshis, 618 Sri Lankans, 1,693 Bhutanese, and 1,739 Nepalese.[62]

Mustafa, his post-1980 peers, and their families live in Gwinnett County, while the more affluent desi communities live in DeKalb and Fulton Counties. The young men in my study moved across Atlanta to manage work, family, and leisure. Places of employment are spread across Atlanta in some instances and concentrated in other cases. The high-profile financial firms like Sun Trust and Wachovia and corporations like Coca-Cola are located in downtown Atlanta and hire many of the post-1965 athletes who are professionals in the field of finance. The South Asian American finance professionals with families live in the affluent suburbs in DeKalb County, Fulton County, or Cobb Country while the hipsters live in recently gentrified areas in Midtown Atlanta or East Atlanta. In contrast, the service industries are located on the outskirts of the city proper. The lower-middle-class and working-class South Asian communities live in Gwinnett County. Not only does this population consist of gas-station and convenience-store workers, it also includes those laboring at various hotels and motels[63] and those managing kiosks at all of the Metro Atlanta shopping malls. I traversed across many social sites, and this is thus a multisited ethnography as performances of masculinity take place across many realms.[64]

Players perform a plethora of practices as "manly" or as "what a man does." In the course of their everyday lives, in and out of basketball, I noticed that they do not routinely use the terms "masculinity" or "gender." Instead, players use terms such as "man," "husband," "father," "playa," and "toughness," to substitute for the term masculinity. Desi men often use the term "man up" on the court to distinguish certain acts as less manly, more feminine than others. Players blurted this exhortation out on several occasions on and off the court. Using it to gauge, mark, and evaluate acts on and off the basketball court, desi basketball players articulate specific boundaries of acceptable, negotiable, and unacceptable gender practices. But, as we will see, the deeds on the court never gain substance or meaning in isolation.

Book Structure

Desi men engage with masculinity as they consume, appropriate, and perform popular cultural and racialized representations on the basketball court and relevant leisure spaces. The United States's multibillion-dollar sporting culture stretches into many aspects of their social life, from recreational activities to amateur ranks to professional sports. Yet sport has not been adequately studied in South Asian America. All the young men I met during the course of my fieldwork had to take up sport whether or not they liked it. As physical education classes in elementary, middle, and high school are mandatory (unless one has a medically documented disability), players admit to the street cred and "symbolic capital" (Bourdieu 1984) of being an athlete on high school, collegiate, and professional teams. Mustafa's younger brother, Ali (in his late twenties) relates that he "got lots of respect and girls wanted to talk to me" when he played varsity basketball in high school. For the young men in this book, sport is part of their socialization into American-ness that is already gendered, raced, and sexualized. This book is one of the first anthropological investigations of sport in South Asian America, as well as one of the few ethnographic texts critically interrogating masculinity formation in South Asian America.

This volume takes the reader on the less-traveled analytical paths of South Asian American masculinity and racialization while staying attuned to how ethnicity, class, and sexuality inflect these gendered practices. In these exclusive male-on-male social spaces, the peer group sets the stage for South Asian American identity. What do these expressions of masculinity look like? How are they related to mainstream racializations? And what do these iterations of masculinity tell us about identity formation? As gender proves critical to these processes of racialization, players utilize the category of masculinity and its respective practices to reinsert themselves into both American-ness and normative masculinity.

Instead of conceptualizing identity formation as a clean, linear progression, this book shows that identity formation—masculinity making—is always messy, uneven, and structured through contradictions. The main contradiction that becomes evident throughout this book concerns how players expand their conceptualization of South Asian American identity even as their expansion comes with exclusions. Although sport has long been ideologically consolidated as neutral, it never exists in a vacuum. Sport embodies greater social issues and contains its own brand of politics. Similarly, brown-out basketball is often constructed as heterosexual, middle-class, and racially closed to mostly African American men. Accordingly, certain persons generally considered "inside" South Asian America, such as desi women and desi queers, are then cast out as "outside" of South Asian American masculinity.[65] Therefore, various symbolic binaries, and their respective exclusions, have to be affirmed in order to give substance to desi masculinity.

Subversive acts like creating co-ethnic-only leagues challenge notions of American citizenship and expand the meanings of South Asian American-ness. While players fight the stigma given them in U.S. society, they also, intentionally and unintentionally, stigmatize and exclude various other groups. Therefore another set of important questions also governs this book: How do practices of masculinity in basketball realms produce marginalizations and exclusions? And how can we understand these exclusions at the crossroads of masculinity, race, sexuality, class, and ethnicity? The chapters in this book are set up to elaborate not only upon the productions of South Asian American–ness at Chicago IPN and in Atlanta's desi basketball scene but also on how gender saturates everyday racialized encounters in U.S. society. Reconfiguring racialized masculinities and performing cultural citizenship for the desi men require the implementing of exclusion.

In order to capture the complexity of the South Asian American engagement with popular culture, basketball, and other forms of leisure, the chapters are ordered to resemble the typical routine of players. When players congregate on the court, their homosocial bonding carries over to other realms such as the local dance-club, bar, and strip-club scene. Through delving into these various social sites chapter by chapter, the book structure reflects the social lives of many basketball players and how they navigate gendered racializations across the cityscapes. For these young men, their initial foray into basketball took place in the loosely organized recreational games known as "pickup" basketball. This is where the book begins.

Pickup basketball, with its structure, space, and temporal organization, contrasts with organized, standardized tournament basketball such as that prevalent at the Chicago Indo-Pak National Tournament or in the Asian Ballers League. Chapter 1 asks how young desi men negotiate masculinity between the social realms of work, family, and leisure. Recreational basketball stands as a counterpoint to other aspects of work and family life by giving some players the training for high-level basketball while opening up pleasure-laden opportunities to socialize with co-ethnic men. At the same time, recreational basketball players accentuate an identity in opposition to other men, most particularly the African American residents of the neighborhood where the players rent out the public gym.

Chapter 2 asks how masculinity is managed when we move away from the individual-centered activities of pickup basketball to the more formalized and standardized forms of Indo-Pak Basketball. Although players claim sameness around the rubric of "Indo-Pak," the competition between teams fleshes out ethnic differences in conceptualizing gender. In this setting, there is the interplay of sameness—the act of browning out, by claiming a South Asian American–ness or desi-ness, and by making the physical gym a symbolically South Asian American place. Teams and players adjudicate their own versions of masculinity through team names and through high levels of competition that position them in relation to other categories such as Sikh masculinity, Hindu masculinity, Muslim masculinity, Gujarati masculinity, and Malayalee masculinity. Within Indo-Pak Basketball there exists a set of exclusions. Several of the tournaments dictate that only players of "Indian descent" can play. I frequently noticed that African American men are constituted as "outside" of South Asian America even though players appropriate cultural tropes of black masculinity as a way to shed effeminate identities.

Chapter 3 looks to answer the following questions about South Asian American participation in the Asian Ballers League and other Atlanta ethnic leagues: How are Asian American–ness and South Asian American–ness understood and negotiated? How is racial brownness managed in the presence of Asian Americans and Latinos? How is racial passing in ethnic leagues also a site of gendered identification as a certain type of man? South Asian Americans are constantly racialized, but that does not mean that they are easily read racially or immediately legible within the black-white racial logic. In the Asian Ballers League, South Asian American men resist narrow conceptions of Asian America but also share in sameness as "Asian Americans" based on histories of emasculation and non-normative subjectivity in the United States.[66] The young men use this kind of illegibility and ambiguity to maneuver through different ethnic leagues, but not all racialized men have that kind of mobility.

Acts of making desi masculinity in relation to other racialized masculinities do not solely transpire in sporting venues. Through the course of this research, I noted basketball players frequenting other leisure spaces with their fellow athletes/comrades. Cultural identities, as a result, are not static, fixed, or located in one physical territory but, rather, performed through various spaces.[67] Chapter 4 traces the movement of players from basketball spaces to local heterosexual nightlife, following Atlanta's South Asian American players to parties and clubs. The tropes of toughness and aggressiveness on the basketball court translate into alternate notions of toughness and aggression in the dance-party scene. Aggressively seeking out women, partaking in physical fights, and pursuing sexual intercourse with women constitute key traits of a man with swagger.

Chapter 5 takes a closer theoretical look at the subjects whose voices are elided in basketball and in the club scene. When homosocial interactions govern leisure spaces, heterosexuality is then inflected into this space in relation to gay men and women. Players cannot simply manufacture distance from homosexuality without in some ways engaging with it. This chapter examines how players engage in same-sex desires and play up gay subjectivity in ironic ways. Players give substance to homosexuality in relation to femininity only to disavow both. Yet the force of abjection does not leave queer subjects and women as hopeless victims. Instead of essentializing them as powerless dupes, this chapter demonstrates the means that women and queer subjects employ to express their own sets of agency within the arena of heterosexual sporting masculinity.

The concluding chapter examines how South Asian American basketball players, especially in Indo-Pak Basketball circuits, articulate visions of a future in which their bodies are read as normative both in South Asian America and in larger U.S. society. Using their social and financial capital to create exclusive basketball venues as the most pleasurable and safest way to offer their own renditions of American-ness does not open up these practices for recognition in larger society. Dismantling the current systems of racialization does not, as we will see, guarantee liberation.

1

Everyday Play

The Formation of Desi Pickup Basketball

Kumrain, a fellow student at Emory University, invited me to play with his South Asian Muslim peers, Mustafa and Qamar, in 1994. Kumrain arrived at my home in Decatur (DeKalb County), and we drove about forty minutes northwest of Atlanta to get to Mustafa's parents' home in Gwinnett County. Gwinnett County, in the Atlanta imaginary, was discursively understood as white and thus hostile to communities of color. Once at Mustafa's house, I noticed him, his older brother Qamar, his younger brother Ali, and their friends Salim and Malik in the drive way shooting on a dilapidated basketball goal. With each shot the goal shook with sad abandon.

As I joined them to play, I found that I had underestimated the skill level of the other desi players, including Mustafa. I was asked to guard Mustafa, and I remember chuckling a bit as I assumed it an easy task. However, to my surprise, he repeatedly found ways to score on me. His left-handed shot initially caught me by surprise. Soon, his quick and smooth release made it difficult for me to time my jump to block his shot. My own stereotypes of and experiences with several South Asian American men at Emory University had clouded my judgment. Little Sheik, another Emory University student, soon joined us and brought two of his peers. With the first dribble and shot from Little Sheik's crew, it was clear that they lacked basketball skills that would provide any competition. They also did not have the physical aptitude to compete as Little Sheik was literally little and short and his two friends did not have any appreciable athletic capacity. These three men did embody my stereotypical perceptions of most South Asian Americans.

As Mustafa continued to score, I thought I would be able to use my offensive skills to keep up. However, he could also play defense. He stole the ball from me several times and blocked my shots. Such competitive play against Mustafa and Ali only amplified my desire to win. Each successful maneuver on offense or defense was a source of joy for me. This basketball court was immediately transformed into a site of pleasure since Mustafa, Ali, Malik, and Kumrain could all play basketball well. Mustafa's impressive basketball acumen and a commendable set of physical qualities enticed me to play harder. Seeing talent that not only equaled but exceeded my own, I was excited about playing basketball with these young South Asian American men. Since Little Sheik and his friends could not provide any formidable basketball adroitness, they would not ultimately be integrated into this basketball community. I was invited to play basketball numerous times at Mustafa's house, at local gyms, and in organized basketball such as Indo-Pak Basketball tournaments.

South Asian American men do not encounter basketball and form intimate ties to sport and citizenship merely through spectatorship. In the above vignette, Kumrain and his Muslim South Asian American peers, including myself, experience basketball at a quotidian level. It is an everyday engagement with sport as a meaningful representation of self. Since the time and organization needed to play regularly in Indo-Pak Basketball tournaments such as Chicago IPN are far too demanding for young men who have other commitments to work, family, or college, they most often encounter basketball through recreational "pickup" games. My initial foray into this community of young Muslim desis took place through such a pickup game at Mustafa's house. Although pickup basketball might seem loosely organized and whimsical, it is a ritualistic practice with its own sort of protocol. Based on where one plays, rules, time limits, structures, and organizations of the teams vary. Even the pickup games at Mustafa's home are strategically organized, utilizing a social network, and serve to form a South Asian American community in relation to other social formations. Like the complex social milieu evident in the Balinese cockfights illustrated by seminal anthropologist Clifford Geertz, in *The Interpretation of Cultures* (1973), these desi sporting venues provide important information about the organization of communities and production of communal notions of self.

Although there are a variety of reasons for playing pickup basketball, these young men and I play it for two main reasons: Some of us come to develop our skills as we train for tournaments, and some come to take pleasure in socializing with co-ethnic peers through basketball activities. However, there are other, perhaps unintended, outcomes of this leisurely activity. Regular recreational play allows young South Asian American men to develop a community that both enforces and challenges norms of masculinity, class, race, and citizenship. On the pickup basketball scene, players strengthen and maintain their social bonds over time. As we will see, their expressions of manliness on the basketball court and subsequent constructions of a fraternity are always informed by their personal histories, their communal histories, their consumptive practices, their racialized experiences of marginalization in other sporting circles, and their conceptualizations of masculinity. In the process, the athletes produce their own acceptable cultural arrangements of South Asian American masculinity.

Pickup basketball provides a different structure of play, social interaction, and athletic possibility than organized tournament basketball, such as Chicago IPN, or other pickup venues at multiracial basketball courts. At the same time, like organized basketball, it facilitates the affirmation of meaningful social bonds with co-ethnic and co-religious men. The very nature of its flexibility and fluidity allow men of various skill and ability levels to access sport in pedestrian, but intimate, ways. Pickup basketball is one way to ensure a daily encounter with the sport and respective sporting cultures. With that said, not all people have the material resources to perform masculinity through sporting channels. Even pickup arenas are political sites where not everyone is guaranteed entry and membership. Little Sheik and his peers are no longer part of this sporting community. While young men like Mustafa and Malik might celebrate the boundaries of this sporting desi community, they simultaneously police and regulate the space, displacing some persons. Forms of ethnic and minority nationalism and diasporic social formations can contain politics of inclusion and exclusion.[1] Even in sites with a majority of South Asian American participants, these pickup venues are structured in ways that can marginalize certain working-class South Asian American communities and other communities of color. Each type of play comes along with a set of boundaries, expectations, and limits on who can and cannot play. It is a formation of a community in which some co-ethnic bonds as Muslims and as South Asian Americans are strengthened simultaneously with the joys of sport. The sporting expressions of South Asian American masculinity expand the possibilities of a desi identity while delimiting the entrance of various Others. Players create some of these South Asian American pickup basketball venues, intentionally and unintentionally, as ethnically, racially, and gender-based exclusive sites in order to reinforce their social connections and express their identities.

Mustafa, Ali, and some of their peers, who played back in 1994, continue to play pickup basketball today, but in a variety of pickup basketball arenas. Whereas mostly Muslim men congregated at Mustafa's house to form the Atlanta Outkasts, Atlanta's South Asian American pickup circuit is heterogeneous, with players coming from many ethnic, religious, and class backgrounds. Players from various socioeconomic backgrounds place significant importance on playing pickup ball with their co-ethnic peers and set aside time weekly to play. This participation is part of their daily performance of self in conversation with the other social spaces they inhabit during the course of their week. In fact, players often posit sport as an alternate to the everyday grind of life. It represents an important place where they perform practices of masculinity that are not easily realized in other realms of their lives, such as in their community, in their homes, or in their places of work.

To examine how pickup basketball is taken up by young Muslim Pakistani South Asian Americans like Mustafa, Ali, Kumrain, and Malik, we must investigate the history of their engagement with basketball. Their life histories make evident a long-standing involvement with basketball that originally began at their mosque, Al-Farooq Masjid. With their sporting histories tied to the Masjid, they were able to conflate American-ness, Muslim-ness, and masculinity. Once we gain an understanding of this interesting history of religion, citizenship, and gender, we will have a basis for exploring the specifics of identification and social formations as they took shape within the Atlanta Outkasts. While the team contains its own particular social identity, the larger religiously and ethnically heterogeneous South Asian American pickup basketball circuit also provides important information on race and class identities. The racializations of desi men, as nerdy and foreign, put limits on the entry and pleasures these young men were able to garner in other multiracial pickup circuits. Paradoxically, they manufactured and policed their own ethnically exclusive pickup circuit in order to celebrate their athletic feats and merit. Even such loosely organized pickup basketball in multiracial formats, as we will see, never operates solely by merit.

Playing Recreational Ball at the Mosque: Religious Identities and Masculinity

Most of the South Asian Americans I have met in the local Atlanta basketball scene and those in the larger North American Indo-Pak Basketball circuit share with me the intimate connections between their respective religious institutions, their religious identities, and sporting masculinity. For example, Max, a key figure in the North American Indo-Pak Basketball community and founder of Chicago IPN, developed an affinity for basketball through Malayalee associations in and out of Chicago.[2] Similarly, several players in Atlanta formed close male bonds through sporting interactions at their churches, mosques, mandirs (Hindu temples), and gurdwaras (Sikh places of worship). Most of the young men playing pickup basketball at Mustafa's home that day in 1994, other than me, initially played basketball together at Al-Farooq Masjid, the first international, mainstream Muslim mosque in Atlanta. Contrary to common perceptions about the incompatibility between Islam and American-ness, the mosque instituted various activities, such as basketball, seeing them as key ways to spiritually train Muslim American subjects. However, the problematic perceptions of Muslim Americans as outsiders and "terrorists" have continued to haunt Muslim communities in Atlanta, as well as in larger U.S. society and other Western nations.[3] There have been many examples of Islamophobia. For example, nativist opposition surfaced in 2009 with regard to proposed construction of a cemetery to accompany the Dar-e-Abbas Mosque in Lilburn, Georgia.[4] The responses that appeared in the *Gwinnett Daily Post* newspaper and on the "CBS News" revealed a predominantly racist, exclusionary reaction to the proposed plans:

This is about hurting our community, this is about hurting our kids.

I just don't like Muslims and I don't want them taking over our neighborhood.

> This is not what Lilburn needs. This is a Christian community, and they are anti-Christian.[5]

The use of "our" with a clear connection to Christianity (and whiteness) marked Muslims as bodies out of place both locally and nationally. Racial discourses of this sort combine nation, citizenship, and religion to project categories of "us" and "them."[6] Mosques (masjids), on the contrary, are not places of irreconcilable difference with American-ness and American masculinities. Rather, the experiences of pickup ball at Al-Farooq Masjid reveal the synergy between these supposed opposing cultural poles.[7] Masjids are sites where South Asian American young men can make the association between masculinity and American citizenship. At Al-Farooq Masjid, members of the Atlanta Outkasts, Atlanta Rat Pack, Camel Jockeys, Atlanta Franchise, and Sand Brothaz teams congregated to bond and play ball over the years. There, basketball, American-ness, masculinity, and Muslim-ness exist on the same plane.

Malik, whom we met in the opening vignette, provides an interesting insight into this connection: "When they [Muslim elders] were building the masjid, my father and other uncles [a term of respect for South Asian elders] wanted to include a basketball court to help their kids find ways to assimilate into U.S. society. They did not want us [their children] to struggle like they did." Muslim elders recognized that U.S. society does not guarantee entrée to all immigrants, even those deemed the "model minority," and they wanted to create spaces where the American-ness of their children would never be in doubt. Those perceived to be the "model minority," who arrived as part of the post-1965 immigration act, did not want their children to endure racist exclusions as they had. The basketball court was seen as one way to enculturate young Muslim men into that American-ness that has evaded the older generation. With this goal in mind, I asked Dr. Said, a key figure in Atlanta's international Muslim community, about the basketball hoop on the grounds of Al-Farooq Masjid. He thought deeply, paused for a few seconds, smiled, and replied, "We noticed the youth playing on the court at Homepark [a learning center adjacent to the mosque] during breaks from their spiritual training." Muslim elders, in their efforts to facilitate Quranic scripture, recognized the need to engage with bodily and leisurely activities. As "muscular Christianity" proved to be critical to the Christian ethos of U.S. society and its imperialistic reach (España-Maram 2006), a muscular Islam provided an entrée into American-ness and consolidated masculinist ideals of diasporic subjectivity alongside Muslim identities. Sultan (Dr. Said's son and a close friend of Mustafa and Ali) reported that, in between Islamic camp sessions, "Me and Ali would hoop during the break . . . that is all we did. We did not want to go back [to the masjid for spiritual training]."

Elders saw merit in basketball as training for Muslim-ness and American-ness. Dr. Said alluded to the many reasons for installing the basketball goal: "We put basketball goals at the masjid because one, it was inexpensive, two, all the youth are attracted, three, you don't need many people, and four, it's not dangerous but still *manly*.[8]" By legitimating basketball as masculine, his reasoning paralleled the foundational reasons given by Dr. James Naismith, who invented basketball in 1891 to facilitate a national muscular masculinity without the out-of-bounds "toughness" he thought inherent in American football.[9] Naismith instituted a game structure and flow that accentuates muscularity within the confines of a middle-class aesthetic, positioning a respectable man in opposition to the football-playing barbarian. The middle-class aesthetic contains religious contours, via muscular Christianity, that have also played out at Al-Farooq Masjid. The institution of a basketball court on the mosque premises is part of the sporting cultures in Atlanta, where large Christian churches in Atlanta have their own private basketball gymnasiums. Furthermore, Dr. Said talked about the interrelation between Islam and American basketball by emphasizing the key role Muslim National Basketball Association players—such as Hakeem Olajuwon, Atlanta's own Sharif Abdul-Rahim, and Mahmoud Abdul-Rauf—have as "indirect role models" for the heterogeneous Muslim youth at Al-Farooq Masjid. Given their examples, basketball (American-ness) is within the repertoire of legitimated Muslim-ness, and vice versa.

The original small outdoor court at Al-Farooq Masjid suited Atlanta's minute South Asian Muslim community in the 1980s. Most lived nearby the masjid in DeKalb and Fulton Counties and were inside the perimeter of intracity Highway 285 (see Figure 1.1). Dr. Said firmly stated that most international Muslims did not live "OTP" (a term for "outside the perimeter" demarcated by Highway 285 that held within it the city "too busy to hate"; see Kruse 2007: 41). The early Muslims were

Figure 1.1. Metro Atlanta Counties with Atlanta inside Highway 285. Courtesy of the Atlanta Regional Commission.

the post-1965 professionals who worked at various Atlanta hospitals or were scientists linked to the Georgia Institute of Technology and Emory University. Their communities lived close to their places of work and in mostly white residential neighborhoods. When Mustafa's family arrived in the early 1990s, however, they were part of a wave of South Asians who could not afford to live inside the perimeter. Mustafa's family, when I met them for the first time in 1994, lived in Grayson, a city in Gwinnett County and past the city of Stone Mountain (once the home of the Ku Klux Klan). He, Ali, and Qamar would drive south on Highway 78 or Interstate 85 to meet up with peers at the mosque. There were not many mosques at that point. However, as a result of the restructuring of financial landscapes in Atlanta in preparation for the 1996 Atlanta Olympic Games and the increased visibility of Atlanta on the global stage, both the South Asian American and Muslim community grew.[10]

The instrumental role in acquiring the 1996 Summer Olympics brought international visibility to Atlanta, and it quickly became a new destination city for South Asian immigrants and South Asian Americans.[11] In fact, the U.S. South contains a growing South Asian diasporic community. A close examination of the 2001 Census data reveals that "26.2% of South Asians in the U.S. live in the South" (Joshi 2006: 2).[12] South Asian Americans in Atlanta have outpaced other populations of

Asian descent.[13] Mohammed of the Atlanta Rat Pack (and formerly of the Camel Jockeys) notes this trend, "It was hard to see desis before. Now, I drive to Gwinnett County and see them walking across the street at a stoplight."

With the growth of the Muslim community due to increasing waves of South Asians moving to Atlanta, Al-Farooq Masjid underwent reno- vation in 1995. This renovation took place alongside the major prep- arations in Atlanta for the 1996 Summer Olympics. The renovation included an expanded, full outdoor basketball court painted in a for- est green to fit Muslim aesthetics. Additionally, with the dispersal of Muslim communities both inside and outside perimeter highway 285, local neighborhood mosques took shape across Fulton, DeKalb, Cobb, Gwinnett, and Clayton Counties. Even Al-Farooq Masjid has a neigh- borhood mosque, Omar Masjid, which boasts a fully furnished indoor basketball court. These courts are primarily used by young Muslim men. Assimilating to American-ness has not been facilitated equivalently for men and women. Mosque elders spatialize gender by specifying certain activities, like basketball, as suitable for boys in their transition to man- hood. Therefore, South Asian American femininity in general and Mus- lim femininity in particular has to be constructed outside of the realm of basketball in order to validate basketball as masculine.

Restricted Play

Owing to the symbolic conceptualization of basketball as an activity for men, South Asian American women have been dissuaded from these pickup circuits. Young men, like Mustafa, Ali, and Sultan, are given a "patriarchal dividend" (Connell 1995) whereby they enter the desi court without any objection. When asked about his interactions with young women at the masjid, Sultan responded frankly, "They [women] weren't there on the court. Girls played in the playground or hung out together in the hallway. They never played sports." By invoking the playground and hallway, liminal spaces within the larger sporting environ, Sultan made the distinction between the symbolic categories of masculine and feminine concrete by solidifying which bodies could legitimately claim core sporting spaces. He evoked a difference between "sports" and "games," validating basketball as a sport and therefore out of reach for girls,[14] who play games. Games are not seen as having elements of toughness, aggression, and competitiveness as do sports; women are perceived as lacking the physical traits and corresponding abilities to play sport. Discourses of this sort take for granted the notion that there are clear binaries of sex and respective performances of gender instead of complicating the "dueling dualisms" (Fausto-Sterling 2000) that blanket the wide biological diversity and respective classifications between sex and gender.[15]

Although Sultan interacts with Muslim sisters at the masjids, the basketball court continues to remain a place for men by men. When he is not playing pickup ball in gender-segregated courts, he plays with his younger brother Imran and Imran's Muslim South Asian American friends and college mates at their parents' house. After Friday jummah (prayer), the young men gather at 5 p.m. to play into the night on the immaculate outdoor half court at Sultan's parents' home. They get a chance to talk about the week's activities and catch up on their social lives while playing basketball and videogames.

Pickup basketball, as a sporting practice, has become the way for young men to socialize into many versions of Muslim American–ness in a symbolically constructed masculine space. During the period of my research from 2006 to 2009, various Muslim basketball tournaments either took place at the masjids or were hosted by them. Basketball, Islam, and masculinity intersected for the young men but existed on parallel planes for women. Men could play and women could only watch. The South Asian American practices of gender segregation in Atlanta limits the presence of women at Muslim tournaments. However, these practices cannot be generalized to all Muslims as Muslims of other racial, class, and national backgrounds practice religious identities with their own gender sensibilities.[16]

As Al-Farooq Masjid is a Sunni mosque, their practices of gender segregation are more rigid than those of most Shiite mosques and also more rigid than predominantly African American mosques (see Karim 2009). Muslim women do play basketball, but in gender-segregated spaces and rather infrequently. There is not the same attachment to basketball by Muslim South Asian American women, nor do the elders see this an important activity for them. Other South Asian diasporic populations, like Samaya Farooq Samie's (2013) Muslim South Asian Brits, use basketball to affirm heterosexual femininity. Additionally, various women's basketball leagues exist in India. In the United States, however, active leagues for South Asian American women do not exist in the same manner; in the United States there is a strong discursive substantiation of basketball as masculine. As a result, the terms "queer" and "butch" get mapped onto women's bodies when they play basketball. This is a strong disincentive for already marginalized populations, such as South Asian American women, to play a sport that will only further alienate them in U.S. society. South Asian American men, on the other hand, utilize pickup basketball as a site to legitimate their bodies as male with the exclusion of female athletes, and their actions on the court are more readily read as masculine in the presence of other men.

Outkasts! Representing Possibilities and Racialized Experiences

Through participation in male-dominated pickup ball and subsequent tournament play, Mustafa's community of ball players formed the team Atlanta Outkasts. The formation of teams is voluntary. This type of voluntary organization highlights the pleasures of co-ethnic socialization while providing a social critique of racialized structures in U.S. society.

> Once we had sweated through our T-shirts after two hours of playing basketball at Mustafa's house, Mustafa's mother, Asma auntie [the use of "auntie," like "uncle," is a sign of respect in South Asian communities and not of filial relations], invited us into their dark, air conditioned family room. Basketball trophy after trophy adorned the walls and corners of the room. Asma auntie brought us fruit-flavored drinks as we discussed potential team names for our cohort of young desi men. Various names were tossed around. Everyone emphasized that the names had to sound "tough" and "cool." Mustafa suggested "Outkasts" but I heard it as "outcasts." As I am a Christian Tamil American and the other men are Muslim Pakistani Americans, both our communities were the quintessential "outcasts" in the Hindu Indian imagination. Thus, the team name outcasts resonated with me. It was then that Mustafa and Qamar informed me that "OutKast," with a capital "K," was the name of an emerging hip-hop group in Atlanta. These young men were actively engaged in Atlanta's hip-hop culture; it was part of their identity, but not necessarily mine. Everyone found the name exciting, tough, and cool.

> We decided on "Atlanta Outkasts" as the team name. We played as team Atlanta Outkasts for the first time a few weeks later at the Greenville Indo-Pak Tournament in South Carolina.

The choice of "Outkasts" as a team name located this group of young men in a diverse representational field that encompasses their complex engagements with both U.S. popular culture and their ethno-religious identity while offering their renditions of (dis)location within the racially stratified realm of U.S. citizenship. By contrast, the literature on South Asian America overemphasizes the influence of South Asian popular cultural forms such as Bollywood, bhangra, and cricket in identity formation.[17] In suggesting the team name Atlanta Outkasts, Mustafa demonstrated a simultaneous affinity with hip-hop and basketball. Indeed, hip hop bass tones frequently resonate at Mustafa's house, during car drives to tournaments, and at tournament games. These young men knew of the hip-hop group OutKast long before the group's mainstream appeal in the late 1990s. Like the South Asian Americans in anthropologist Nitasha Sharma's (2010) book, *Hip Hop Desis*, they have a long-standing affiliation and identification with hip-hop. However, unlike Sharma's subjects, their consumption of hip-hop did not fully translate into embodying all of the political possibilities in black cultural forms. Mustafa's and Qamar's identification with hip hop is partly an expression of their own marginality in larger U.S. society, but it is also an act of claiming their American-ness through black cultural forms.[18]

The affinity to hip-hop is part of the claiming of an urban cool that translates into a "basketball cool." Such acts of appropriation of cultural blackness and its concomitant masculinity invert racialized stereotypes of South Asian Americans as nerds and effeminate.[19] The young South Asian American men, through their bodily comportment, linguistic choices, and ways of identification, counter the markers of assimilation that demand white cultural forms as evidence of successful assimilation. Although the common perception is that consuming white aesthetics provides a pathway to American-ness, black cultural forms are prevalent throughout U.S. society. As hip-hop is seen as a quintessentially American musical form and genre (Dyson 1993; Rose 1994), it offers claims to citizenship for ethnic subjects whose racialized bodies limit the possibilities of claiming whiteness as American-ness.

Mustafa and Qamar positioned their identity as "cool" and "urban" men in relation to black stylistics *without* claiming to be African American. Claiming corporeal and political blackness would relegate these men to a different racialized masculinity that they did not want to occupy. Instead, they embody black stylistics. By doing so, they could still lay claim to normativity without the fear of being racially represented as dangerous, thuggish, uncontrollable subjects, common stereotypes of black men.[20] As we will see in the pickup basketball venues, performing South Asian American masculinity entails a rejection of and distance from black masculinity.

Their choice of team names inserts Mustafa, Ali, Malik, and their peers into an urban, cool lexicon that is compatible with basketball identities; beyond this, the term "Outkasts" has additional meanings for this group. Because Mustafa's and his friends' families are composed of post-1980 immigrants, the choice of "Outkasts" references a particular class position. Mustafa, Qamar, Ali, and their peers intentionally and unintentionally contest the singular association of South Asian America identity with the "model minority" status. The "model minority" moniker is a complex racial formation that stems from U.S. racial hierarchies and geopolitical exigencies of the racialized U.S. state.[21] It is a product of racial workings in the United States and tends to flatten the lived diversity of South Asian America. Identifications with underground hip-hop work against the image of the clean, passive, and respectable model minority subject who is projected as consuming only South Asian cultural forms. Consuming aspects of cultural blackness interjects toughness to the effeminized body of the "model minority." Young South Asian Americans turn to a wide repository of U.S. popular cultural forms, including hip-hop, to mold notions of themselves that challenge the not-so-cool and "forever foreign" (Lowe 1996) meanings associated with "model minority" moniker.

Mustafa's family members experienced life in the United States differently from their peers in the post-1965 wave of professional immigrants. When Amin uncle got a job in Houston in the early 1980s during unstable economic times, Mustafa and Qamar played pickup basketball with and against Latinos and African Americans in a multiethnic working-class neighborhood. Mustafa expressed his surprise about the residential space: "I didn't know what the ghetto was till we moved to Houston.

Man, we were in the ghetto." This was Mustafa's first encounter with basketball and it shaped his subsequent interactions with men. There was a sense of camaraderie and pleasure in male bonding on the court with other working-class and lower-middle-class communities of color. That love of basketball is evident in his transient family history.

To survive in a tumultuous economy, Amin uncle took jobs in various parts of the United States. Each job took the family to the remnants of a struggling economy: They moved to industrial towns, the symbolic vestige of post-Fordist shifts away from industrial centers, in places like Detroit, to small non-unionized towns around the country.[22] The family moved many times, from Canada to Memphis, Tennessee; to Houston, Texas; to LaGrange, Georgia; to Grayson/Lawrenceville/Stone Mountain, Georgia; to Dalton, Georgia; and back to Lawrenceville, Georgia. Each move was to an area outside the city of Atlanta but in nearby counties with new industrial bases. LaGrange is 80 miles southwest of Atlanta in Troup County, while Dalton is 70 miles northwest of Atlanta in Whitfield County. Both Lawrenceville and Grayson are to the northeast corner of Atlanta in Gwinnett County. The majority of the moves put the family in working-class and lower-middle-class communities, often working-class white communities in Georgia. Only the final move to Lawrenceville gave Ali a chance to attend a prestigious majority-white public school in Gwinnett County. Ali exclaims that, in each new town, "the first thing we did was put a hoop up." During such uncertain times, putting up a hoop to play basketball gave these young men a stabilized point around which to socialize. Staking that basketball post into the ground and attaching the basketball backboard and net normalized their lives during turbulent times. The social interactions around the basketball hoop helped to create a sense of community. Each basketball encounter reifies the shared experiences of life for a cohort of young Pakistani American men that stands in opposition to other South Asian American men.

The children of the post-1980 wave of immigrants, like Mustafa and his siblings, did not generally have the same access to education, professional status, and social mobility as their post-1965 peers.[23] Mustafa and Qamar attended working-poor white public schools, while Ali was lucky enough to attend an elite public school during the final move back to Lawrenceville, Gwinnett County. Although various children from the post-1965 waves would play on the Atlanta Outkasts, including Malik, Kumrain, and Sultan, the main members and key figures are mostly children of the post-1980 immigration waves. Mustafa is the captain; Ali and he are the primary figures on the team.

Playing pickup basketball with and against their post-1965 peers presented opportunities for men like Mustafa and Ali to invert the disproportional symbolic status given to the model minority subject. Through their level of basketball play, Mustafa and his peers empower themselves and "man up"; they dominated other men with their aggressiveness, toughness, and basketball skill sets. After one Monday night pickup game in 2009, Daniel, a Malayalee American professional whose mother, a nurse, came in the post-1965 wave,[24] acknowledged his idolization of Ali. He told me, "I didn't think Indians [Ali is Pakistani American] could play like that. Ali can play."

Ali, however, is not immediately respected in multiracial basketball circuits unless the other participants have already seen him play. He and his teammates have endured stereotypes as "not-athletic enough" by both white and African American ball players in other basketball arenas. Sultan explained the experiences of marginalization: "You [South Asian Americans] are not seen as American, not American enough to play basketball. We are seen as *scrubs*."[25] In basketball, "scrub" is a vernacular identification of a person seen as inferior athletically and less-capable masculine subject. When non–South Asian American players marginalize desis in basketball venues, creating exclusive pickup spaces provides one way for them to avoid feeling like outcasts.

African American and white internalization of stereotypical images of South Asian Americans can be traced to common representations of South Asian athletes in the U.S. media. South Asian men surface in only a few instances in U.S. sports coverage. In one instance, ESPN showcased Indian American men celebrating in California after India won the Cricket World Cup in 2010. Yet this feature only served to dislocate South Asian Americans from the American imaginary and solidify their position as South Asian (Indian in this case). Other elements of sports coverage have also emphasized cricket, with a brief mention of the Indian cricketer Sachin Tendulkar getting his 100th century in 2012 and the coverage of two Indian cricket players trying out for the Pittsburgh Pirates in Major League Baseball.

Media coverage of cricket does not dispel the perception of South Asian Americans as "perpetual foreigners"[26] and as less-than-American men. Other than cricket, South Asian Americans do, however, receive disproportionate coverage in one other area of competition. Young South Asian Americans gain national "sporting" visibility every year through ESPN's coverage of this realm, the Scripps Spelling Bee. South Asian Americans appear annually and often win. Yet coverage of this sort does little to dismiss, challenge, or reconfigure stereotypes. Even in this realm, it is the "brain" that centers their identity as the body is almost completely negligible in the Spelling Bee.

Representations at the Spelling Bee perpetuate the depiction of South Asian American as "nerds." One prime example, both humorous and tragic, illustrates this problematic association. At the 2003 Scripps Spelling Bee championships, 13-year-old Indian American Akshay Buddiga got up to spell "alopecoid," but sheer mental exhaustion led to his swaying to his left and stumbling down in front of his opponents.[27] His body failed him. There was a pause. The viewers could see the surprised faces in the audience as well as at the judges' table. Buddiga stood up uneasily. He moved to the microphone and still correctly spelled the word. His mind did not fail him. Disproportional focus on desi participation in the spelling bees flattens out the numerous other sporting venues where South Asian American gendered identities take shape. In my initial pickup game at Mustafa's house, I was equally guilty of having harbored stereotypes of South Asian American men as not athletic enough for basketball even though I am myself a South Asian American basketball player. Playing intensely against skilled co-ethnic peers forced me to rethink this stereotype, and I found pleasure in celebrating multiple brown sporting bodies.

The normal media coverage of basketball as black or white additionally reinforces the stereotype of the South Asian as physical outcasts in the realm of this sport, even in recreational games. Ethnographies and research on basketball sometimes follow this black-white racial trajectory. The sociologists Scott Brooks (2009) and Reuben May (2007) have published rich ethnographies on African American engagement with basketball in large U.S. cities, Philadelphia and Atlanta respectively. Both these cities contain considerable South Asian populations. These scholars offer deft analysis of pickup basketball, known as "playground ball," in relation to organized "schoolyard ball," but only through black-white racial interactions.[28] Only recently have scholars started to examine other communities of color within basketball.[29] The young men in this book have had an enduring relationship with basketball even though they feel marginalized in some multiracial basketball gyms.

Their experiences of being "Outkasts" in basketball fit with their marginalization in U.S. society. Because members of the Outkasts team live in Metro Atlanta, they face particular racializations that come with living in the U.S. South. The team consists of primarily Muslim South Asian American men whose very presence contests the religious, racial, and cultural ethos of the Bible Belt.[30] The "Bible Belt" is both a symbolic and material boundary that cinches the national waist as middle-class, heterosexual Christian. For Muslims, their faith alongside their brown skin is imprinted as a racial category of difference (Rana 2011). The racial hysteria following September 11, 2001, intensified the symbolic connection between religion and race with material consequences. In a 2002 issue, the *Atlanta Journal Constitution* reported: "Georgia ranks 12th in the nation for the number of employment discrimination cases filed by Muslims, Arabs, South Asians and Sikhs—or those perceived to be from these groups—because of alleged Sept. 11 backlash."[31] Discrimination based on religious-racial markers has additional disastrous material effects for Muslims. Muslim Pakistani American communities are disproportionally deported in relation to other communities (see Maira 2009; Afzal 2010; Rana 2011). Through participation in pickup basketball, players manage the messy terrain of identity by complicating depictions of masculinity. However, not just any pickup arena will suffice to counter these stereotypes. African American and white players propagate these stereotypes in even the most causal pickup basketball courts. In order to evade such stereotypes lobbed at them by African American and white players in multiracial basketball venues, South Asian American men participate in their own exclusive and carefully managed pickup ball.

Monday/Thursday Night Brown Out

Other than the pickup basketball games at Mustafa's house, I came across two other important pickup basketball venues. One consisted of pickup games after Friday jummah at Sultan's parents' home. His younger brother Imran arranged this setting, and players included the South Asian

American and Middle Eastern Muslim peers he had grown up with at the local mosque. Most of the young men were children of the wave of post-1965 professionals and were themselves finance professionals or college students. The other pickup games took place every Monday/Thursday night at designated public gyms. For the latter, the crowd was composed of a heterogeneous religious and ethnic group of South Asian Americans in their mid-twenties to their late thirties. Although Mustafa and Ali play at the Monday/Thursday night pickup, it was originally organized by middle-class desis. A couple of finance professionals, Daniel (Christian Malayalee American) and Harpreet (Sikh American), along with Jonny (Sikh American), put together a weekly pickup ball night for their community of friends. They invited Malik to play as he is linked to both their professional and social circles. Additionally, all three attended highly rated universities in Atlanta. Malik then invited his peers on the Outkasts to play. When Malik brought Mustafa into the fold, Mustafa in turn invited me to play. In addition to incorporating a diverse non-Muslim population, the pickup games on either Monday or Thursday nights differed from games at the mosque with regard to their high level of institutionalization. Daniel and his peers created an affluent social network, had access to resources to secure a gym, structured their own rules for play, and established their own criteria for membership. Partaking in this form of pickup basketball came with its own types of class and race politics.

Driving to play pickup basketball on Monday night in April 2009 involved crossing different class and racial terrains of the city. I rented a room in a lower-middle-class Asian American and Latino neighborhood in Chamblee, a city adjacent to Doraville and in DeKalb County. To get to the gym, I crossed Buford Highway, which was seen as the quintessential ethnic space in Atlanta. I passed through mostly Asian American and Latina/o businesses and came close to the Brookhaven Subway Station near Peachtree Street.[32] I had to drive through an emerging white neighborhood that had previously housed African Americans and immigrants from Asia, Africa, and Latin America. Store signs in Spanish, Vietnamese, and Khmer gave way to English signs. New homes, boutique shops, yoga studios, fusion restaurants, and wide walker-friendly sidewalks existed uneasily with a neglected liquor store, a remnant from an earlier time.

A Pilates studio greeted me as I turned the corner and saw young white women with yoga mats walking inside. The white middle-class and upper-class community morphed into a not-so-easily definable neighborhood. A stop sign signaled the halting of gentrification, at least temporarily. The 2008 economic downturn had limited new construction in the historically immigrant and African American neighborhood. Although far fewer whites and middle-class denizens were buying houses here, the working-class African American community continued to feel the push out of this neighborhood as a result of the increased property taxes with the new builds. A mismatch of newly built homes stood across from the original crumbling, small homes with disintegrating paint. The working-class African American community occupied many of the small homes.

I soon came upon the gym with its drab beige paint, weathered brick, and randomly placed shrubs. I parked my car and saw Daniel in his yellow Corvette. Once inside the gym, Daniel conversed with the African American woman who managed this public gym. He gave her the check to cover the rental fee for the two hours. About six young African American kids, local residents of this neighborhood between the ages of 8 and 12, were on the court and enjoying themselves as they shot on the standardized goals of 10 feet and the adjustable side hoops that were 6 and 7 feet high. They challenged each other to dunks and blocks on the small baskets. Soon other South Asian American players arrived.

With only nine players there, we did not have enough to form the required two teams of five. Daniel reached out to a young African American resident who was working at the gym and asked him to play. Daniel then asked Tim (a white player) and me to pick teams. At this time, one of the young African American boys lost hold of his basketball on the side court and it came onto center court. The youth chased the ball down and took a shot on the main goal. Vivek, a regular South Asian American player, was visibly agitated by the presence of the African American boy. With a sneer on his face, Vivek looked over at his South Asian American peers and yelled, "Come on, get that little Kallu[33] off the court!" Vivek laughed off his own comment. Daniel, however, did not find it amusing and retorted, "Don't call him a 'Kallu.' That is a little kid!" Our game began and Vivek pleaded with Daniel, "Don't make me guard that guy [the 17-year-old African American male Daniel had asked to play]."

The organization and level of detail that went into Monday night basketball betray any assumptions about recreational basketball as whimsical and meaningless. Daniel and the other men did not randomly show up on Monday nights (games were on Thursday nights when I first began my research in 2006) to play. Not anyone can play. Rather, Daniel, Vivek, Joe, Tim, and the other players are there because they have various degrees of connections with each other. They are part of a social network. They both intentionally and unintentionally form a sense of fraternity that does include non–South Asian Americans. When these players arrive at this public gym, their movement across the city to this sporting venue provides important details about Atlanta and its South Asian American communities.

The desi pickup players interact with each other and also with the local neighborhood each week. The presence of South Asian Americans in this neighborhood at this historical moment signals gentrification, or what anthropologist Martin Manalansan (2005) refers to as "neoliberal governance," where private (real estate and construction firms) and public (city government) collusion leads to the continual displacement of working-class communities of color. Both the liquor store and the older public gym are remnants rich with histories and politics antithetical to the gentrifying white aesthetic. They symbolize a period of change in the 1950s and 1960s, when African Americans entered the majority white neighborhoods by Oglethorpe University. The move engendered white flight, in which capital, businesses, jobs, and homeowners moved to the suburbs in Cobb, Fulton, DeKalb, and Gwinnett Counties.[34] DeKalb County remains as a minority-majority county, while Cobb and Gwinnett Counties are predominantly white.[35] Daniel and Harpreet lived in established middle-class and upper-middle class (majority white) communities in DeKalb and Fulton Counties—both their parents are the professionals of the post-1965 wave. Vivek, Amit, Karthik, and Joe were transplants to Atlanta. They resided in the trendy neighborhoods in Kirkwood, Midtown Atlanta, and Atlantic Station (near the Georgia Institute of Technology) that were majority working-class African American but transitioning since the mid-1990s.

When I first met the pickup crew in 2006, they were playing at a public gym in Doraville. This suburb was a key landing site for most of the early post-1965 professionals and their families. Malik, Sultan, and Harpreet acknowledged that post-1965 immigrants, including their families, initially lived in Doraville and played at the gym. In the early 1980s, Daniel and his middle-class peers moved to the affluent part of DeKalb, Fulton, and Cobb Counties—emblematic of the larger aspects of white flight. However, since the mid- to late 1990s, there has been a reverse trend of affluent (mostly white) denizens moving back into the city center.[36] Coming back to these gyms constituted for desis and their middle-class and upper-class peers a usurpation of certain cityscapes from working-class communities of color.[37]

The move back has been due to city-center rejuvenation/gentrification projects. At the same time, immigrant communities, especially the lower-middle-class communities that Mustafa and his class of peers belong to, have been moving increasingly into the suburbs.[38] Mustafa's and Ali's family lived in lower-middle class suburbs in Gwinnett County. Their neighborhoods were mostly lower-middle-class white and Latina/o. These young men owned homes in this county, but in the poorer part of the county. In contrast, affluent new arrivals bought homes in the predominantly Asian American neighborhood known as John's Creek—which has one of the stronger public school systems in the state. Within a span of a few decades, Gwinnett County drastically changed its racial face. Unable to afford the mortgage of homes in John's Creek, Mustafa and some of his lower-middle-class and working-class peers now live in areas near Pleasant Hill Road (the location of the Global Mall, a hub for South Asian business), where the schools cater to a working-class Latina/o migrant community (see Tarasawa 2009). Mustafa expressed anxieties about living here: "Look man, the signs for Sara's [his daughter] school are in Spanish. Her school is not good . . . I want to find another school, maybe establish residence somewhere else." While racializing local schools through the prevalence of Spanish (Latina/os), he projects a particular racial and class geography to his residence in Gwinnett County. As a result of the shifting structure of schools and neighborhoods, Mustafa's children attended weaker public schools. Yet, his class position, as lower-middle-class South Asian American, differed from that of the African Americans in the neighborhood of the gym.

While South Asian American players came to play ball, affluent consumers were buying up houses in the black neighborhood. African Americans were being pushed out because of inflated property taxes and loss of jobs in sales, service, and industry. In his examination of Atlanta during and after the 1996 Olympics, political scientist Michael Keating (2001: 26) contends that "black men, too, have entered the job market in large numbers, but the percentage of black men holding the best jobs relative to their overall numbers in the workforce has actually been declining, and their proportions in the least desirable service and blue-collar jobs have increased." If not for the economic downturn in 2008, most of the original African American residents would have been evicted sooner. As a result, the underground economy[39] and the entertainment industry offer the few opportunities that exist for social mobility.[40] Moreover, the growing trend toward privatization of public services such as public gyms has meant that local residents have lost access to the pleasures of public play and to even the minimal possibilities of social mobility via sport. Unlike private gyms, there are strict hours of operation, and the desi men and their peers foreclose a key period of playtime from 7 p.m. to 9 p.m. once a week. This public facility was made private through the collusion of desi racial and class networks.[41]

South Asian American pickup players are able to privatize public gyms in communities of color as the facilities are in dire need of funds. "The diversion of dedicated revenue to the stadium [the Olympic Stadium, now known as Turner Park] meant less money in the Recreation Authority's budget that could be used to rectify the segregation era's unequal distribution of facilities" (Keating 2001: 99). During my ethnographic research from 2006 to 2009, the Doraville gym closed down. The historian Kevin Kruse, in *White Flight*, details the racial politics of public spaces with his case study of Atlanta at the height of the integration movement in the 1960s.[42] He argues that, with the fear of sharing public facilities, such as golf courses, swimming pools, and gyms, white citizens left the city center, and the capital flight left the public recreational facilities, such as the gyms used by my informants, in shambles. There was an erosion of public services that continues to resonate today.[43] When the public gyms closed because of renovations or structural issues, Daniel first found the gym by Oglethorpe University, and then when that gym faced its own structural issues, he sought out another gym and found a church—a private venue—in a mostly white, middle-class DeKalb County neighborhood. The move to the church had financial implications for some of the lower-middle-class desi players. When I ask Ali why he did not play anymore, he mentions the time demands to care for his two children but additionally added, "Man, they play too far out and its costs too much. I can't justify $10 for ball." Professionals in the field of finance such as Vivek and Joe, embodiments of the prized labor of neoliberal times,[44] had greater financial stability and purchase power during the economic downturn. In February 2009, a larger corporation bought out Ali's place of employment. For a period of five months Ali managed without an income while looking for employment opportunities. At the public gym, the cost of $5 a week to play did not overwhelm Ali's budget. However, the shift to $10 could not be easily justified. Although Ali does not play often, he continues to be part of the social network. Most of the other desi players commit themselves to this weekly ritual of basketball as an expression of identity. Yet players never use the language of "masculinity" to describe their sporting practices. They find masculinity inappropriate in describing sport but use it to talk about their identity in other realms of their social life.

Playing between Social Spaces: Leisure and Masculinity

For many desi ballers, the pickup format engenders co-ethnic homosocial bonding that differs from the co-religionist bonding at their respective religious centers. It further provides an alternate to gendered expectations at work and at home. When I inquired as to why they play, some of their responses were

KHURRAM (Muslim): Basketball is a great way to escape normal life and work—it gives me the opportunity to have fun.

AMIT (Hindu): I love playing basketball, and it's a good way of getting to meet others.

JOE (Christian Malayalee): One is for the exercise and enjoyment of playing basketball. Second is to meet new people (having just moved to Atlanta [from the Northeast]).

HARPREET (Sikh): A grasp of the past, grasp of youth, enjoyment with friends, Enjoy the game.

ABDUL (Muslim): Basketball is my vacation in the middle of the week. Gives me something to look forward to all week. Basketball provides leisure to busy men who may not have much time for themselves. Very healthy for men to have such an activity. Prevents break downs of any sort by providing a healthy outlet for energy and stress.

Ali's childhood friend Abdul started playing pickup basketball in February 2009. Abdul is a medical professional who did not originally know about this community of desi players until Ali introduced him to them. By playing, he could spend quality time with Ali while tackling his own obesity. These two men, as a result of their different class statuses, would not necessarily meet in other social spaces other than the mosque or community-wide cultural events. Abdul would not play basketball with Ali in tournaments or other competitive formats as Abdul had minimal basketball abilities.

Abdul and Ali maintained close social bonds through their weekly meeting for pickup basketball. The basketball court represented a "male preserve" (Theberge 1985) in which men could be men without the company of women. It also represented a reprieve from the demands of everyday life. In his answer above, Abdul conflated sport and masculinity with his allusion to basketball as "leisure" for "busy men." I noticed that players like Abdul frequently alluded to pickup basketball and its related social interactions as a most welcome "escape" and "vacation" from the grind of "normal" life. Basketball constituted part of the spectrum of masculinity not available in other settings. At home they could claim the title as the "man of the family" by securing the status of the "breadwinner." Young men like Abdul and Ali could not compromise the expectations of masculinity at home and at work that involve titles/roles as "father," "husband," and "employee"; any compromise would have a detrimental effect on how they are received in their communities. When they played on pickup nights, they invoked desires and pleasures in homosocial bonding that were constitutive of their understanding of masculinity but outside the realm of gender practices at home or at work.

Sport is simultaneously a break from work and family life and yet is informed by those other spaces. When players are scheduled to play but have work or family issues that prevent them from attending, they express their discontent to the community of ballers through their e-mail Listserv. For example, one of the white men, Patrick, sent the following e-mail on one game day: "Sorry for last minute notice. . . . I'm stuck at work . . . won't make it tonight." Work is an obligation where he is expected to perform a certain type of masculinity. On the basketball court, in the presence of just other co-ethnic men, they can affirm a tough masculinity through a gamut of movements, expressions, and creative abilities.

While Abdul understood this relation of masculinity to leisure, other players rejected such an ideological connection. In fact, for some of them, masculinity has nothing to do with sport. Instead, their work lives and family obligations are considered the epitome of masculine ideals and obligations. Accordingly, most players emphasized manhood in relation to their professional worth, "responsibility," and family (which was read as heterosexual). They rarely let the category of masculinity slip into the leisurely arenas of sporting cultures. When I prodded them about definitions of masculinity, they responded:

VIKRAM (Hindu): It's [the acts of being masculine] about being responsible; taking responsibility for your actions. It's your job to provide for your family, to keep your family name alive and proud. Basketball doesn't really relate, except that it helps you build camaraderie with others guys and keeps you healthy.

SIVA (Hindu): I just enjoy playing basketball and competing—to me, it doesn't relate to being a man or anything like that.

KHURRAM (Muslim): I think a man is somebody who respects himself and those around him. More importantly, he takes care of his family. I wouldn't say basketball relates to a man because I believe the game is for everybody, including women and children.

Vikram, Siva, and Khurram define activities around family life and work as masculine where others' dependency on them creates a sense of responsibility. In fact, the connections between masculinity, respect, responsibility, and family life were evident in the way these men carry themselves in community-wide events. They displayed masculinity in how they deferred to and showed respect for elders and family members. Within the family unit, they positioned themselves higher in relation to their female counterparts. They emphasized a take-charge attitude that is about caring for the family/community. For example, Mustafa expressed discontent when his wife, Fatima, did not clean the house according to his specifications. While sweeping the floors, he tells me, "Man, look at that [how clean the house is]. I am the one that cleans well. She [Fatima] is messy." The young men at times sweep the floor on the basketball court to make sure no one falls during games. Yet they do not see that as feminine work within the confines of sporting space. When I asked them about what they deemed masculine on the court, their responses demonstrated how ridiculous they believed the connection between masculinity and sport to be.

Nevertheless, pickup players actively participated in ascribing masculinity to their bodies and actions. Vivek clearly explained this connection between gender identity and sport: "I define manhood as the ability to take care of your business as well as your obligations. I think the ability to be there for your family and your significant other is what it means to be a man. I think going out without your wife and just spending two hours with a bunch of guys and working in a team environment is related to being a man." Once these men completed what they deemed the requirements to be a man in the workplace and in their respective families, they found masculine pleasures of homosocial bonding. In this instance, Vivek was not distancing this sporting masculinity from those gendered practices at work and at home. Rather, he emphasized that this was *another* important element of being a man. On the court, one could express manliness through a multitude of basketball gestures and social interactions that receive affirmative praise. Masculinity has to be constantly performed and judged by other men.[45] However, only a certain kind of social network has the opportunity to enter this sporting community.

"Who's Ballin'?" Creating the Social Network

The public basketball gym in the neighborhood was privatized for a definite time and made an exclusionary space when Daniel rented time for the pickup games. Although players articulate how sport is structured through meritocracy, the creation of their social network says otherwise. Although they form their own space to escape racializing discourses in

other sporting formats, they partake of their own forms of social policing. E-mail Listservs maintain boundaries and privacy in ways that
facilitate the construction of an exclusionary public with very particular
gendered, racial, and classed contours.[46] Every week Daniel sends an
e-mail invitation to the group of more than 50 men, asking, "Who's ballin' on [Month, Day]?" In order to get a spot to play on Monday night,
members of this social network must respond immediately to Daniel's
e-mail to secure one of the 15 spots to play, and they pay Daniel to cover
the fee for the gym. The e-mail format makes this type of sporting community different from that of pickup games at other gyms. With the
e-mail, there is already a community in play with social bonds, relationships, and expectations. Other pickup games can be much more random
in their demographics, with various newcomers taking part—anyone
could enter the space.

Private gyms with a multiracial clientele, such as LA Fitness gyms in
Atlanta, have long lines of players waiting to play. There is no guarantee
that players will even get to play a single game, as the waiting time could
be upward of two to three hours. With their class resources, Daniel and
his peers secured a *public* gym for their *private* basketball pleasures with
the guarantee that all 15 players would play several games within a two-
hour period. Establishing a limit of 15 players facilitated having many
games within the time period as it breaks down into three teams, so
only one team waited to play instead of six or seven teams or more at
LA Fitness. On Monday nights the first team to reach 24 points won
(each basket counts for 2 or 3 points). This point limit made it possible
to get through several games in the two-hour period. Local residents,
who were already there and would be there after the games ended at
9:00 p.m., did not have the opportunity to play at this time. Only with a
shortage of players did the players reach out to the mostly young African
American neighborhood men at the gym.

When I asked Monday night players why they continued to play
weekly with their co-ethnic peers, Daniel answered, "I have to play a
role when playing at LA Fitness, not *here*."[47] This "role" refers to the
web of racialized discourses and basketball stereotypes faced by South
Asian American players. Daniel complained that he could not use his
athletic gifts and talents to play pickup basketball the way he wanted to
at LA Fitness. Other white and African American players did not afford

him the same kind of creative freedom and expressive opportunities in basketball as they did for African American players. Black and white players read Daniel's body as unsuitable. They constrained him by refusing to pass him the ball. Other players saw him as a weak link that had to be contained and limited his presence on the court by asking him to just primarily play defense. Being constrained to the defensive role falls short of the very core of pickup ball, as the sociologist Scott Brooks shows brilliantly in *Black Men Can't Shoot*, where games match individuals against individuals, players set defenses around man-on-man play instead of zone defenses, and the highlights are either steals and defensive blocks or offensive proliferation.

Getting a chance to showcase one's offensive skills is a key part of laying claim to the space. When black and white players see South Asian Americans on the court, there is often a stereotypical projection of South Asian Americans as "nerds" who are not suitable for such an athletic enterprise. Inherent in this perception is the assumption of inferior and failing masculinity. At the Northlake Mall LA Fitness, I witnessed and experienced such emasculation. Once I was the only non-African American on the court, but I was praised as one of the better players. When the team I was playing on lost, another African American, who had not seen the previous game, came to pick teams and chose African American players who were much less skilled and less athletically gifted than me. I just shook my head with frustration but also familiarity with this pattern of social relations on the basketball court. The ball players who had seen me play chastised the new player who picked teams. In contrast to this LA Fitness experience, I was not typecast into a *racialized role* on Monday night pickup basketball. In fact, on Monday nights, I took pleasure in dominating some of the other players and having the freedom to play a variety of positions. When playing in organized games, I could not play the point guard, shooting guard, or small forward positions. In organized basketball, the teams I played with needed me to play the role of key defender and match up against the taller/tallest players.

On the pickup circuit, I could literally play with a cornucopia of basketball moves on the pickup court and not worry about staying within a demarcated role in organized ball or about the racialization in other pickup circuits. Other equally skilled, more-skilled, and less-skilled desis also encounter such racialized logic on the multiracial court. South

Asian American men use resources, financial and symbolic, to overcome their constant marginalization in other social realms. Players are able to buy gym space, restrict the presence of threatening Others, and thereby play their way into (athletic) American-ness.

Team Making and Fairness

Not all players equivalently endure marginalization. Mustafa stands out in various pickup basketball circuits and garners respect due to the level of his basketball skills, his athletic abilities, and his swagger. He finds ways to enter the sporting realms of American-ness and athletic masculinity much more easily than some of his desi peers. Unlike some of the children of the post-1965 wave of immigrants, Mustafa plays with and against other communities of color, thus achieving greater basketball "cred." In addition to his deft basketball toolkit, he also understood and embodied the major premise in other pickup basketball circuits—domination, domination, domination. As a result of the ways other pickup games are structured along particular notions of limited time and space, Mustafa tossed ideas of middle-class aesthetics, such as fair play and parity, aside in order to win and remain on the court. When he played Monday night pickup, he wanted to assemble the members of the Atlanta Outkasts and dominate the time on the court. Such a move would contrast with the middle-class respectabilities on the brown-out court. If Mustafa, Ali, Malik, Sultan, and I played together on a team, the games would easily be swayed in our favor. However, Daniel and the other players structured the teams and the type of play in a different manner, in contrast to LA Fitness and other gyms. Just the very act of asking the top two players to pick teams created parity across teams.

When Daniel separated the skilled players into different teams, it increased the competition between the teams. No one knew for sure who would win and dominate on a given night. Each player came with a real possibility of winning against another team. This stood in counterpoint to the structure of play and team formations I observed at the LA Fitness gyms at Northlake Mall (in DeKalb County with a mixed-income crowd and close to African American neighborhoods) and Perimeter Mall (in Fulton County with a younger, middle-class clientele) from 2006 till 2009. The high level of basketball talent at the Northlake (with some players having played professional basketball overseas) and the sheer numbers of people waiting meant that a small window existed for people to play. If one loses, one might have to wait hours to play again. Players at LA Fitness tried to maximize court time by forming elite teams that repeatedly won against the other teams. As players had to sign in to play at LA Fitness, those in the know signed in with skilled peers instead of being in a group of five with average or below-average athletes. On the Monday night desi pickup scene, through intentional structuring, players artificially constructed competitiveness and were able to enjoy its concomitant pleasures of intense, close, and hard-fought games that could produce feelings of achievement and pride.

By constructing parity and delimiting who can play, Monday night players "man up" through middle-class norms of fairness that work both with and against masculine norms of domination. The format of play is fairly dynamic. The top two players do not always act as captains and pick teams. When more than ten players are present at the start of games, players shoot free-throw shots from the top of the rectangular box on the court to make teams to ensure that everyone has a chance to make the first two teams. The first five players to make baskets form the first team while the second five to make baskets constitute the second team. All others, failing to make baskets, constitute the third team that plays the winner of the first two teams. Yet if an imbalance occurs on the teams, in which one team dominates the other two, the players willingly choose to rotate and rearrange certain individuals to create a more-level playing field. Whereas we might think that individualism flourishes in such a sport setting, the contradictory impulse for parity also contains individualism for communal joys of better competition.

Individualism and individual merit have a key role in pickup basketball. On Monday nights, making a basketball shot from the free throw line on the court could put an inferior player on a team ahead of a better-skilled player. Any one of the 15 players who signed up and paid to play could make the first two teams by "sinking" (successfully making) a shot. One's "merit," making the shot, allowed one to play immediately. Yet these moments of merit worked only for those with the capital and social network to privatize this public gym. The African American residents of this neighborhood could not use their "merit" (basketball skills) as currency to play.

The South Asian American pickup players got to expand upon their basketball expressive practices by owning the public gym for two hours. They were able to indulge in basketball creativities that extend the limitations set forth by the dominant racialized discourses about race and ability (Gilbert 2010). Although players with exceptional basketball ability, such as Ali and Mustafa, dictate the kind of play on the court, other players can play a variety of positions. At 6′2″, Vivek, who would normally be forced to play a power position when playing at other gyms, would thus not be allowed to partake of acts such as dribbling as it is usually given to shorter, quicker, more-experienced players. In the company of his desi and financial professional peers, however, Vivek dribbled the ball and attempted to make fancy passes. Each attempt at difficult and *cool* basketball moves facilitated trash talking as a form of male bonding and praise from one's peers at the venue.

A "call-and-response"[48] cultural decorum existed whereby players appraised, judged, evaluated, and policed the movements and actions on court. For those attempted plays that were outrageous and out of bounds of common basketball sense, the other players chastised the guilty party. When Vivek carelessly went crashing for a rebound on a missed shot without accounting for other bodies in that space, he landed on one of Ali's teammates. He could have severely hurt the player. Vivek just wanted to showcase his vertical jumping abilities and use that as a means to move up this gendered sporting hierarchy. He used his jumping ability to claim the sporting space. Ali responded firmly, "You are such a fuckin' retard! Watch what you are doing!" The term "retard" connected (dis)ability with Vivek's physical and intellectual grasp of the game. Saying such things did not diminish the sense of community as players still spent time with each other before and after games. The historian Robin Kelley (1997), in *Yo Mama's Disfunktional!*, demonstrates the process by which trying to one-up each other with verbal flair, jokes, and creative puns are forms of intimate community building in African American communities. In a similar vein, the players used the already established social network to tease and challenge other men while reaffirming their notions of community. As a result, they constructed jokes that involved queering other men as gay or feminine. For example, during one e-mail conversation among members of the Listserv after a game, Paul (one of the original Malayalee players in this circuit alongside Daniel) took to poking fun at another player, Ram, by providing six "bitch moves" that invalidated Ram's basketball abilities. The "bitch moves" included acting "retarded" and being familiar with "two-dad" households. Discourses of this sort rarely led to the severing of social bonds but instead consolidated them through such intimate verbal positioning.

This Is How We Ball

The young men on the pickup court displayed a spectrum of basketball movements, both spectacular and ridiculous. Each gesture gained meaning and was understood within the masculine hierarchy in relation to the other men on the court. Although an expansive set of basketball moves transpired on the court, they all shared one key element: All games, even though consisting of teams playing against each other, eventually filtered down to matchups between individuals—a man-on-man offensive and defensive scheme. Thus one was judged individually in relation to one's opponent. Players determined games not by a shot clock but by a score clock. The games were compressed within two hours of playing time. Scoring a basketball earned players praise. With games determined by which team scored 24 points, the participants overemphasized the individual acts of scoring and spectacular defensive plays, such as blocking a shot. This invariably highlighted certain individuals at the expense of other individuals.

As a result of the one-on-one format, the lack of defensive zones and offensive plays manifested itself in transforming a team game into moments of one-on-one play. Sometimes players would rotate and assist their teammate on either defense or offense. Players, accordingly, frequently came into contact with each other and engaged in what the communication scholar Lawrence Wenner (1998) classifies as "forceful and space-occupying ways." While playing, the young men forced themselves into their opponents' personal physical spaces after spectacular plays such as blocking a shot. According to the sporting vernacular, they "got in someone's face." Spatial intrusions served to highlight the individual whom his co-ethnic peers judge, based on movements, as strong, innovative, and forceful.[49] During one of the games, Vivek got a rebound off his teammate's missed shot. He assumed he had a wide open hoop to make an easy shot. Out of nowhere came Daniel, standing at 5'9" at best, who out-jumped Vivek to block his shot and then ran side-by-side with Vivek and jovially taunted him, "Get that shit outta here!" With this exaltation, Daniel proved his momentary dominance over Vivek. He had out-jumped and overpowered a taller opponent. As Daniel received praise, Vivek got the brunt of the teasing. Thus masculinity, as is the case with South Asian American identity, is always performative, fleeting, fragile, and in need of constant iteration.

In the pickup circuit, the players put their names and status on the line against their peers with their styles of (physical and verbal) play. Pickup basketball does not just individualize the expressive practices of athletes but also bleeds into the individualized enforcing of rules. As a result, players are equipped to challenge each other's moves as "foul" and out of bounds. Unlike the major tournaments and standard organized basketball, this type of recreational play does not have officials on hand to oversee the play on the court. The responsibility of the style of play falls on the players. With a format like this, players exert very clearly the limits of certain types of toughness, physicality, and creative basketball moves.

Amit, as one of the shortest players on the court, accrued symbolic capital with his 3-point shots. He did not possess the dribbling acumen to create distance from another player. Instead, when his teammates outmaneuvered their opponent and entered the "lane" (the term for the box by the basket) to score, other defenders were compelled to leave their primary defensive assignment to help out. An opening would emerge as Amit's defender left to offer help, which would enable the ball to be passed to Amit for a 3-point shot. His high arching shot, which looks like a rainbow, would frequently go smoothly through the net without making any contact with the rim. This shot, vernacularly called a "swish," garnered high fives and pats from his teammates. Each successful 3-point shot counts heavily in a game when reaching 24 points signals victory. The winning team would stay on the court and play the next team in wait. As 3-point shots are the most point laden and the most difficult shots, several players attempt them, regardless of size or skill level. Khurram, Amit, and Paul (Christian Malayalee American) showed that they could successfully execute basketball shots with their smaller, less-athletic body frames.

In addition to making difficult shots, players took joy in attempting difficult passes and creative dribbling. Since teams still want to remain on the court and play instead of sitting out a game, certain limits on such creative flair existed. Yet players could freely venture out and confidently attempt basketball maneuvers such as long passes across the court, passes through tight spaces, and intricate dribbling moves. Vivek's skill level and athletic aptitude might limit the types of opportunities given to perform difficult basketball moves in other pickup circles. However, on Monday nights, Vivek tried out the difficult passes to his teammates. Others like Paul, Joe, and their peers attempt such passes fairly frequently. They all witness firsthand the brilliance of Ali's passes and try to replicate his moves.

Creative dribbling and difficult passes secure athletes status with "basketball cool"—a type of confidence and self-assurance. With each made shot, successful pass, or creative dribble, players would walk slowly with an elongated stride as an embodiment of swagger. However, not all athletes choose, or have the bodily abilities and skill level, to perform the creative maneuvers. Instead, they take to physicality and athleticism, as with Daniel's block of Vivek. Other players would try to grab the rim to showcase their athletic ability. With the basketball rim at a standard height of 10 feet, it is a remarkable achievement to grab hold of it. As one of the taller persons on the court at 6'2", Vivek constantly jumped at the rim after his teammate's shot. He hoped to grab the rebound in the air and slam it through the 10-foot rim. This was more fantasy than reality, but it was part of his weekly ritual. Vivek took pleasure in making that jump frequently to showcase a (perceived) dominance over the other players on the court. He showed his bodily capabilities even though most other players acknowledged Daniel, Brandon (a multiracial person of various racial heritages), Vincent (a white professional) and his white friends, Mustafa, Ali, and me as the athletically gifted persons. Vivek could still illustrate his jumping abilities and position himself as manly in relation to other players like Abdul. Thus, when he blocked my shot on numerous occasions during one game, he received praise. He had outmanned me, and other patrons teased me. I then reassured my place within the sporting hierarchy by using my muscularity to push and physically control Vivek on the next set of plays. The other players ranked me in their basketball universe, and I had to perform my basketball ability in order to secure rapport as both a participant and researcher.

Sanjeet (a Sikh American whom I introduced to Monday night pickup) and Abdul used their sheer size to their advantage. As Abdul was already obese and athletically limited, he used his girth to his advantage in unacceptable ways on the court. Although Abdul would take and make certain 3-point shots, most players recognized him for his hijinks and comical toughness. He failed to keep up with the speed of most of his opponents. To make up for this shortcoming, he intentionally grabbed, held, and fouled players. In this co-ethnic community with strong social bonds, his acts, regardless of the deliberate nature, did not ostracize him from the community. His presence there was part of the community building and perpetuation of social bonds among the young men. Even when Abdul took part in the most outrageous and unwarranted of basketball plays, his opponents displayed minimal annoyance and laughed it off.

Abdul also chose the young men on the lower rung of this social milieu on whom to commit his outrageous fouls. On several occasions, his opponent would drive past him, and Abdul, with his size and power, would stretch his hand out and "clothes line" the opponent. The shots he inflected on others were a nuisance, without a doubt. As the other players knew him and respected his kinship with Ali, his acts were interpreted as humorous and absurd. They did not, however, damage the pattern of social relations on the basketball court. The toughness and bold disposition of Abdul affirmed a certain status that his basketball skills could not secure. He had a certain freedom, as a result of close co-ethnic social ties, to partake in such lunacy on the brown-out court. That same freedom would not be possible in other public pickup basketball settings, where a "clothes line" move would result in conflict and fighting and could permanently damage his membership in that particular sporting community.

Sanjeet, in contrast, had a formidable skill set but also used his 6′2″ and over-220-pound frame to his advantage. On various occasions he would box in and trap defenders under the basket, as they could not get around his massive body. This would lead to easy scores. I often had to guard him, and it was a herculean task, but we both took joy in trying to outplay and overpower each other. There was a certain laxity mixed in with intense competition that accentuates a sense of South Asian American identity among the players. They could revel in the joys of interpersonal competition while demonstrating the gamut of basketball moves. Since players called the fouls against each other, this led to a larger set of acceptable basketball moves than one would normally see in organized basketball.

Cultural Blackness and "Playground" Ball: Invoking Race

The young men consumed varieties of what the cultural critic Nelson George, in *Elevating the Game*, calls "playground" basketball. As there are many varieties of playground basketball that are context specific and differ from organized basketball, the acceptable athletic moves found in playground ball might be called violations in organized basketball. Some of the fancy dribbling was closer to a "carry," where one's palm, instead of lying flat on top of the ball, turns over and cradles it. It is a stylistic move that requires knowledge and experience to execute properly. In general these moves carry particular racialized values as working-class black aesthetics, but these racialized meanings were not mapped onto the bodies of the middle-class athletes at the pickup gym. They also contained racial meanings, a certain blackness, that desi players simultaneously embraced and displaced onto other racialized bodies.[50]

Vivek and others in this basketball community indulge in creative practices that were not read equivalently when performed by African American men. Black participation in "playground/pickup" ball and it respective creative practices produced notions of black men as uncontrollable, unregulated, and deviant.[51] In contrast, "organized" ball (tournament and league games) contains meanings that map it as a standard, pure, and controlled (read as white) version of basketball.[52] On Monday nights, South Asian Americans partook of the creativity and status-quo pushing elements of playground ball associated with working-class African American communities without carrying the burden of blackness that African American players experience. Such acts involved difficult passes, fancy dribbling, and other stylistic movements that might be whistled as "fouls" in organized basketball. Improvisation took center stage at Monday night pickup, but within its own set of limits. Players disciplined each other so that certain levels of creativity were accepted without diminishing a core set of basketball rules. At various times players would shout out "you walked," "you double-dribbled," "you carried the ball."

Blackness was always part of this space and seeped into the ethos of desi basketball in many ways. It was one of the foundational elements of making South Asian American identities through which to invoke toughness to escape the nerdy bodily representation. Players consumed various elements of cultural blackness as it displaced representations of them as too foreign and too nerdy. Most of the players came from affluent suburbs in DeKalb County, Fulton County, and Cobb County, but they entered the public gym near Oglethorpe University while blasting hip-hop music. They consumed elements of cultural blackness as urban cool—a certain type of belonging as a denizen—by which to signify their athletic movements as "basketball cool." Along with hip-hop music, many of the players sported other elements of black stylistics on the court.

Desis, more so than their white counterparts, pay considerable attention to their sporting attire. The items of clothing that are part of a "basketball cool" consist of clothing popularized by certain African American athletes like Michael Jordan, LeBron James, and Kobe Bryant. Other than Khurram and Daniel, who did not appropriate elements of black style and mainstream basketball style into their sporting outfits, most other players, including myself, arrived with clear ideas of sport fashion. Most players wore expensive Nike basketball shoes, which is the top-selling basketball sneaker company. Karthik (who played for the Tennessee Volunteers Indo-Pak team but moved to Atlanta for work), Vivek, Amit, Sanjeet, Abhijeet (Sanjeet's friend), Joe, and Ali came with fashionable clothing that consisted of, in several cases, matching T-shirt, shorts, and shoes. The T-shirts were often sleeveless to showcase their muscular arms. Their bodies constituted a site of desire for themselves and their peers. On a couple of occasions, I ran into Vivek at local gyms as he worked out with his friends. Thus, the basketball court was a place where he could show the products of his hard work—his muscular arms. The clothing, music, and type of walk captured a "basketball cool" linked to cultural blackness. As a commercial commodity, the blackness was part of the swagger they embodied and the "basketball cool" they claimed. Consumption of black style and music functioned as a way to desire the brown sporting body and provided a social critique of expectations of South Asian American–ness as linear progression to white American–ness. Desi players consume black stylistics, but one, thits existence in the larger marketplace, devoid of its political embers. Black style could travel across social spaces in ways that black men could not (see Maira 2002). This contradiction illuminates the workings of race in desi sporting cultures. While South Asian American basketball players see their consumptive practices as part of a "basketball cool" with no relevance to race, their interactions and policing of community boundaries displaced race onto the bodies of African American men. This displacement often took the form of the South Asian idiom "Kallu."

Vivek's use of the term "Kallu," in the vignette above, was part of a larger racialized hierarchy of gender, class, race, and sexuality. The term "Kallu" is specific to languages in the Indo-European language family. It originates from Northern India and served originally to stigmatize South Indians with darker complexions. As a result, those of us with ancestral links to South India, Malayalee, or Tamil ethnic heritages are the original Kallu subjects. On the pickup court and in South Asian America, this term is commonplace regardless of one's ancestral linguistic background and foregrounds another hierarchy determined by race. Daniel, an ethnic Malayalee who also speaks Malayalam (a language in the Dravidian language family), told me, "My dad used this term, that surprised me. I thought it came from people who spoke Hindi or Urdu. My dad must have gotten it from other [North] Indians." On the basketball court, "Kallu" referred to African Americans in particular and blacks in general. When I e-mailed Daniel to ask about Vivek's use of "Kallu" and why he objected to Vivek's reference to the young African American boy as "Kallu," his answers showcased how black bodies are read by some within South Asian America:

> DANIEL: Kallu to me means colored / black/ african american [*sic*]. The way it was said seemed a bit derogatory. . . . I would have preferred he just said make the little kid leave, no need for *Kallu* to be used as all the other kids were black right ☺.
>
> STAN: Can you please explain to me what you mean when you say, "no need for *Kallu* to be used as all the other kids were black right." When should one use that term and in what context?
>
> DANIEL: "Every little kid out there was black. The only time I've heard the term used is to refer to someone whose [*sic*] black but there are different folks around. So why say make the little black kid move if

there are only black kids around. Why not say make the kid on the court move or just make the kid move. . . . I do think brown folks (us indians [sic]) are ignorant in the fact of using the word *Kallu*, people aren't stupid and will pick up on the word. Plus other indians [sic] telling their friends what it means."

"Kallu," as a stigmatized term in South Asia, adds stigma to dark bodies (in the United States, read as black bodies). The term essentializes black communities and fails to get at the heterogeneity of blackness.[53] Players do not similarly stigmatize whites with a South Asian lexicon. Although the term "gora" exists for whites, it does not surface in basketball contexts as white players enter this pickup community without much objection. Some white peers of South Asian American basketball players know the term, but very few African Americans know of its meaning. Intimate knowledge of the meanings further illustrates how whites are ingratiated as part of the community in ways that African Americans are not. Furthermore, the potent racial meanings ascribed to "Kallu" locate black bodies in different positions in contrast to white bodies. Vincent, one of the new white members of this social network who played beginning in Spring 2009, did not come to know of this pickup ball through professional connections like the other white athletes: "I live near the gym and stop in frequently to find pickup games. When I discovered that a group rented the gym on Thursdays, I was more than happy to chip in so I could play with them." He was one of the people who lived in the new homes being constructed as working-class African American communities are being pushed out with higher taxes and evictions. As African American residents felt the push of gentrification and middle-class tastes, they equally encountered a racialized marginalization on the basketball court that was at the crossroads of race, gender, and class.

Black bodies were read by participants, both South Asian American and white, as out of place at the pickup gym even though these same African American men live in the neighborhood and play there when the desi ballers leave. Though the pickup players depict African American men as innately built for sport and physical activities,[54] the working-class black men in the local neighborhood were not welcomed into this desi community. By ideologically constructing sport as an arena governed by merit alone, the African American presence was perceived to threaten the supposed sanctity of the game. Pickup ballers took pleasure in their co-ethnic bonding in a racial milieu mostly free of a "threatening" black presence. There were, however, two middle-class African Americans who played on a Monday night. Brandon, a mixed-race finance professional, played every week, but he was not considered "black" by the other athletes. His class position and phenotype (light skin without kinky hair) allowed for a certain racial passing. However, the working-class African American men could not so easily pass and override their racialization to enter the court.

Athletic identities on the pickup court take shape with the stigmatization of black bodies. This was evident when Vivek would not guard the young African American Daniel invited to play. The young African American was on my team. Vivek had a few choices as a result of his height and athletic ability: guard me, guard the young African American man, or guard someone else much shorter. In a tournament format, Vivek would succumb to pressure to guard the tall man on the opposing team. I knew Vivek would not guard me as I am too aggressive for him. It made sense that Vivek, as the tallest player on one team, would guard the tall young African American. But Vivek deliberately chose not to guard him. Instead, Vivek, at 6′2″ chose to guard Amit, who was close to 5′6″, which made for quite a comical match up. This deliberate move to avoid guarding the young African American man demonstrated the processes of racialization at work. Whereas whites and blacks *underestimate* the athletic worth of and make assumptions about South Asian American men in multiracial settings, Vivek assumed and perhaps *overestimated* the athletic ability of the young African American man. Such an overestimation of athletic ability came along with a judgment of moral and intellectual aptitudes. For example, when Vincent, the young white man from the area, lost his new basketball, Vivek quickly suggested that the young African American boys had stolen the ball. Sultan found the ball in a dark corner of the gym and returned it to Vincent, but this revelation did not change the ways in which some young desi men represented African American communities. By invoking innate strength, danger, and defunct moral compass, Vivek positioned black masculinity in opposition to South Asian American masculinity. The abjection of black masculinity opened the door for South Asian American sporting practices to constitute the domain of normative masculinity.

Brown-out pickup ball is a venue in which co-ethnic and somewhat uniform class lines among participants are intentionally enacted. This type of basketball differs in the structure of play from the multiracial leagues. Through peer-group structuring of this space, the young men took part in multiple expressive practices of masculinity that were accompanied by the joys of performing masculinity through many bodily possibilities. They were able to perform a wide assortment of symbolic actions of masculinity without enduring racialized stereotypes. In the process, they instituted pickup basketball as a routine expression of their selves, a quotidian practice of manhood. By doing so, the men, even though they did not explicitly state it, integrated basketball into their everyday articulations of South Asian American–ness. However, as we have seen in Vivek's and Sultan's statements, the performances of sporting masculinity can only take place through constant policing of the brown-out space to deter women and African American men from joining. Any opposition, be it women or the figure of the Kallu, helps to give shape to South Asian American masculinity.

The various elements of class, race, and gender that played through the creation of exclusions in pickup basketball spaces also surfaced at Indo-Pak Basketball tournaments. At these tournaments, South Asian American players expanded the realm of masculinity with their competition against their co-ethnic peers. It was no longer a man-on-man style of play that governed Indo-Pak tournaments but, rather, teams (as emblems of one's ethnicity, religion, and city) that competed against each other. In this case, the category of ethnicity proved critical in multiplying South Asian American masculinity. The difference between organized basketball, such as Indo-Pak tournaments, and pickup ball demonstrates different gendered expectations and highlights the alternate set of allowable performances of masculinity.

2

"Who Is Desi?"

Understanding Organized Brown Out Basketball

Words that aim to define
Never fit like skin on fruits,
There is always some space
Accommodating other meanings.
Definitions, as any skin, ages
But like the mythic dragon
New skin replaces old,
The question re-invents itself
And answers take the field
Against weapons of definition.
—Stanley Greaves (2002)

As I entered the air-conditioned gym on a very balmy, hot Chicago summer day in July 2006, I proceeded to the court where the Virginia Playaz team was playing against the New York Ballaholics team. The premier tournament in the Indo-Pak Basketball U.S. circuit, the Chicago Indo-Pak National Tournament issued only 17 invitations to teams across North America, two of which had gone to these rivals. During lay-up lines before the game, players from both sides took practice shots while using creative gestures to make baskets. Viraj, a light-skinned South Asian American playing on the New York Ballaholics team of mostly dark-skinned Malayalee[1] Christian men, captured the gazes of fans with his ability to soar above the basketball rim and throw the ball down forcefully in seemingly effortless ways. He made his dunks look commonplace and yet spectacular. As the white and African American referees blew the whistle to start the game, the young men readied themselves.

The New York Ballaholics played a closely contested game and, led by Viraj's athletic prowess and one forceful mid-game dunk, pulled out a win over Virginia Playaz. With the win, New York Ballaholics moved on to the next round of play. The Virginia Playaz team had come to the end of their tournament journey this year. The win for the New York Ballaholics was important, but most participants were talking about Viraj's dunk. After the game, news of his basketball skills spread quickly through the Indo-Pak Basketball grapevine. His ability to soar in the air, his over 6' frame, his muscularity and chiseled figure, and his strength had already endeared him to this sporting community. Several Chicago IPN organizers and players from other teams who were watching the game approached Viraj with accolades and urged him to continue playing in Indo-Pak Basketball tournaments.

While other players and Chicago tournament organizers were talking to Viraj, I walked over to Andrew, the captain of the New York Ballaholics. When asked about why he plays in Indo-Pak basketball tournaments, Andrew responded, "Everyone is trying to have their own identity. I played other tournaments, other leagues; the competition is different. The kids [an affectionate and vernacular term for young men][pause], there is just a sense of community [here], absolutely." When I inquired about Viraj and how he, as a tall, light-skinned desi, ended up on a team of dark-skinned, shorter Malayalee Americans, Andrew explained,

We found him playing underground [not in desi spaces]. Especially in the Malayalee community in New York, there's a bunch of church tournaments, a bunch of interdenominational tournaments, a bunch of youth tournaments, and they [the Malayalee and larger desi community] tried to keep it that way. We got to see how people play, we get a lot of scouting done . . . it is getting tighter [formalized] with the search, it is almost getting professional [by creating groups that go out to various events to scout for new talent].

We then came to the topic of Indo-Pak Basketball tournaments in general, and I asked, "How do you form teams for the tournaments?" Andrew thought it over for a second and then stated emphatically,

They [tournament organizers] make it [membership in Indo-Pak Basketball] real sophisticated. Our search is narrowed to the South Asian community. We had a couple of other players that are eligible for our other tournaments on the East Coast, but they [Indo-Pak tournaments such as Chicago IPN] don't want to recognize them here, such as Trinidadians and Jamaican people. As long as you have Indian descent, East Coast tournaments will allow you to play, but here things change, so we had to come, find people that fit that description [of South Asian American-ness] to be allowed to play.

The poem above by the Caribbean artist Stanley Greaves opens up the dilemma of definitions. He refuses to settle for static productions while elaborating on the ongoing process of defining. His poem, when coupled with the vignette, helps to problematize monolithic understandings of South Asian American–ness. If identities are understood as definitions of personhood that rely on one or two essences, then they tend to flatten the heterogeneity while failing to account for the constant "becoming" (Hall 2003) that is part of identity formation. When athletic identities are defined through feats such as dunking, African Americans and whites are frequently represented as successful practitioners of basketball. Definitions therefore fail to "accommodate other meanings" and the "spaces" that allow for identities to always be in progress and re-invented. The athletic feats on display by Viraj can be found on many basketball courts across the United States. Acts such as dunking, especially over another opponent, receive praise in basketball communities across the racial and gendered divide. However, one must not assume equivalence and singular definitions of sport across ethnic and racial communities.

The desi basketball players at the Chicago IPN demand a rethinking of mainstream representations of sport. The relationship young desi men have to basketball, identity formation, and citizenship is different from those of black and white men. The echoes of the ball bouncing off the wooden floors, the sweet sound of a "swish" shot, the physicality on the basketball court, and a multitude of other athletic pleasures are derived from a variety of basketball movements that are not commonly associated with South Asian American communities. Most common associations, as we saw earlier, are with the game of cricket. Pukh, a Sikh American basketball player and finance professional from the team NJ/Cali Soormay Franchise, explains, "A lot of people say, 'oh you know' when you talk about Indians, 'you guys are really good at cricket.' . . . They don't know that here in the United States and Canada we got a huge community of players where they [South Asians] *actually*

play basketball."[2] By evoking cricket, the United States mainstream public continues to position South Asian Americans as invested in South
Asian cultural forms and incapable of assimilating into American-ness.
Such problematic associations continue to haunt U.S. "belonging" with
strong racial and cultural meanings. Symbolic associations with cricket
play an instrumental role in foregrounding what poet Stanley Greaves
philosophizes as static "definitions" that are continuously challenged
and re-made. If one looks only at cricket as the epitome of sporting
South Asian American identities, then South Asian American–ness is
read only through a singular definition always located and contained
within the category of "South Asia." By emphasizing South Asia instead of South Asian America, there emerges a form of "cultural racism"[3] that biologizes and naturalizes cultural practices as irreconcilable
forms of difference. As a result, certain cultural practices are evoked to
foreground racial difference, even though race and culture are different social registers with their own unique histories.[4] In the case of my
interlocutors, their stories highlight how their experiences of marginalization in institutionalized sport constitute one form of their exclusion,
"cultural racism," in mainstream U.S. society. As a result, the actions that
transpire on the Indo-Pak Basketball court complicate how we understand South Asian American racialized identity in 21st-century America and corresponding performances of "cultural citizenship" (Rosaldo
1994; Maira 2002).

The tournament space described above does not easily fit into a singular definition of "American-ness" or "South Asian–ness." Rather, the
ways in which the young men perform cultural citizenship show the
multiply inflected categories of race, gender, and class that defy simple
definitions of American-ness.[5] The link to cricket and other South Asian
cultural forms is a racial register through which South Asian American
men are projected as "forever foreign" and not suitably man enough to
play U.S. sports. Yet, the activities on the court and subsequent conversations open up definitions of identity where "new skin replaces old
[definitions]" through bodily practices of skill, toughness, aggression,
creativity, and domination.

Each basketball act on the court, such as Viraj's dunk, is a simultaneous engagement of self in relation to other men while it constructs an arsenal[6] of "weapons against definition." The teams perform South Asian

American identity through "difference" and not through equivalence,[7] even though they share similar stories of marginalization and racialization. By delving into the history of Indo-Pak Basketball, how young desi men express their ethnic and religious identities through basketball, and into the means by which South Asian American communal identities are iterated along racial and class lines, we can see how South Asian American identities are performed in and in relation to the institution of Indo-Pak Basketball. In the first instance, the participants construct a desi place out of the physical space while sharing a sameness in appropriation of American popular culture. In the other instance, they challenge and mark ethno-religious difference from other men through their sporting practices. Finally, they challenge singular conceptions of identity at the very moment that they essentialize and exclude African American men. Within this arena of sport, young South Asian American men fashion and refashion definitions of desi masculinity that challenge mainstream racializations while concurrently enforcing parameters of belonging within the diasporic communities.

Marginalizations within Mainstream Basketball

Indo-Pak Basketball tournaments, such as the Chicago IPN, stand in contrast to pickup basketball. Highly organized basketball circuits, like Indo-Pak Basketball, afford young South Asian American men and their peers an opportunity to rearticulate a South Asian American identity that is not welcomed in other highly institutional realms of organized sport. For instance, several of these young men played high school and collegiate basketball. Although sport is often sanctioned as a safe space and place of resistance to racism in the larger world,[8] South Asian American athletes intimately endure the marginalizing processes in structured, organized, and revered realms of basketball. K-Rock is a Hindu American of Gujarati background who was a sophomore collegiate point guard playing at a Division II collegiate basketball program. At the 2006 Chicago IPN, he played for a heterogeneous ethnic and religious Indo-Pak team known as Philly Fay. K-Rock, like several of the other Indo-Pak players, shared stories of racist taunting, boundary maintenance of American sport by whites and African Americans, and increased essentialism with negative connotations after the 9/11 terrorist attacks. He described the racism he felt at nationally sanctioned games by the National Collegiate Athletic Association (NCAA).

Instead of these games taking place in a neutral space governed solely by merit, he lamented that "there is racism elsewhere [in opposition to Indo-Pak Basketball]. At one of the games, [opposing] fans were shouting, 'Go back to Afghanistan!'" The racial formation of "Muslim looking" (Ahmad 2004) envelops South Asian men, whether of Muslim, Hindu, or other ethno-religious backgrounds, into a vague and expanding racial category physically grounded in the symbolic landscape of the "Middle East" or "Arab land."[9] The comments by the opposing fans are part and parcel of the production of the "patriot" and the unassimilable "terrorist" embodied in a dangerous brown body. The opposing fans police, regulate, and expel certain players from the national fabric while ingratiating themselves into that very same American-ness. "As strategies of surveillance, the panopticon and the profile work simultaneously to produce the terrorist and the patriot in one body, the turbaned body" (Puar and Rai 2004: 82). Here the fan defines himself/herself as the "patriot" through the racialized figure of K-Rock's body. The global "war on terror" is interwoven into the social relations, on the court and in U.S. publics, between what is deemed mainstream America and its abjection. Organized basketball—be it in high school, college, professional, or Olympic formats—is a forum for representing one's community, one's city, one's alma mater, or one's nation. K-Rock's dislocation is a refusal by fans to allow South Asian Americans to be defined within American-ness in collegiate sport.

However, we must not fall into the trap of assuming that such racial dislocation of South Asian Americans from U.S. sport began to take place only after 9/11. The Arab American studies scholars Amaney Jamal and Nadine Naber trace a long historical trajectory of shifting racializations and exclusions of Arab Americans.[10] They do not point to 9/11 as a starting point of problematic racial formations but as a "turning point" at which certain passionate racist discourse and nativist sentiment becomes easily mapped onto "Muslim/Arab/South Asian/Mexican/Native American/African American" bodies.[11] Harpreet, whom we met earlier, played with a majority Sikh American team at the 1994 Greenville Tournament. His experiences of racialization and racist depictions while playing high school baseball and basketball included umpires asking him if he spoke English and opposing (white) fans in basketball chanting "sand nigger."[12] The epithet points to the racial boundaries of 21st-century American sport that position certain men as more deserving of citizenship. Institutionalized sport is thus a site of "racial formation"[13] where racial categories, through performances of cultural citizenship, are constructed, managed, negotiated, challenged, and sometimes destroyed in relation to "belonging" and American-ness. The young men challenge their racialization by positioning themselves as a certain type of (athletic) American man.

(Re)-Defining Desi-ness

Even at the moments in which the specter of the "terrorist" affects South Asian American participation in mainstream sport, other stereotypes also exist. The flattening of South Asian Americans specifically and Asian Americans in general as nerds plays out in mainstream sport and in South Asian American communities. Even in their own South Asian American communities, which we might overstate as safe spaces, the young men do not always have the opportunity to offer their versions of South Asian American identity. Sanjay, of team California Shockwaves, shared that within the South Asian American community there are not opportunities, as there are in Indo-Pak Basketball, to synchronize sporting identities with South Asian American cultural identities. He recalled, "When I was in high school . . . early 90s, there was no such league. . . . You didn't even think there are other Indians there [basketball spaces], that's kind of how it is. . . . I was an aspiring young athlete when I was younger, because of our culture. . . . The athletic part of our genes, as you were saying earlier, is not really expressed. . . . You are an individual, lost person, in this large world of sports." Sanjay then moved into the contemporary moment, "There are so many ways we can celebrate our culture, and that includes basketball. It [basketball] hasn't been part of the Indian community till IPB [Indo-Pak Basketball]." Sporting practices are part of the cultural toolkit of identity formation, even though the hegemony of professional success and academic achievement—the "model minority"—limits those articulations of identity. Sanjay was able to find his way and expand the possibilities of expressing South Asian American–ness through participation in Indo-Pak Basketball. Indo-Pak Basketball represents a site for the continuum of basketball excellence that extends beyond adolescence and is woven into the fabric of desi identity.

Other participants in Indo-Pak Basketball have had a long historical affinity to basketball; their participation at the Chicago IPN is part and parcel of a longer process of identity formation. Rathi, a female Chicago IPN organizer, offered her perspective: "I'm not sure if it [Indo-Pak Basketball] gives them a new [masculine] identity, but I do believe it has given another identity that wasn't so dominant before. I think about 10 years ago or so, many parents only wanted their sons to focus on their education and didn't see a need to make time or have any interest in anything else, especially sports." For certain segments of the South Asian American community, Indo-Pak Basketball is institutionalized as a key site of socialization, while providing an alternate to the means of identity formation in the larger South Asian American community.

Mainstream sport, as a reflection of U.S. society, continues to be a site negotiated through a myriad of racial politics. As young men like K-Rock and Harpreet endure socially marginalizing racializations, their own ideas of membership in sport is then governed by the racialized politics of exclusion at intersections of masculinity, respectability, and ability. When the young men from across North America arrive to play at the Chicago IPN or the other big Indo-Pak Basketball tournaments in Dallas, Washington, DC, and San Francisco, they bring not only their team uniforms but racial baggage that is a part of American sport. As South Asian American men desire competitive basketball forums, they are able to secure their desired athletic setting by taking part in the politics of exclusion and inclusion simultaneously. In fact, New York Ballaholics captain Andrew attended to this fluid racial identification in the opening vignette by addressing how the categories of membership shift in various sporting arenas. For him, the racial makeup of his team depends on the tournament they plan to attend. Thus, Andrew could not take certain players who are of mixed-race heritage to a few tournaments where the "definition" of South Asian American-ness has racial contours that disallow his peers to be, in his words, "recognized."

How does race then play out in Indo-Pak Basketball? What are the ways in which performing race is also a means of delineating masculinity? These questions govern the experience of sporting cultures. For desi athletes to invert their racialization, they invoke race and class to position themselves as certain types of men in opposition to other racialized masculinities. Desi players appropriate and produce versions of athletic swagger and make their bodies into sites of desire for the occupants of the gym. Players rejoice in the success of their African American basketball idols and take up aspects of black stylistics/aesthetics, but they create a racial difference from the everyday African Americans and working-class desi men they encounter as a way to delineate themselves as respectable types of men. As a result, the invocations of race are fluid, contradictory, dynamic, and intersectional. At the very moment in which they negotiate identities in relation to other co-ethnic desi men, they also adjudicate the racial boundaries of South Asian American masculinity. When teams arrive to play at the Chicago IPN, their social formations are signs of intimacy and long histories of male bonding.

"It was Michael Jordan's City": The Birth of U.S. Indo-Pak Basketball

For many players within the South Asian American basketball community, the Chicago IPN symbolizes the pinnacle of desi basketball. Winning it promises substantial symbolic capital within the Indo-Pak Basketball community. Teams fly in from various cities across the United States and Canada. There exists a whole cadre of organizers and volunteers who give time to structure the tournament. The players financially cover their flight, tournament fees, hotel, food, and other leisure activities (such as going to local dance clubs at Chicago IPN, Dallas IPN, Washington, DC, IPN, and the California [San Francisco] IPN). The tournaments are a way to celebrate the desi sporting body as athletic spectacles, as hope, and as affirmations of American-ness.

The players believe that Chicago IPN differs in significant ways, both logistically and symbolically, from other South Asian American basketball formats and multiracial U.S. basketball leagues. Players emphasized that Indo-Pak Basketball brought in a higher level of talent and prestige than their respective localized desi basketball venues, such as Monday/Thursday night pickup basketball in Atlanta. To explore its importance further, I met with Max, whom participants recognized playfully as the "godfather" of Indo-Pak Basketball. He is a Chicago Protestant Christian Malayalee man who is also a high-level tech and finance professional. During our first conversation, I asked him about his love for basketball. I mistakenly assumed that he had always loved basketball. He quickly responded, "Well, I didn't play basketball initially. I loved *baseball* and that was what I played. . . . All my friends started playing basketball."[14] He paused for a second and provided me with a "duh" moment: "I am from Chicago; it was Michael Jordan's city. I couldn't escape it. I loved the competition." Max's take to basketball is indicative of a larger turn by sporting communities toward basketball locally, nationally, and globally. With the figure of Michael Jordan as a cherished commodity, the NBA colluded with various corporate partners to market the NBA/Jordan brand globally.[15] Max encountered basketball intimately through the local Boys and Girls Club in Chicago, as well as within his ethnic Malayalee church. As youth across the country were taking up basketball in greater numbers in the late 1980s and early 1990s, young South Asian American men, like Max, likewise created their sporting affinities through African American sporting heroes like Michael Jordan. However, their desires to emulate professional basketball icons, consume "basketball cool," and take up basketball met resistance in the greater U.S. society, where these young men were seen, in the 1980s and 1990s, as lacking both the racial (bodily) constituency and appropriate cultural competency to play.

Despite the ideological grounding of basketball as black-white, an increasing love for basketball emerged in immigrant communities alongside Michael Jordan's global iconicity. Even the local Chicago Malayalee Association and Malayalee churches took up basketball. Max explained, "They [the Malayalee Association and church] would break up the teams and have tournaments. But [pause], they would stack the best players on two teams. There wasn't any competition; it wasn't fair." At the church, the cliques and politics within led to minimal competition. Without the uncertainty of who would win on any given day, the lack of parity frustrated Max and deprived this sporting space of the pleasure of competition. Winning at the Malayalee events could not guarantee or shore up his conception of a sporting identity that paralleled the competition in the NBA among the Chicago Bulls, Los Angeles Lakers, Detroit Pistons, and Boston Celtics.

With a desire for competition and parity, Max instituted the first U.S. Indo-Pak Basketball tournament in 1989. He used his connections in Malayalee churches and Malayalee cultural organizations, such as FOKANA (Federation of Kerala Associations in North America),[16] as well as the informal system of "word of mouth," to attract South Asian American communities from Houston and other parts of the United States to compete against Chicago's heterogeneous South Asian American community. The federation provided a strong foundation to reach Malayalee communities across North America and advertise the tournament. Although the tournament is named "Indo-Pak National," it is not shorthand for just India and Pakistan. The use of "Indo-Pak," although it encapsulates the hegemony of India and Pakistan in South Asian politics, stems from the ways in which heterogeneous communities use this lexicon for easier reference even if they are from Sri Lanka, Bangladesh, or other diasporas.[17] The binary of India-Pakistan does not necessarily surface on the ground as Indo-Pak Basketball participants identify as desis, which connotes a greater multivocal, multilocal conceptualization of South Asian American–ness.

Max instituted a game structure at the initial Indo-Pak Basketball tournament that players appreciate. It corresponds to the type of play in other U.S. basketball venues: "No one [other desis] had a tournament like this [Chicago IPN]. The Malayalee Association used to take $110, didn't give us refs, had an outdoor court, and the trophy was this big [motions with his hand to an object that is small]." He added, "First tournament was $35 and I gave everyone shirts. The Malayalee association charged $110. What are you guys doing with the $500 [you raise]? I used to work at the Boys and Girls Club, and I had a gym there. So, basically, I said, 'Hey can I borrow the gym for the tournament and I'll give you the profits coming in.' They gave me the gym for the weekend. . . . We made $400 and gave it to the club." With a borrowed gym and outdoor courts, Max initially held the Chicago IPN twice a year with trained referees and an awards ceremony. He and other organizers eventually made it into a once-a-year tournament. The first tournament in 1989 had Malayalee American teams, Sikh American teams, and Muslim American teams from Chicago while reaching out to teams from Houston, Texas. Now teams come from U.S. and Canadian cities with large South Asian populations. With the borrowed gym from the Boys and Girls Club, Max, other volunteers, and teams were able to make the basketball court into a South Asian American place. Organizers of the Chicago IPN worked diligently to transform the gyms into a meaningful South Asian American communal place. It was hermeneutically reconfigured to celebrate the passions and achievements of South Asian American male athletes.

Making a South Asian American Place

Through strategic planning and careful manipulation of space and time, Chicago IPN is a type of institutionalized basketball that garners great reviews from players. The tournament both resembles and differs from other basketball tournaments in the United States. The Indo-Pak Basketball tournaments' structure corresponds to the format for collegiate basketball, with two halves and a strict code of high school rules uniformly shared by referees. The two halves, unlike collegiate basketball halves of 20 minutes, are either 18 minutes or 16 minutes in order to increase the number of games played in a certain day. The games have a running clock, which does not stop at every infraction except during the last two minutes of the game. Shorter games allow the Chicago IPN organizers to maximize time in the rented gym in order to finish as many preliminary and playoff games as possible within the limited time span of an extended weekend. As a result, the game duration is significantly shorter than that of official collegiate games. Before the start of the tournament, Max and other organizers meet with referees and volunteer staff to go over the format of the games, the rule guide they will follow, and how to direct player questions/concerns to organizers. After the conclusion of the Chicago IPN championship game, large trophies and medals are handed out to teams as well as individuals. The basic tournament format is equivalent to that at other basketball tournaments around the United States. However, subtle and explicit manipulations of the physical space exist to make over the space with a sense of South Asian American–ness.

The 2008 Chicago Indo-Pak National tournament organizers Max, Rathi (Max's wife and co-organizer), and Jake (a white peer) invoke contrapuntal cultural motifs to inscribe South Asian American–ness onto the built environment. The sport scholars C. Gaffney and J. Bale contend that "the senses of belonging not only to history but to a larger collective identity are vital components of the stadium experience" (2004: 37).[18] Various sensory cues are intentionally integrated into the stadium experience to underline a desi ethos and facilitate the browning out of the gym. In this instance, the process of browning out involves weaving in South Asian American sporting histories alongside the already present athletic histories, awards, and celebrations at the gym. These historical markers do not erase other histories but effect an integration that makes South Asian American athletic identities a normal part of this urban American landscape.

Indo-Pak Basketball organizers in Chicago do not have access to their own facility to host the tournament. They rent private and public gyms that are not usually coded with any markers of South Asian American-ness. At the 2006 Chicago IPN, Max, Charles (Malayalee American), Rathi, and Jake intentionally arranged the high school gym in a particular manner through their use of banners to inflect South Asian American-ness to a space with a strong black athletic history. Charles mentions, proudly, that Corey Maggette (an NBA player) attended this high school as a young man. He and his co-organizers tried to bring Maggette back to Chicago for the tournament, but to no avail. Alongside narratives about the greatness of black athletes, the organizers simultaneously use various visual cues to claim the space and celebrate desi athletes. On one of the banners at the 2006 IPN, English script is transposed into Hindi stylistics. Participants understand the creative play to incorporate linguistic fonts from both English and Hindi. The mingling of distinct linguistic mediums captures a sense of *sameness*, as a desi community.

High school and college sporting facilities, like those the 2008 Chicago IPN organizers utilize, contain their own corporate sponsors, such as Powerade, Nike, and Coca Cola, on their walls. In 2008, alongside these banners, the organizers juxtaposed smaller but meaningful banners celebrating desi sponsors. At the Chicago City University[19] court, where the playoff games were held, Patel Brothers, a well-known grocery chain with franchises in several cities, was one of the main desi sponsors with a banner. Alongside the banner of Patel Brothers was a banner acknowledging the Chicago Punjabi Heritage Society, as well as individual sponsors. Max displayed on the floor alongside the university court the T-shirts given out to players over the previous 20 years of Chicago IPN.

These T-shirts extend a shared history of desi basketball communities back beyond the 2008 moment. A few players had been at almost all of the tournaments while others either played in or had older brothers/ relatives who played at several Chicago IPNs.

The final T-shirt was the 2008 creative image of a blackened silhouette body (presumed male) dunking and hanging on a basketball goal. Beyond this stood a set of top-20 lists on large posters stands. The top-20 lists next to the T-shirts consisted of memorable moments over IPN's two decades. The top-20 Indo-Pak storylines ranged from athletic feats to funny incidents. The lists elevated the lives of participants of Indo-Pak Basketball and placed the participating men at the forefront of this history, while the huge Chicago City University's banners serve as background, not center stage.

One list recognized the top teams from the last two decades, while another celebrated individual athletic excellence. These accolades serve to position certain groups of men over others and distinguish some as more spectacular than others. The players are situated as part of a longer history of desi basketball even as the space is reworked to celebrate the South Asian American athletic body. Instead of only admiring and imitating white and black athletes, the lists provide a much more accessible pantheon of desi heroes. By creating a list of the top teams, the organizers insert teams other than NBA and collegiate teams into a collective South Asian American cultural memory. The placement of T-shirts and the top-20 lists onto the gym reinforces a sense of shared cultural memory that comes about by creating an exclusionary racial milieu.

Acts of place making additionally transpire when players verbally mingle on and off the court, incorporating South Asian linguistic terms in Punjabi, Urdu, and Gujarati with English vernacular. They tease each other and "talk trash."[20] Using both South Asian and English vernacular, they transform the previous English-only linguistic milieu of this space.

The Toronto Khalsa team had finished their game earlier on Friday. Their Sikh compatriots, the NJ/Cali Soormay Franchise team, had just won the previous game. Players from both teams huddled together in one corner of the gym while I interviewed Pukh, the captain of the Soormay Franchise team. The vocal celebrations and banter made is difficult for us to carry out our conversation. And it was hard to not to be distracted by the fun taking place in the stands. As the interview was ending, a burst of laughter came from the right side of the stands where most of the Toronto Khalsa players had gathered. Singh, a short Sikh Canadian who got little playing time on the court, asserted his manhood by teasing one of the other players, "Come on bauji [father or old man],[21] you got passed [another player sped past you]." He then teased players by appraising their movements. The players from Soormay Franchise moved closer to Singh as they, too, joined in on the appraisals of play. In this moment, Singh had become a spectacle that others enjoyed, even though he was nearly invisible when his team was on the court. The laughter echoed through the hallway as the teams exited for food and preparation for their next game.

The Sikh teams from Canada and the United States congregated in one corner of the gym and teased other players on the court using Punjabi and English idioms. Such teasing and trash talking affirms intimacies among the co-ethnic men while incorporating linguistic means of affiliation that incorporated both English and Punjabi.[22] By carefully switching linguistic codes in the midst of trash talking, Singh elevated himself through his comedic interventions at the expense of other South Asian men. As players switched linguistic codes, other audio cues infiltrated the court. The deep bass tones of hip-hop anthems resonated against the brick walls of the building. Many heads bobbed up and down to the beats on the speakers during time-outs and between games. When hip-hop songs were not playing, the tournament organizers infused the beats of Panjabi MC and his global hit "Mundian To Bach Ke" (Beware of the boys) with hip-hop artist Jay-Z's voice on the remix.[23] Hip-hop and elements of cultural blackness infiltrated this space and were instrumental in the making the physical structure of the gym in a South Asian American place.

In addition to these visual and audio cues, senses of smell and taste served critical roles in facilitating a sense of shared collective identity.[24] Chicago IPN organizers offered a cornucopia of food including both traditional American sports fare and South Asian delicacies. At the gym's food stand, participants could purchase pizza, hot dogs, various sodas, and Gatorade. At lunchtime, tournament organizers brought in food that 2006 Chicago IPN organizer Charles labeled "desi" food. The "desi" food f(l)avored certain hegemonic "North Indian–ness" as the site for constructing desi-ness. Even though several of the key organizers were Malayalee Americans, traditional South Indian food was not brought to the event. This was one instance in which food is emblematic of how North Indian bodies, cultures, and histories often stand in as the template of South Asian American–ness. A local Chicago South Asian restaurant offered South Asian delicacies like naan, biriyani, chicken tikka masala, naan, tandoori chicken, and saag paneer.[25] At the gym, the distinctive smells of the South Asian dishes mingled with the smell of pizza and hot dogs and the crisp artificial fruit smell of Gatorade. One could be an athlete, have Gatorade, and eat some biriyani with saag paneer. Although these actions might not be seen as harmonious combinations in many sporting spaces, here they combined South Asian and U.S. cultural artifacts to confirm a shared sensibility as South Asian Americans.[26] That shared sensibility through the manipulation of the physical environment worked alongside the particular team histories and corresponding team names that inflected other meanings upon the space.

Managing Histories and Team Identities

The meanings of South Asian American–ness through visual cues, sounds, and smells nurtured for players, organizers, volunteers, and spectators a sense of a cosmopolitan-ness through their multiply located consumptive practices of South Asian and American cultural forms. Other elements of consumption played vital roles in identity formation and representation. A close examination of team names reveals the level of self-awareness of masculinity and reconfiguring of racial identity made possible through consumption of popular cultures across national and diasporic spaces. The trend, however, both in the social world and in the academy, has been to conflate South Asian American consumptive practices with South Asian cultural forms, especially Bollywood. When I asked Ali of the Atlanta Outkasts if he watches Bollywood films, he quickly shook his head. "No man, I don't watch that. I got no interest in that. That is what the uncles and aunties [older generation] and FOBs [a pejorative term for new immigrants; i.e., "fresh off the boat"] do." Even though Indian cinema is a global phenomenon and one venue for expressing diasporic identities, Ali chose to deliberately distance himself from Bollywood to showcase the nature of his performances of South

Asian American–ness. Players in Indo-Pak Basketball consume U.S. popular culture on many levels and use aspects of it to signify their place as ethnic Americans by displacing the racialization generally conferred on new immigrants and their parents' generation. The consumption of U.S. popular culture, ironically enough, also constitutes one way to detail their own ethno-religious histories.

Teams and players at the Chicago IPN appropriated various forms of U.S. popular cultural artifacts, such as movies and music, to signal their (social) location, on and off the court. Max, the "godfather" of Indo-Pak Basketball, played on the Chicago Untouchables team. The team name, "Chicago Untouchables," is polyvalent and highlights the complex, multiple terrains of representation. Chicago is home to specific mafia history that has been represented in the wildly popular cinematic depiction *The Untouchables*.[27] The movie highlights the conflicts between the mafia and the police in Prohibition-era Chicago. A strong, aggressive, and tough masculinity is valorized in the movie that celebrates violence by both the police and the mafia. Although a general sense of "cultural blackness" (Kelley 1997; Vargas 2007) weaves through the fabric of South Asian American sporting masculinity, the choice of "Untouchables" demonstrates a clear engagement with localized popular cultural forms and white aesthetics through which to depict one's community in relation to Chicago's history. In line with the acceptable and celebrated depictions of white masculinity on film, it is now understandable why Indo-Pak participants refer to Max as the "godfather." The reference conjures up images of respect, toughness, and manliness. In a similar vein, the team name, Chicago Untouchables, is woven through with this thread of a tough, dominating, and imposing masculinity. The name additionally represents "basketball cool." By using the name "Untouchables," Max and his teammates link it with the basketball idiom "can't be touched." In this sense, a player or team's continued dominance over another positions them as greatly superior, thus *untouchable*. The play on words allows the players to appropriate elements of U.S. popular culture and translate them into the realm of basketball to represent themselves at athletic, strong men.

Although members of the Chicago Untouchables creatively delve into an aspect of U.S. popular culture to reference their identities, the team name also implicates South Asia and South Asian histories. The team name additionally references the players' ancestral identities as "untouchables," who are the lowest rung on the caste totem pole in conservative Indian politics. Some Dalits[28] ("Dalit" is the self-identifying term for "untouchable") find liberation from the rigid caste system through their conversion to Christianity. Max and some of his teammates on Chicago Untouchables are Malayalee Christians whose ancestors were some of the earliest Hindu converts to Christianity (particularly to Catholicism).[29] The team additionally contains some Sikh and Muslim players whom high-caste Hindu Brahmanic politics additionally brands as untouchables. These three religious-ethnic identities contest the hierarchical Hindu structure and reflect a vision of South Asia beyond the Hindu-Muslim binary while inserting a new social ranking, through sport, that positions these "Untouchables" above Hindu men on the basketball court.

The voluntary nature of team formation in Indo-Pak Basketball further exemplifies social intimacies constructed through, but not limited by, one's caste, religion, and national background.[30] In his elegant examination of Cuban baseball and spectatorship, anthropologist Thomas Carter elaborates upon how sport presents "not just venues for representation and participation but also solidarity and fraternity" (2008: 74). Similar to the Cuban baseball spectators who evoke a sense of Cuban identity, *Cubanidad*, through their engagement with baseball, the South Asian American basketball players re-signified the physical venue and articulate an athletic identity that did not resemble the usual patterns of ethno-religious segregation in South Asia.[31] Players shared a sense of fraternity or brotherhood that is encompassing of their ethno-religious background as differently racialized American men but not limited by it. One of the New York teams at the 2008 Chicago IPN was the New York D-Unit team. Similar to the Outkasts, D-Unit team members turn to cultural blackness to invoke tropes of tough masculinity and urban "cool." New York City is home to hip-hop star Fifty Cent (Curtis Jackson III) and his posse and corporate brand G-Unit (the "G" is for "gangsta"). For young desi men who experience emasculation in mainstream U.S. culture, their consumptive practices of "cultural blackness," through team names, provide one way to recoup a tough, "cool," but distinctly South Asian American masculinity. The "D" in D-Unit stands for "desi." With four Sikhs, four Hindus (one who identifies as Guyanese), and one Muslim, D-Unit captured one element of the ethno-religious heterogeneity of desi men through shared consumption of black aesthetics. [32] Unlike much of the immigration literature that sees assimilation as the loss of ethnicity,[33] the choice of team names in Indo-Pak Basketball demonstrates an active engagement with ethnicity and American-ness. Sporting cultures, such as that present at the Chicago IPN, are spaces where ethnicity, manliness, and American-ness are collapsed. Team names like D-Unit, Outkasts, and Untouchables provide evidence of how South Asian histories and corresponding ethnic identities are carefully woven into team/communal names.

The New York D-Unit team was not the sole set of players to appropriate black cultural forms to represent their South Asian American identity. Part of the browning out of the organized basketball court was the allowance, preponderance, and performances of black stylistics. Players across teams embraced this form of expression in a myriad of ways. Through their clothing choices, players constructed images of a personal and collective "self."[34] Players judged each other on style as did fans. The sociologist C. J. Pascoe, in her examination of gender formation in high school, theorizes the complexity of masculinity formation not only in its performances but also in its reception: "It is important to attend to the manipulation, deployment, and enactment of varieties of masculinity, not just as what men do, but as how respondents recognize it" (2007: 166). Mary, a white spectator dating Sean on the Maryland Five Pillars team, received and recognized a relationship among clothing, race, and masculinity:

> If I were to date a white guy, for example, and taking Sean, a big Indian, he wears a lot of athletic wear, what you would see a black guy wear, for example. If I were dating a white guy who's wearing the same thing I wouldn't like that because it seems inauthentic; I really don't like it when white guys think they are another ethnicity, especially black. For some reason, when Sean wears or any other person in Indo-Pak league wears athletic stuff. . . . It seems authentic to me, it doesn't really bother me. . . . These males adopted an urban identity, a black identity, and it's working for them. I think they make it their own. . . . It doesn't seem inauthentic.

Mary's statement underscores how articulations of "authenticity" and "urban identity" for certain populations depend on consumption of black aesthetics. South Asian American–ness, as explicated by Mary, exists in relation to whiteness and blackness. Although she did not conflate African Americans and South Asian Americans, she did open up possibilities to think about complicated processes of racial identification. As racially non-white, some South Asian Americans utilize urban stylistics and black aesthetics to simultaneously collapse the category of "American" and "South Asian." Simple consumption of white aesthetics does not always do this type of recuperative work as basketball has been racially indexed as black, regardless of its long white historical past. Although whiteness is ambiguous, multiple, contradictory, and dynamic,[35] desi consumption of white aesthetics does not translate into full American citizenship unless one attempts to appropriate a much more universal theme of tough white masculinity—such as that creatively used by the Chicago Untouchables. For the most part, the invisibility of whiteness is part of its power to stand in as the norm through its continuous projection of the hyper-visible non-normative man. For this community of men who have faced emasculation alongside stereotypical projections as "terrorists" in other circuits, their racial position as "perpetual foreigners" makes it impossible to effectively use the whiteness that slips past their grasp. Whiteness is the foundation of their abjection, and thus they are not able to hold onto it. However, the valences of "cool" and "toughness" associated with black stylistics, already translated as a valuable commodity in the marketplace, affords entry into American-ness as more masculine men. By appropriating black cultural forms, the browned-out court was open for desis to stake an alternate mode of belonging in the urban milieu. Once they come up with team names, paraphernalia, and other symbolic representations of a team identity in a South Asian American space, the teams then took on the task of differentiating themselves from each other through the physical activities on the court. Basketball moves could position certain teams and individuals higher on the athletic hierarchy.

"Beat That Shit!"

Although team formation is an instrumental first part of representing one's self and one's community, it is through athletic feats and intricate, creative maneuvers that participants most clearly set themselves apart from other men on the desi basketball court. Physical domination on the court is the epitome of one-upping and manning up against co-ethnic peers. In this sense, basketball skill matters very much. In the opening vignette, Viraj's dunks set him apart from his opponents and his own teammates. He became an exemplar in a setting with proficiently skilled basketball players. His feats became even more remarkable as the tournament format traditionally highlight teams, not individuals. Thus Viraj's ability to stand out in this sporting ethos foregrounded his athletic excellence. He was put on a pedestal, and the community of men admired him. However, those moments of standing out can also come with certain racialized judgments. For example, players, who often are trained through middle-class networks of organized sport, such as club teams and summer camps, would chastise certain other players for being too individualistic, or selfish, or for being primarily concerned with their style and not the team outcome. Nevertheless, the contact between players, even in a team ethos, led to opportunities in which the team could shine alongside the celebration of a few individuals.

For players Viraj, Mustafa, and Ali, their individual recognition carried a lot of social capital in a sporting space inhabited by other deft basketball players. In addition, the style of play in organized basketball added a new set of challenges to individual excellence. At Chicago IPN, as in other organized basketball circuits, teams employed team defenses, zone defenses, and strategic defensive schemes. With trained officials at Chicago IPN and the Washington, DC, IPN, players do not have the same kinds of creative freedoms as they do in pickup ball. The lax rules in pickup basketball allow multiple types of dribbling styles that would be violations in organized basketball. "There are clear limits, however, for the improvisation of these movements, as they must be recognizable within the limits of a system of movements" (Brown 2006: 164). To garner individual recognition and praise in a setting with limited man-on-man opportunities, players must creatively employ their bodies within the uniform protocol of rules established by the tournament organizers and officials while attempting to set themselves apart from the competition. The symbolic dividends are enormous and resonate within the Indo-Pak Basketball community long after the act—as was the case of Viraj and his dunking. When I first met up with Max at the 2006 Chicago IPN, he remembered Mustafa and Ali as a result of their exceptional basketball feats in Indo-Pak Basketball even though they had not played against each other in over a decade. Both Mustafa and Ali were prolific scorers; Ali garnered additional praise for his dribbling and passing skills. But Max did not remember or recognize me, even though I was a starter on the Atlanta Outkasts. He did remember our team and its history of basketball success in the Indo-Pak Basketball circuit. For players like me, the team recognition spills over as I could take pleasure from our team's success. In a similar vein, Indo-Pak Basketball players knew many of the players on the Maryland Five Pillars (a team of mostly [Ahmadi] Muslims and Hindus) not primarily as a result of their individual athletic prowess but, rather, because of their success as a team. Maryland Five Pillars won the 2006 and 2008 Chicago IPN.

The display of basketball skills and corresponding bodily movements stood out as the key site for the politics of difference among teams and among individuals. At Chicago IPN and other Indo-Pak Basketball circuits, players had the opportunity to demonstrate skill in order to set themselves apart from other athletically talented men.[36] This venue was a safe space, unlike other multiracial basketball gyms where they are racialized as unfit and not man enough for basketball.

Daniel, whom we met earlier in Atlanta's pickup circuit, alluded to the freedom of not having to "play a (racialized) role" in desi-structured pickup ball. That same kind of freedom to play a variety of positions does not always exist in organized, tournament basketball. The player positions (such as point guard, shooting guard, small forward, power forward, and center) are not as fluid in organized basketball as there are demands by their team to stay within certain roles on the court. Indo-Pak Basketball players more readily accept a role on the team in order to succeed in organized basketball. Thus, when I played in the 1998 Chicago IPN with the Atlanta Outkasts, I had to play the role of "defensive stopper," thereby limiting my touches on the offensive side of the game.

As players sacrifice the glory and recognition that individual accolades bring, there still existed a strong desire by players to "show out" (excel and dominate) their opponents through their personal and collective bodies. "The performance of identities is not always a straightforward replica of the social self, but a mobile exchange of bodily movements, looks, gestures, feelings and personal constructions of social space" (Dudrah 2002: 378). South Asian American basketball players utilized their bodily abilities and basketball training to signify their place, amid the mainstream racializations and their localized experiences, in this sporting hierarchy. The acts of signification involved various movements, gestures, and acts of athletic swagger. While the players practiced exemplary basketball movements similar to those found in other venues throughout the United States on the Indo-Pak court, the South Asian American men did not have the same relationship to basketball as black and white men. Mary, the white spectator whom we met earlier, alluded to how the participants of Indo-Pak Basketball reconfigure the common racializations of their brown bodies: "You associate basketball more with the black population and, I think, people from India, Pakistan, and Southeast Asians have a reputation for not being really athletic. . . . I had a hard time believing Sean was Indian at 6'6"." Being athletic and physically intimidating are not features generally ascribed to South Asian American male bodies, which are generally seen as frail. Sean's bodily integrity, at 6'6", countered such stereotypes. But his body alone could not recuperate the long history of emasculation. Rather, his body had to demonstrate highly skilled basketball moves alongside toughness, aggression, and victories. Sean and his co-ethnic peers actively had to use their bodies, within basketball rules, to dominate other men in order to be evaluated positively.

The act of "palming" the basketball represents one such activity that inverts the stereotype of desi men. Some players palmed the ball before dribbling or after dribbling it. They would not palm the ball while dribbling as that is called a "carry," a basketball violation. When performing the act of "palming," the athletes placed their palms on top of the ball and held it with their palm. The ball then hung down from their palms. Palming the basketball is a common practice, but not all men can do it. The act highlights the large hands of certain South Asian American men, countering the stereotype of desi men as petite, who have neither the large frame nor muscular ability to palm a basketball. As Michael Jordan is well known for this move, demonstrating this skill allows players to take joy in "being like Mike" (a famous McDonald's advertising slogan [Andrews 2000]) and in being able to be part of a larger discourse of sporting "cool" and masculinity.

Each challenge by team against team and individual against individual incorporated a diverse set of basketball plays, not just "palming"

the ball. One specific basketball practice that won praise from participants consisted of blocking an opponent's shot. Mustafa, of the Atlanta
Outkasts, bragged about how he "beat that shit," referencing the act of
blocking an opponent's shot. Mustafa spoke with much delight: "I guard
the weak guys on the team. I can leave my man and come from behind
and *beat that shit*."[37] Mustafa's teammates, like me, would play the role
of defensive stoppers while he floated around to come to our assistance
in case we struggled to defend. Blocking is an act of physical domination
in the midst of a heated game. The defender physically and symbolically rises above his opponent and blocks the shot. In this sense, as in
dunking the basketball, the player mans up by literally elevating himself
higher than his opponent. The same was especially true of Viraj's dunk
in the opening vignette. Sociologist Scott Brooks, in *Black Men Can't
Shoot*, explains that "dunking [like blocking] on another player is very
impressive because it is a notable physical feat, jumping and slamming
the ball through a basket that is ten feet high, and it is also a show of
dominance over someone" (2009: 31). Brooks explains how dunking and
blocking incur tremendous symbolic worth as it pits one player against
another with reputations at stake. When Indo-Pak players display such
vertical jumps and the forceful throwing down of the ball through the
hoop, they showcase athletic swagger and bravado not commonly associated with South Asian Americans. Viraj received accolades for his
ability to dunk the basketball. Not all men at the venue had the skill,
basketball acumen, or physical gifts that Viraj had to dunk a ball.

Macky, a Sikh player on the NJ/Cali Soormay Franchise team, was
praised for both his ability to dunk the ball and "beat that shit." At almost 6'9", his surprising agility and quickness made him a dual offensive and defensive threat. His spectacular abilities and skill allowed him
to play a variety of positions, unlike his teammates. He found ways to
control both ends of the court. Just when the opposing team's players
thought they had an easy shot, Macky would come running, extend his
lanky frame, jump forcefully, and block it, sending the ball flying into
the stands. This act elicited positives coos, "wows," and "whoas." With
the significantly better competition at Chicago IPN than that found in
local desi pickup ball, each act of dunking and blocking garnered greater
appreciation. Macky exhibited significant levels of timing and physical
ability to block his highly skilled opponents. Each time Macky blocked

an opponent's shot, he could bask in the glory of towering over his peers. At the end of the 2006 Chicago IPN, his continuous spectacular play was rewarded when Macky received the tournament's prestigious "defensive player" trophy.

The trophies were material evidence of Macky's basketball spectacularity. In the midst of a game, there are opportunities for defenders and offensive players to one-up each other and garner status. Defensive players accrue status by blocking shots, taking offensive fouls, or stealing the ball. These tactics are made possible by occupying the physical space of the opponent. During tournament play, Mustafa, of the Atlanta Outkasts, cut down the distance between himself and the offensive player in order to block the shot of his opponent. The offensive player deployed the opposite approach; he tried to create distance from the defender so as to score the ball. However, there are intimate bodily moments when an offensive player is praised for his scoring even with the defender in a tightly contested physical space. The "and 1" play highlights the strength and physical dominance of the offensive player. "And 1" is basketball vernacular for a play in which the offensive player is fouled in the act of shooting and still successfully makes the shot. The basket counts, and a free throw is awarded. During play, K-Rock, the point guard of the Philly Fay team, attacked the rim (opponent's goal) with fervor to either draw fouls or "dish" (pass) to his prolific shooting teammate Suresh. On one drive to the basket against the NJ/Cali Soormay Franchise team during the 2006 Chicago IPN playoff game, he was fouled hard by Rukh (a Sikh American who was the team's "tough" man). Rukh grabbed K-Rock's left hand and forcefully pulled him down in order to prevent an easy lay-up shot. Despite the physicality displayed by Rukh, K-Rock managed to score the basket with the ball in his right hand. The officials blew the whistle to call the foul and awarded K-Rock a free throw. K-Rock turned around, stared back at the players and audience with a concentrated, menacing look. He then let out a short but strong yell. His teammates gave firm high fives while Suresh bumped chests with him. Instead of having defenders contain him with their bodies, he had managed to use his strong upper body to facilitate physical contact but still score the basket. This moment changed the result of a tight game, and the momentum swung over to Philly Fay, which then went ahead to win the playoff game.

Alongside toughness and physical domination, some players accrue symbolic capital with creative basketball maneuvers. Instead of simply laying up the ball for an easy shot during lay-up lines, they take the ball to one side of the basket and float their bodies in the air across the goal to make the shot on the other side with the alternate hand. These ostentatious acts are performances of difficult skills validated through flawless execution and legitimated by the other people in this arena. During lay-up lines, there are no severe consequences, such as winning or losing, so players can delve into a wide assortment of creative gestures. Furthermore, the players train their bodies to make the difficult plays seem routine. Young men compete against each other to showcase their jumping ability, bodily balance, and finishing ability.

Creative dribbling and difficult passes also engender tremendous praise when performed in the midst of a game. Moves such as the "cross-over," spinning around the defender while dribbling, and demonstrating tight control of the ball receive positive appraisals from other players, spectators, and officials.[38] The cross-over, when done with speed and deft control of the ball, is a figurative crossing over of players into their renditions of normative sporting masculinity. When successfully executing the cross-over, one gains respect on the court and crosses over into the class of talented athletes, even if one's stay in this category is only for a short period. The move consists of a gamut of intricate maneuvers in which timing and bodily control are of utmost importance. There are a variety of ways to execute a cross-over. In general, the foundational elements of a successful cross-over consist of the offensive player dribbling the ball to one side of his body while pushing forward in one direction. Then the player suddenly shifts directions by bouncing the ball to the other side of the body. In this instance, the offensive player positions his body one way as a way to signal a move in that direction. The player then takes a dribble or two in that direction before swiftly changing the trajectory of the ball to the other side of his body. As a result of the swift unexpected move, the defending player is at the mercy of the offensive player. A well-executed cross-over destabilizes the defender and gives the offensive player room to get past the defender or to create space to take an uncontested shot.

Executing such difficult moves in the traffic of defenders demands a keen sense of one's placement on the court in relation to other players. Furthermore, one must have both the bodily ability and skill set to keep control of the ball while making rapid moves. Finally, players need to know when best to cross someone over. It is not an act one can script onto the court in advance of the game. These moves are spontaneous. They demonstrate the organic creativity players embody. Creative moves, such as the cross-over, often stand in as an exemplar of masculinity.[39] For example, when Macky, the nearly 6′9″ player on the NJ/Cali Soormay Franchise team, leaned down and pushed forward with his right hand dribbling the ball, he quickly swung the ball across through his legs to his left hand, pivoted his right foot, and spun around with his body rotating counterclockwise against the body of the shorter 6-foot defender. The sequence of events opened a lane for shot as the initial cross-over destabilized his opponent while the spin put the defender behind Macky, thus making it impossible for the defender to block his shot. Once Macky executed this complex set of actions in one smooth move, the players in the stands stood up and shouted in praise. Several put their fist to their mouth shouting, "Damn!" The move confused his opponent, who fell down, and Macky made his way to the basket for an easy "finger-roll" shot. Moves such as this aim to confuse the defender and make him lose his balance. If the defender actually falls to the ground, this comical act is known as "breaking someone's ankle." The offensive player's moves make the defender look athletically diminished, like someone who broke his ankle and no longer has the ability to compete at that moment.

Moves such as the cross-over demand a certain level of skill, commitment, and knowledge of the game. Several of the Indo-Pak players have years of training, so they are able to execute these moves spontaneously and flawlessly. Training of this sort means that some players sacrifice time engaging in other leisurely pursuits in favor of their love of basketball. Ali, of the Atlanta Outkasts, explains his commitment to sport: "When Qamar and Mustafa [his older brothers] went out to the [dance] clubs, I shot baskets and practiced for hours. I loved it; I would work on my shot and my dribbling, again and again." Through a dedication to practice, immersion in high-ranking basketball club teams, and frequent basketball interactions, some players like Ali rose in the localized ranks of South Asian American basketball players and in the larger local basketball landscape. Although players like Ali enjoy dominating the local desi basketball scene in Atlanta, he, Mustafa, and members of the

Atlanta Outkasts garner higher emotional rewards from playing against tough competition. In a way, they reflect their images of self while playing against equally skilled players. Indo-Pak Basketball represents a site in which other players understand the complex basketball movements on the court; there is bodily communicative competence. The participants desire the competition of Indo-Pak Basketball, in a way desiring their own bodies and abilities in a realm of athletic parity. K-Rock, a collegiate basketball player on the Philly Fay team, explains: "Our college was mostly Caucasian, so we don't know that many Indian people. . . . I was really surprised by how good the players were [at Chicago IPN]. Growing up you're always like 'I'm the best Indian player around,' that's what everybody thinks cause you don't know there are good Indian players around." Experiences at the North American Indo-Pak Basketball tournaments made K-Rock and his peers rethink their exceptionality and move toward normalizing South Asian American men in basketball. I also found this sentiment among players in Atlanta's South Asian American basketball community.

The level of play at Chicago IPN is much more competitive than localized play, as some players, like K-Rock, have played high school and collegiate basketball. Sean of Maryland Five Pillars played in the premier Amateur Athletic Union (AAU), a top-tier basketball league for youth, with the likes of DeMarr Johnson and Joe Forte, both young black men who played in the NBA. Sean and some other players had competed and succeeded in multiracial settings and then tried to dominate in this brown milieu. Even as these moments of individual success garnered recognition and respect, teams also displayed swagger with their victories in the tournament. At these moments, individual players were subsumed into their teams, and players represented their cities and communities when they battled on the court. In the process of setting themselves apart from their opponents athletically, they invoked ethnoreligious histories to further differentiate themselves.

Wearing Religion on Their Sleeves

In other basketball venues, the young desi men are not always valued for their skill and style regardless of what they are able to do with a basketball. Hindu American K-Rock of Philly Fay emphasized that the marginalizing experiences elsewhere do not necessarily materialize at Chicago IPN: "Nobody really wears their religion on their sleeves, you know you are respected. . . . Everybody here is just cool. . . . It is always about respect here. . . . Even in the heat of the game you would never think of fighting in these tournaments just because the atmosphere, the culture, it is more than just being a game." Indo-Pak players experience brown-out basketball as a space in which to articulate sameness as desis that is always interjected with various points of ethnic, religious, linguistic, class, and bodily difference. K-Rock is correct that religion does not solely structure the nature of social interactions among teams. Players, in the cultural milieu of Indo-Pak Basketball, do not sustain conflicts of Hindu vs. Muslim or India vs. Pakistan. While the place making involves imbuing a sense of a shared communal identity, the marking of ethno-religious difference, the charitable giving, and the racial significations negotiate, manage, and challenge South Asian American identity. Accordingly, the players articulate a difference from other teams and individuals at the same moment they claim the basketball court as South Asian Americans.

Although the players do not position religion as a divisive aspect of South Asian American identity, at Indo-Pak tournaments religion is part of the socialization on the court. Social interactions among participants of Indo-Pak Basketball cross religious and ethnic boundaries. But this does not mean that religion and ethnicity are not important in team formation and social interactions. One mode of religious expression takes the form of tattoos. Some players literally wear their religious identity underneath their sleeves. Players' tattoos embody ethno-religious difference and masculine toughness. Although there is a strong presence of collegiate and professional basketball players with tattoos who index their own specific locations, desi players' choices of tattoos intentionally represent themselves at the intersections of gender, race, class, and ethnicity. Most Muslim players, however, embody Muslim respectability and piety through their choice not to tattoo.[40] Although contemporary tattooing practices in the United States surfaced originally in lower-class working communities and communities of color as a class-based aesthetic,[41] it is commonplace now across the class divide in basketball circuits, including Indo-Pak Basketball. This inking up constitutes one way to appropriate lower-class aesthetics, the racial meanings of black "cool," and their respective valences of toughness to man up and disrupt the uniformity of South Asian American masculinity. In addition, the wearing of tattoos allows players to carry their ethno-religious histories with them when they compete in North American Indo-Pak Basketball tournaments.

Certain Sikh players wear religiously influenced tattoos that mark them explicitly as tough Sikh men. One such tattoo consists of two swords bent in to overlap at their tips. Another sword comes through the center with a shield in the background engulfed in flames. The iconic marker of Sikh masculinity is directly related to a Sikh military, nationalistic masculinity. The players with these tattoos are on Sikh American teams with similarly symbolic team names. The NJ/Cali Soormay Franchise team is made up of Punjabi Sikhs who met at the gurdwara (Sikh place of worship) and originally competed in North American Sikh basketball tournaments. The team name "Soormay" denotes "warrior." The community of Sikh men, soormay, is emblematic of the "panth," or community (Axel 2001). The Sikh tattoo is an embodiment of soormay masculinity.

The soormay constitute the soldiers who make up the Sikh army— Khalsa. The Toronto Khalsa team explicitly identifies ethno-religiously with their reference to the Sikh army. With the team name "Khalsa," they represent themselves as the protectors of the imagined homeland of Khalistan and as representations of their diasporic communities. Although the tattoo has the purpose of marking the wearer as Sikh, it simultaneously serves to position Sikh men in a different class from other desi men. During an interview with Sanjeet, a Sikh American player in Atlanta's desi basketball scene, he explicated, with pleasure in his voice and while using his 6'2" body as an example, this difference within South Asia and South Asian America: "My dad told me that we are Sikh, we are man enough for two!" He insinuates that Sikhs have twice the power and strength of other desi men. In doing so he appropriates the racial logic used by British colonial powers who disproportionately employed more Sikhs and Muslims, which they deemed "martial races" (Burdsey 2007; Rana 2011). Such appropriations are also common in the United Kingdom, where Sikh men accentuate their sporting masculinity through a reference to the panth and the original British colonial discourse.[42] Sanjeet recalled his own understanding of Indian history in which the Sikh Khalsa, on behalf of various communities on the Indian subcontinent, fought back the Muslim invaders. In this telling of history, Sikhs were man enough, as a numerically small minority, to successfully defend the Hindu majority and hold back the dangerous Muslim specter. Sanjeet's tattoo embodied a gendered, ethnicized, and religious difference that created distance from the tattoos worn by white and African American athletes.

Some Hindu players sported tattoos as well. A few chose to sport the Hindu om symbol. Krush, a Hindu American on the primarily Muslim team of Maryland Five Pillars, had a tattoo of the Hindu lord Ganesha on his arm. During our 2008 pickup basketball games in Maryland, Krush showed off his newest tattoo through his sleeveless shirt. It stretched from almost his shoulder to his elbow, showing the image of Hanuman, who has simultaneously monkey-like and human-like qualities. As an aid to Lord Rama, Hanuman is known to literally move mountains. To accentuate this characteristic, Krush's version exaggerates the masculine consistency of Hanuman. Muscles came out of every part of this image. The muscularity of Hanuman stood as a clear marker of Krush's expression of self through Hindu sensibilities.

Sanjeet and Krush intentionally used tattoos as a way to foreground the "cool" associated with basketball and urban life, underscore their religious identity, and assert a politics of difference within South Asian American masculinity. While this is an individual practice and does not necessarily diffuse across a team, some teams mark their religious identities explicitly through their team formations. In ways similar to Sikh players on the Toronto Khalsa and Soormay Franchise, other players use team formation to address religious difference within Indo-Pak Basketball. The Chicago Sher team had many Sikh players, with the name "Sher" denoting the lion, a key emblem of Sikh masculinity. Muslim players with ancestral ties to India, Pakistan, and Bangladesh played on the team Chicago Pak-Attack. The team formed based on what the anthropologist Ahmed Afzal calls a "Muslim heritage economy."[43] In Afzal's rich ethnographic study of the Pakistani diasporic communities in Houston, Texas, he illuminates the changing contours of community formation. Whereas persons of various religious, ethnic, and South Asian national backgrounds initially congregated in the more expansive category of "South Asia" and established a "South Asian heritage economy," a shift in community formation subsequently took place.[44] Increasing

South Asian and international Muslim immigration to Houston led to respective religious insularity. As a result, Afzal contends that regardless of ethnic or national backgrounds, Muslims from various regions of South Asia as well as Muslims from other places form a community based on their Muslim cultural heritage, a "Muslim heritage economy." When I asked player Abid about Pak-Attack's formation, he responded, "It is a team of just Muslims [with ancestral ties to Pakistan, India, and Bangladesh], we like playing with guys who share our culture. We had more in common with each other." Chicago Pak-Attack operated with a Muslim heritage economy through which their victories were against men of other religions. In this sense, they asserted a politics of difference as Muslim men. They chose to compete against other teams as Muslim men with shared ideas of Muslim masculinity and Muslim respectability. For the Chicago Pak-Attack and Cali/NJ Soormay Franchise teams, their politics of difference were expressed through the outwardly symbolic manipulation of ethnicity and religion—that is, through their team name or tattoos. Yet their invitation to play at the tournament set in place a classed negotiation of South Asian American identity that not all men within South Asian America are privy to. Within an organized tournament structure, class politics lay the groundwork, through racial language, for positioning middle-class respectability in opposition to other masculinities.

Philanthropy: Creating the Contours of South Asian American–ness

Class constitutes one key element of differentiation within South Asian America.[45] Organizers of the Chicago and Washington, DC, Indo-Pak tournaments conveyed a sense of self through their philanthropic efforts, which set them apart from other desi men. The act of giving is a variety of masculinity that is not available to all men. Aadil, captain of the Maryland Five Pillars team, is a member of a sect of Islam known as Ahmadiyya. The Ahmadiyya community has a long history of interaction with African American communities and social justice projects.[46] Ahmadis (members of the Ahmadiyya community) are not always recognized by the dominant Sunni branch of Islam as Muslims. They have a dual commitment to refrain from extremist practices of Islam and to maintain an obligation to perform, zakat (one of the five pillars of Islam that centers on charity and social service). At the annual spring Washington, DC, IPN, Aadil directed all tournament fees to "Humanity International," the philanthropic branch of the Ahmadiyya movement that provides funds for communities facing catastrophic natural and social disasters. This commitment to philanthropic giving positioned the DC organizers apart from the Muslim South Asian American basketball tournament organizers I knew in Atlanta. Various players deemed masculinity, "being a man," as "giving back" to one's community. As masculinity is dynamic, players did not see aggression on the court as the only way to secure manliness. They engaged in acts of caring and giving. The major Indo-Pak Basketball tournament organizers advocated giving as emblematic of a cosmopolitan manhood. Not all South Asian Americans, however, had the same relationship to brownout basketball and charity.

Suleiman, of the team Atlanta Franchise, for example, hosted Indo-Pak and Asian American tournaments in Atlanta. He did not have the same professional status or financial standing as Aadil or other organizers of the North American Indo-Pak Basketball circuit. The main organizers of the Indo-Pak Basketball tournaments in Chicago, Washington, DC, Dallas, and San Francisco are the children of the post-1965 wave of professional immigrants; the tournament organizers themselves are professionals. Suleiman, however, in Atlanta, is a child of the post-1980 waves of families who reunited with siblings in the United States. He channeled the money raised at the tournaments back into his own pocket. Some Atlanta players, like Ali, consider Suleiman "suspect," not trustworthy, and outside the realm of acceptable masculinity.

Although Suleiman took home the revenue from the tournament, the major North American Indo-Pak Basketball tournaments bridged philanthropy and benevolent masculinity. Max, the founder of Chicago IPN, incorporates philanthropy into the very fabric of Indo-Pak Basketball. During his telling of the formation of Indo-Pak Basketball, he mentioned, "I was involved with the Boys and Girls Club early in life. I wanted to give back. All the money raised at Chicago IPN goes to the Boys and Girls Club. . . . Not a single penny from the tournament goes into our [organizers'] pocket." At the 2008 Chicago IPN, Max celebrated the work of the Boys and Girls Club when he announced his retirement from Chicago IPN organization. Players from various generations of Indo-Pak Basketball came to honor Max and his 20 years of service. During his announcement, Max introduced the Indo-Pak community to Carlton, an older African American man. Carlton worked at the Boys and Girls Club and had known Max as a much younger man. The two had kept in contact for all those years. The Chicago IPN annually donated money to make sure that all young people at the club received opportunities to succeed in life as Max did. With key cuts in city budgets and diminishing funds for public services, and especially with the financial crisis and sub-prime debt crisis of 2007–2009,[47] the Chicago IPN funds greatly supplemented the monies at the Boys and Girls Club.

Max's commitment to the Boys and Girls Club is part and parcel of middle-class respectability. To give back is an expression of one's role as a man, a breadwinner and provider. Members of the post-1965 waves, for the most part, had the financial wealth and stability to be able to partake of philanthropy while other young men like Suleiman consider Indo-Pak tournaments as a source of income. At the North American Indo-Pak Basketball tournaments, the foundation of philanthropy ran through the core of the tournament. Thus most members of the North American Indo-Pak circuit celebrated South Asian Canadian player Parambir for both his athletic abilities and his acts of social service. Parambir has played with Vancouver Indo-Pak teams and is recognized in the larger North American Indo-Pak Basketball circuit. His fame is also due to his time with the Canadian junior national team and his short period in the premier Atlantic Coast Conference (ACC) collegiate basketball conference in the United States. In addition to admiring his physical stature and basketball skills, which set him apart from other men, players revered Parambir's commitment to working with youth, especially in the realm of sport. He worked with organizations to reduce violence among youth and provided sneakers for youth in Africa.[48] Through basketball, men like Parambir and Max were able to offer aid to their respective communities.

Such middle-class aesthetics of charity are infused with other class respectabilities of "manning up." Class constitutes a way to regulate which men can claim membership and how often they can claim it in this cultural milieu, and it marks differential access to resources—both in greater U.S. society and within South Asian America.[49] For example,

Chicago organizers limited the participation of teams, frequently affiliated with the post-1980 immigration waves, whom they deemed to have
a propensity for fighting.[50] As a result, there is a politics of difference
based on class between the professional classes and their lower-class
co-ethnic peers. Max iterated, "Some of these teams are good, but we
don't allow them in if they get into fights. There are teams that fight too
much, we don't invite them." The masculine traits of aggressiveness and
toughness that are celebrated on the court existed within set limits that
represented class respectabilities, managed through a racial lexicon. In
this case, players utilized racial categories of "black" to identify South
Asian American men with traits of toughness outside of the boundaries
of middle-class respectability.

Their use of "black" is an appropriation of the historical projection
of "blackness" upon African slaves and African American bodies that
stands a key element of difference from white, middle-class, Christian,
heterosexual normativity.[51] The participants in the Indo-Pak space reconfigured racial meanings to position certain South Asian American
men as non-normative within South Asian America. Professional South
Asian Americans labeled desis with a propensity for fighting as "black"
while self-identifying as "white." Players never referred to themselves as
black. Although Indo-Pak participants displayed aggressiveness on the
court, Mustafa's peers of the post-1980 immigration waves were disproportionately discursively represented as "thuggish"—as fighters. The identification as "white" holds up the men of the post-1965 wave as the ideal
representations of South Asian American masculinity. "Malik is white. . . .
Mustafa and Qamar [his brothers] had it tough. They had to fight to survive. . . . Mustafa and Qamar are black," explained Ali of the Atlanta Outkasts. Moments such as this demonstrate the "intra-ethnic Othering"
(Abelmann 2009) that requires "racial grammars" (Bonilla-Silva 2007) to
foreground class difference among South Asian American men.

For men like Mustafa who did not have a four year college education or a high-level professional job, they understood "blackness" as
an alternate way of getting respect. Mustafa teased out the significance
of fighting: "Also in our community, when you are ghetto,[52] you have
more respect. People are scared you might beat them up. . . . This is
why they [South Asian American men] take on a black role." Using fluid
concepts of race to map difference outside of black and white bodies

but within that racial lexicon, Mustafa highlighted the different ways in which members of the South Asian American community engage with U.S. life. When "white" and "black" are taken up, it is critical not to reify these concepts as particular to only certain racial bodies. They are not biological facts. Rather, they have become shifting, fluid markers of difference that structure American life.[53] The cultural theorist C. Patrick Johnson admits that "'authentic' blackness is most often associated with the 'folk' or the working-class black" (2003: 22), and South Asian Americans use it to classify working-class desi communities. As a result, for some working-class and lower-middle-class South Asian American communities, basketball and its respective physicality are more than just about play but embodiments of racialized American life. Their status, reputation, and masculinity are at stake in tournaments. By displaying toughness, working-class and lower-middle-class desis claim status at the moment they fail to live up to the gendered, classed, and racial connotations of the "model minority" category. Often players with such a *blackened* reputation did not receive invitations to Chicago IPN.

During one of my interviews with Mustafa, he referred to himself as "black in the past." He admitted, "I remember back in the days when Outkasts used to be out there, we were pretty ghetto. We got into fights. And now you look at the teams coming out of Atlanta, they are goodie goodie. Look at Rat Pack, they will run before they fight [big laugh]." The courts constituted a realm where fisticuffs could invert the hierarchical symbolic structure of South Asian American identity. Through aggression and violence, *blackened* desis manned up over *whitened* "model minority" co-ethnic peers. At a Florida Indo-Pak tournament in the mid-1990s, Outkast players got into a major fight. Mustafa recalled that the physical escalation led to threats of gun violence. As a result of the severity of this fight, Outkasts were banned from future Florida Indo-Pak Basketball tournaments. Only after showing athletic excellence over the course of many years without fights was the team invited to other tournaments, including the 1998 Chicago IPN. Outkasts had to perform toughness *within classed boundaries* in order to play in the prestigious tournament.

Most teams at the major Indo-Pak tournaments came from socioeconomic backgrounds similar to members of Atlanta Rat Pack. Among Atlanta Rat Pack players and others, the term "white" referenced young men who had the luxury to play but could not defend themselves physically. Whiteness marked access to safe spaces and training in middle-class respectability. Players would self-identify as *white* since it did not push them out of bounds of normative conjugations of South Asian American identity. Although U.S. history clearly demonstrates the violence inflected by white men upon other men that contests the sterility of whiteness,[54] South Asian American players still use identification as white to condense class status (profession, immigration wave, and education) and middle-class respectabilities. Mustafa explained, "White is for those nice guys. You know, guys with an education, they know not to act up. They are not ghetto." Thus he called Rat Pack players "goodie goodie." By so doing, Mustafa contested the hegemonic discourses of the "model minority" moniker by effeminizing "Rat Pack" with their choice to "run before they fight." While marking difference within South Asian America with racial categories of white and black, players invoked race directly to validate South Asian American sporting achievements at the exclusion of racialized black masculinities.

Consuming Cool, Excluding Blackness

African American men are the frequent visible manifestation of the *outsider* to South Asian American masculinity in the pickup circuit. Unlike pickup games in Atlanta where very few African American men play on the court, African American men are frequently on the Indo-Pak Basketball tournament court. Some African American men on the premises are referees. They monitor games alongside their white peers at the major North American Indo-Pak tournaments as well as in Atlanta's Asian American leagues. As officials, they evaluate the style of play, and they additionally control the format and the pace of the game. On the pickup circuit, players call their own fouls. At Chicago IPN, trained officials oversee the game. However, in this role, some African American referees articulated a politics of difference that compromises the sanctity of a co-ethnic basketball court as a safe space, thereby threatening to unravel the corresponding deployments of masculinity. Rathi addressed this issue during our drive to the second day of the 2008 Chicago IPN games: "The black refs are the worst and receive the most complaints from the players. I asked them [black referees] about why they don't make any calls. He [an African American official] said, 'You [desi men] better man up and play hard. We ref and make calls in other leagues in the city where they [non–South Asians] play hard.'" The black referee invoked racial logic that gendered South Asian men as effeminate, classifying them as different from other American men. The literary critic Grant Farred (2006) and the sociologist Kathleen Yep (2009, 2012a, 2012b) demonstrate, in their analysis of former Chinese NBA star Yao Ming, the ways in which Asian athletic bodies are rendered weak in relation to the excessive physicality of black bodies. We see a similar racialized reading of masculinity by the black official at Chicago IPN. Regardless of the physicality of games, he saw South Asian American men as not "manning up" enough to black and white masculinities. When I asked Max why he did not get South Asian American referees, he opined that co-ethnic referees would not be able to break free of the biases that stem from their own ethnic and religious loyalties.

Although African American officials are ever present, desi basketball players have few black peers as co-athletes at the tournament. At the 2008 Chicago IPN, one of the rare African American peers, Jim, provided logistical support for Rathi, Max, and Jake. He is a fixture at this tournament. The seasoned Chicago teams, like the Chicago Domenators, Chicago Untouchables, Chicago Pak-Attack, and Chicago Rejects, knew Jim and greeted him immediately as they entered the gym. However, African Americans and persons with black heritage did not as easily gain entry onto the court to play. African Americans would compromise the racial milieu of the desi court and change the dynamics of performing a normative sporting masculinity. Black bodies in play are imagined to be permanently non-normative on the court. Part of the process of expressing South Asian American-ness has been the process of repudiating blackness (Singh 1998). Thus, Indo-Pak participants employed race to manage the boundaries of who could play and claim a normative sporting masculinity. They relied on malleable and yet consolidated concepts of race.

At the 2007 Washington, DC, IPN, Charles, one of the 2006 Chicago IPN organizers, spoke about the extra surveillance that mixed-race players receive. In particular, he pointed to the presence of a person with black heritage on the team California Shockwaves, who caused some resentment among players on the other teams. Charles dismissed this resentment as silly. He remarked, "They [Dallas IPN] are really strict about your heritage. John [Dallas IPN organizer] will ask you for your papers. We [Chicago IPN] don't care about that stuff. You [a mixed-race subject] can play at the DC and Chicago tournament." Although Charles opened up the category of South Asian America at Chicago IPN, there exists a longer history of racialized exclusion of black men in basketball in general and Indo-Pak Basketball in particular.[55] "Technically, according to the rules, you got to be from India or Pakistan [to play]," explained Sanjay of the California Shock Waves. Indeed, the very notion of "Indo-Pak" is premised on the exclusion of other South Asian nationality groups and privileges a construction of diasporic communities in terms of national origin. Andrew, the captain of the New York Ballaholics,[56] whom we met in the opening vignette, similarly alluded to this history and emphasized the changing criteria of membership. His team makeup would vary based on which tournament they attended. Some tournaments would not let his teammates with Caribbean heritage play, even if they identified as South Asian. The symbolic associations with the Caribbean are racialized in ways that posit *blackened* South Asian bodies outside the boundaries of South Asian–ness. The shifting and fluctuating criteria of South Asian American–ness are unified with the consistent exclusion of black men.

At the 1994 Greenville, South Carolina, tournament, Mustafa took objection to the presence of two tall, robust, dark-skinned Afro–South Asian players. He immediately stated, "Those are Kallus" and made their presence objectionable in this setting. Even though these young men were mixed-race subjects, their *blackness* made impossible their *South Asian American–ness.*[57] In opposition to desis, African Americans are considered naturally athletic, innately gifted for sport, and a threat to the foundations of "merit" that supposedly undergird South Asian American sport.[58] At the same time, players refused to acknowledge any racial politics in basketball as that would mean their own co-ethnic sporting space was racially constructed and corrupted. The institutional levels of play, such as organized basketball, are sites that are taken for granted as being purely meritocratic. Krush, a player on the Maryland Five Pillars team, emphasized that "race has nothing to do with basketball." He refused to see it as a place of racial haunting. Yet the experiences of K-Rock and others tell us that this is a site of symbolic racialized production of the proper (white, middle-class, Christian) patriot. While dismissing the presence of race in the "merit-based" basketball court, players frequently engaged with race by which they "racially displaced" (Andrews 2000) categories of blackness upon mixed-race subjects and other black men.

These mixed-race men were seen as out of place biologically and culturally. One drop of black blood had "corrupted" their South Asian American–ness, being perceived as giving them unfair athletic advantages and compromising an acceptable sporting masculinity.[59] Mixed-race persons with white and South Asian heritage did not receive the same type of racial policing. Players with long light-brown hair, light skin, and a very muscular body played at various tournaments from 1999 to 2009. They were children of white–South Asian unions. These white—or *whitened*—persons were not key bodies subject to surveillance; only certain types of racial bodies receive heightened surveillance.[60] Somehow, the mixed white–South Asian bodies were outside the realm of race and were not a threat to the sporting space.

The word "Kallu" was additionally used by South Asian American basketball players to reference the appropriateness and inappropriateness of certain basketball movements. I heard the term at a 2009 Asian American basketball tournament in Atlanta as Mohammed, of the Atlanta Rat Pack, watched another South Asian American team, Atlanta Franchise, play. He looked over at Mustafa and said with disgust, "They play Kallu style of ball." Although the Atlanta Franchise has one African American player on their team, the word "Kallu" did not just reference his black body; it referenced a style of play.[61] I asked various South Asian American community members about the definition of Kallu. Sharif, who is a professional in Atlanta who self-identifies as gay, candidly responded, "It is used to refer to black individuals. It is racist and not acceptable. . . . It casts broadly, and that is not acceptable. It is used in a derogatory way to criticize somebody about behaviors seen as *less than ideal*."[62] The racial epithet now represents masculine behaviors outside the boundaries of South Asian American respectability. Race, as a result, is no longer located just on *less than ideal* black bodies; rather, it extends to provide racialized judgments on bodily practices and embodiments by other desi men. In particular, the creative practices seen as embodying a lower-class black aesthetic did not receive favorable appraisal in organized basketball. Thus, there were limits to how one could comport oneself through sporting maneuvers. One could not perform a "Kallu style of ball" and be validated positively by one's peers because it mapped out a certain blackness upon desi bodies.

During the 2006 and 2008 Chicago IPNs, players and teams appraised each other. Although these appraisals did not explicitly use the phrase "Kallu style of ball," players utilized a racialized vocabulary to offer judgments of the teams playing. During the Chicago Pak Attack's evaluation of another team, they appraised players "who could play" versus those with "style but no finishing skills." The flashy plays that highlighted the individual at the cost of team success are constitutive of what Mohammed deems as "Kallu style of ball." Although flashy plays are part of the fabric of pickup basketball, those acts, if detrimental to the team, go against the grain of appropriate sporting masculinity in organized basketball. If the plays cost the team a win, this would mean that the team would be knocked out of the tournament for good. Thus, when certain players took part in the flashy possibilities of basketball, the phrase "Kallu style of ball" was a racialized judgment. Through this racialized reference to desi players, African American men were conceptualized as "less than ideal" because they focused on flair and "style" instead of team victories. Thus, players were *blackened* if they embodied this style of play. Yet young desi men embodied styles of play based on their own access to resources and training as much younger men.

Only those with basketball training through institutional avenues demonstrated bodily movements that fit within the class contours of respectable basketball. Ali, who has gone through the formal channels of learning and playing basketball, was revered for his style of play in organized basketball. He played in basketball clubs and went to premier basketball camps in Atlanta, an experience quite different from those of the players on the Atlanta Franchise team. Thus there was a separation of those players trained through rigorous, institutional basketball versus those whose movements were learned from an organic experience at the playground. Those young men trained in organized basketball had greater social mobility and were appraised positively in *any* basketball space. Those men with "Kallu style of ball" in Indo-Pak Basketball received poor evaluations for their actions on the court even if one or two of their acts were deemed spectacular.[63] The style of play had an array of evaluations that sets desi men apart within the category of South Asian America while enforcing an opposition with African America. The anthropologist James Ferguson contends that "to be part of a community is to be positioned as a particular kind of subject, similar to others within the community in some crucial respects and different from those who are excluded from it" (2006: 17). At the very moment in which Indo-Pak players negotiate identities in relation to other co-ethnic men, they also adjudicated the racial boundaries of South Asian American masculinity. While using ethnicity and religion to accentuate difference in a South Asian American sporting place, players found ways to insert race into the equation of identity. Ironically, the invocation of black athletic celebrities and black stylistics was accompanied by various social foreclosures that excluded black men and classed Others from playing on the court. The category of race was regulated to clearly distill which men could be on the court and in what capacity.

While Indo-Pak Basketball players appraised their bodily meanings and movements in relation to blackness, black masculinities and South Asian American masculinities were not the only racialized masculinities in this field of gendered play. In order to improve the quality of play within the local Indo-Pak league, league organizers in Chicago opened their doors to Asian Americans. Similarly, members of the Atlanta Outkasts and Atlanta Rat Pack regularly participated in one of Atlanta's Asian American leagues as well as a Latino league. The next chapter examines the connection between Asian American leagues, Latino leagues, and South Asian American masculinity formation. As Asian Americans and South Asian Americans were conflated as the "model minority" and share histories of emasculation, South Asian American men's participation in Asian American basketball leagues gives insight into how they negotiate the realm of South Asian American masculinity in relation to Asian American masculinity. The different histories of racializations between Latinos and South Asian American men present a dissimilar process of masculinity making between these two communities in Atlanta's Latino basketball leagues.

3

Racial Ambiguity

Hoopin' in Other Ethnic Leagues

At the April 4, 2009, Asian American tournament at Georgia Tech, the Rat Pack team played the Ballz of Fury team (a team of mostly Asian Americans, white-Asian mixed-race persons, and whites). During the customary lay-up lines, Mohammed took off his warm-up pants to reveal his long, black nylon shorts. He then shoved his T-shirt into his shorts. Rather than simply tucking it in, he exaggerated the act by hiking up the waist of his shorts to his chest. Imran, Amir, and Sanjeet (a Sikh American playing with the Rat Pack for this tournament) could not refrain from laughing at his sartorial depiction of a nerd. Mohammed extended the hyperbolic representation by bouncing the ball so hard that it bounced above his shoulders and looked as if it could, at any moment, slip out of his hands. Given the linkage of Asian Americans to popular perceptions of nerdiness, in any other setting, Mohammed's outward appearance and bodily movements would have solidly fixed him as a nerd. At this tournament, his teammates and other people understood the satirical gesture. Even with his shorts hiked up to his chest, Mohammed did not carry out the imitation in full. He continued to make all his baskets by jumping high to shoot the ball off the backboard and slapping the backboard on the way down. He showed off his abilities despite the comedic representation. Once the referees blew their whistle to start the game, Mohammed walked over to the huddle, pulled his shorts down to his waist, and captained the team.

Mohammed caricatured a common stereotype in U.S. society: the nerd. In the landscape of sport, the figure of the nerd stands as a necessary antithesis to the athlete. The athlete is conjured within the confines of acceptable American masculinity, while the figure of the nerd signifies a failing masculinity.[1] In various situation comedies and films, such as the movie *Revenge of the Nerds*,[2] the nerds face their nemesis in the good-looking, muscular, and handsome (read as white) male athlete. The nerd often has his pants/shorts raised high on his chest. He is portrayed with thick glasses, communicating both his undesirable sexuality and his fit within the academic world that is his only domain. In the vignette above, something interesting, contradictory, and complicated takes place. Mohammed's portrayal simultaneously employs and repudiates the nerd-athlete dichotomy. His comedic gestures stand easily within the "model minority" racialization even as he performs them with irony in the midst of a larger Asian American community, which is both inclusive and exclusive of South Asian Americans.[3]

Mohammed indulged in the racialized representation but used his body to mimic and displace the meanings ascribed to Asian Americans in general and South Asian Americans in particular. Displacement of the nerd stereotype was a temporary process and not a complete negation. As a financial professional, Mohammed enjoyed the fruits of his social mobility and resources. In many ways he embodied the "model minority" and nerd stereotypes but collapsed them with athletic success. In this process, his body became a signifier of his individual self and a representation of a larger struggle between mainstream racializations and co-ethnic/pan-ethnic social interactions.[4] Mohammed and the other the young men worked, produced, and received multiple social meanings upon their bodies in the company of other racialized men. They negotiated South Asian American identity in relation to other minoritized masculinities—Asian American, Latino, and African American masculinities. Through their social interactions with other racialized men, they constructed acceptable racial contours to masculinity that challenged mainstream representations of South Asian Americans as nerds.

The nerd stereotype, although common throughout U.S. society, has a special and flexible racial relationship in Asian American communities. The continued essentialism of Asian Americans as nerds has social currency and staying power in the United States. American sports, to some extent, offer a respite of sorts from such racializations. Without a competitive Indo-Pak basketball league that runs year round in Atlanta, many South Asian American basketball players, like Mohammed, turn to Asian American leagues and tournaments, while some basketball players like Mustafa take part in the Atlanta Latino League. Young men like Mohammed and their South Asian American peers participate in the Asian Ballers League, a competitive ethnic league in Atlanta that caters to an inclusive pan-ethnic Asian American community. At the Asian American basketball tournaments and Asian Ballers League, Mohammed reconfigured the nerd stereotype by normalizing athletic excellence in and on the desi body. He contested mainstream racializations and extended the contours of Asian American identity. For Mohammed and some other desi young men, Monday/Thursday night pickup ball or local Indo-Pak tournaments were not the only viable means of performing South Asian American masculinity. They could garner status with victories over other teams and by one-upping Asian American players. Each victory served to rearrange the larger societal and Asian American sub-cultural hierarchies of race, masculinity, and ability. Playing in these heterogeneous racial spaces, however, became one way to reify identities structured through racial exclusions instead of dismantling gendered and racial hierarchies.

With the heterogeneous Asian American population in the Asian Ballers League, it is not possible for South Asian Americans to create desi-only spaces in this league. Additionally, Atlanta does not have enough concentrated desi basketball talent to operate an all-seasons basketball league like the Indo-Pak Basketball league in Chicago. The network is not as expansive or as tightly knit as that in Chicago. Atlanta's most skillful players can easily choose to play in multiracial leagues in order to encounter better competition. Several desi players choose to create all or mostly South Asian American teams in the Asian Ballers League. During the course of my ethnographic study when I was an active participant (player and observer) in the Asian Ballers League, only two South Asian men played on teams composed of primarily Asian American men while the others joined majority South Asian American teams. In this instance, I use "Asian America" to describe East Asian Americans and Southeast Asian Americans, but South Asian Americans have an ambivalent relationship with the category of "Asian America."[5] It is a term fraught with fissures and contestations that open up and close membership to South Asian Americans. In a diverse ethnic and racial milieu, masculinity making for South Asian American players consist of relations of affiliation as well as opposition to their co-ethnic peers and to other racialized masculinities—Asian American men and, as we will see, Latinos. The shared experience of emasculation, as model minorities, means that desi men and their Asian American counterparts share desires to show up their pan-ethnic peers on the court while marking their ethnic group as the most athletic in the league.

As desis, as well as Asian Americans, exist outside the normative white-black racial citizenship in the United States,[6] they benefit from their racial ambiguity and the respective non-threatening gendered meanings assigned to their bodies. It allows them to gain access to various ethnic leagues. Mohammed's caricature of the nerd had real implications in relation to racial legibility. South Asian American presence in the Asian Ballers League does not result from their skill level alone or their immediate, guaranteed membership in Asian America. Rather, their racial legibility and illegibility in the U.S. South is accompanied by gendered valences of *what type of man they are*, which results in greater access and maneuverability in and out of various Asian American and Latina/o ethnic categories. South Asian American players take delight in proving themselves against skilled Asian American players. Even as they share a sense of sameness within the pan-ethnic category of Asian America, I noticed how the players on the Atlanta Rat Pack, the Atlanta Outkasts, the Air Punjab/Hit Squad (a team of mostly children of the post-1980 Jatt Sikh immigrants), and the Sand Brothaz (a collection of mostly children of desi professionals from affluent Muslim, Sikh, and Hindu backgrounds) emphasized difference, involving cultural and biological terms, from their Asian American peers.

Examining the relationships among Asian American, South Asian American, black, white, and Latino bodies is critical to understanding how masculinity is read and written differently across bodies and sporting spaces. The American studies scholars Grace Hong and Roderick Ferguson (2011) argue that "comparative racializations" defy notions of singular racializations and instead emphasize intersectionality and the relationality of racializations. Thus to understand South Asian American racialization, we must see its relationship to Asian American, Native American, Latina/o, and African American racializations. In contrast to desis and Asian Americans, black men are not racially ambiguous but rather racially overdetermined. Black bodies are interpreted not through fuzzy racial categories but, rather, through cemented stereotypes as natural athletes, thereby making black men unwanted in these leagues.

South Asian Americans gain entrée into Asian America and Latino-ness because their racial ambiguity comes circumscribed with palatable gendered meanings for mainstream U.S. basketball—desi masculinity is not perceived to be unmanageable, uncontrollable, or threatening in the same ways as black masculinity.[7] Although Mohammed challenged the nerd stereotype, it is the desi's very racialization as effeminate and nerdy that also promises a racial *passing* into other ethnic leagues.

Opportunities to play in the Asian Ballers League are part of the system of race and racialization that allow for certain levels of racial ambiguity to participants outside the black-white racial binary.[8] In this case, desis are allowed entry into Asian America: they are gendered as different type of men from whites and African Americans. The ethnic basketball leagues, such as the Asian Ballers League and the Atlanta Latino League, decipher athletic ability using racial parameters that are embedded in the black-white binary. As a result, South Asian American athletes are read and valued differently from black men and white men. South Asian Americans are not seen as athletically gifted, as are African American men.

By reevaluating their bodies as capable of intellectual and physical success, players engage their bodies to upend the stereotypes that portray South Asian American and Asian American men as having abnormal bodies, valued only for certain types of intellectual labor. This reevaluation demands the presence of other men of color so that desi men can displace their own racialization upon the racialized bodies of Asian Americans, Latinos, and African American men. As the postcolonial scholars Deepika Bahri and Mary Vasudeva remind us, "Self-definition takes shape not simply against the center but against other marginals" (1998: 25). In the Asian Ballers League and other Atlanta ethnic leagues, such as the Latino League, desi men needed the presence of the other marginalized masculinity to showcase their brand of athletic aptitude. Exploring why South Asian American men chose to play in Asian American and Latino basketball leagues explains the racialization of South Asian Americans that imposes very clearly gendered valences upon the brown sporting body. It also shows us how Asian American, Latino, and South Asian American masculinities are solidified through the marginalization and (sometimes) exclusion of African American men from the sporting court.

Seeking Better Competition

Exploring why Mohammed and some of his South Asian American teammates chose to play in the Asian Ballers League rather than in Monday night pickup basketball or the local Muslim tournaments helps to illuminate the presence of Atlanta's desi ballers in non–South Asian ethnic leagues. Even though Atlanta's South Asian community outnumbers its Chinese, Japanese, Korean, and Southeast Asian communities,[9] the most competitive ethnic basketball leagues are the Asian Ballers League and the Atlanta Latino League. The pickup circuit, Atlanta Indo-Pak tournaments, and Muslim tournaments are not always ideal expressions of a sporting masculinity owing to the diluted competition and poorly organized game structure. Other Atlanta desi men participate in the local Indo-Pak and Muslim tournaments as a chance to socialize with co-ethno-religious peers and for an opportunity to win trophies.[10] For example, the local Indo-Pak Basketball tournaments in Atlanta feature high school and college men with limited basketball skills. The games are officiated by a corps of high school and college volunteers with insufficient working basketball knowledge. Without trained referees, undue physicality and hard fouls ensue. The aggressiveness at these tournaments falls outside the boundaries of competitive but fair play for players like Imran, Mohammed, Ali, and Mustafa.

Atlanta's Indo-Pak tournaments caused frustration for highly skilled players. At the 2007 tournament at the Hindu mandir in Atlanta's southern suburb of Jonesboro, Ali left one tournament complaining that local Indo-Pak tournaments are "a waste of time. . . . I get tired of telling people what to do. . . . It isn't serious." A young crew of Muslim Pakistani Americans, with parents from the post-1980 waves of lower-middle-class and working-class subjects, idolized Mustafa and asked him to play on their team, Atlanta Franchise. Suleiman was the captain but did not play because of his poor skills. Mustafa invited Ali and me to join him. The other players had little working knowledge of organized basketball, and Ali lost his temper on a few occasions explaining to them where they should be on the court. Furthermore, without trained referees to manage the games in a uniform manner, the excessively hard and deliberate fouls by opponents limited the type of creative plays in which Ali could indulge. On one occasion, with hard fouls continuing to mount upon

Ali's body, he took his elbow to the throat of an opponent to both teach the opposing player a lesson and to make the officials blow the whistle. The whistle was blown mildly for the exaggerated violation on Ali's part. His frustration continued to mount before he resigned and went home. In contrast, the Asian Ballers League epitomizes the pinnacle of ethnic basketball in Atlanta for Mohammed, Imran, Sanjeet, and other South Asian American players. Trained and certified high school adult referees oversee the Asian Ballers League and Atlanta Latino League games.

The admittance of South Asian Americans into these leagues mutually benefited desi players, who wanted better competition, and the Asian Ballers League, who got new teams to challenge the status quo. The Asian Ballers League was organized by Kdol, a Cambodian American whose family was part of the waves of refugees from Southeast Asia after the Vietnam War.[11] Cambodian Americans, as well as those who came through refugee waves, are not easily received into the Asian American category.[12] Their identification as "refugees" and their lives of struggle stand contrary to the "model minority" subjectivity. Refugee communities do not generally have the flexible incomes necessary to partake in numerous leisure activities such as basketball. Nevertheless, Kdol considered basketball critical to his self-identification. During one of our conversations, he recalled his reasons for creating the Asian Ballers League: "I wanted to build the identity as Asian Americans . . . make sure we don't get lost in the shuffle in the U.S., give kids motivation. Parents didn't encourage sports." Unlike elders in his community, Kdol invested his time, social networks, and resources in basketball as a passage into Asian American–ness. He said with conviction, "I don't want to work with Asian American organizers who want to hold very exclusive ethnic leagues like Chinese-only leagues. I want to build something that will be for and cater to Asian Americans." However, not all Asian American leagues in Atlanta are open to the heterogeneity within the Asian American community itself. Mustafa mentioned one of these other Asian American leagues with some disgust in his voice: "They won't let brown boys in. Got to be straight out slanty eyed to play." With this statement, he contrasted the sharply delineated racial membership of other Asian American leagues to the Asian Ballers League while articulating his own racial classification of Asian Americans. The doors of Asian America are not immediately and always open for South Asian Americans, but Kdol envisioned an expansive, inclusive membership.[13]

"We Had to Fight to Get In": The Parameters of Asian America

Membership in the Asian Ballers league has never been guaranteed. Membership is shifting, dynamic, and performative.

> On April 12, 2009, during an Asian Ballers game, Rat Pack players and their friends waited to play. Afzal, a student at Emory University and a member of Rat Pack, brought his white classmate along. This young white man sat in the stands with the Rat Pack and made comments that attested to the complicated, contradictory nature of Asian American membership. He commented wryly, "This is a discriminatory league!!" There was a pause. He lowered his voice to inflect a comedic sadness, "You all won't let me in." Players and spectators laughed. Mustafa interjected, "We [South Asians] had to fight to get in." The white spectator responded, "At least you are from the subcontinent. There is no example of Russians being allowed to play."

In this vignette we quickly notice the tension among Asian American identity, present-day American-centric cartographies of the world, and racial classification. Although we could easily say that the white spectator did not understand the category of Asian America, his clear understandings of the cartographic contours of Asia put in doubt the fixed, static notions of Asian American identity. He articulated the contradictory and multiple meanings of Asian America. He brought to light the specific lines being drawn on this court that expel Russia (and subsequent whiteness) from the territorial category of Asia and ongoing practices of Asian American–ness. As the spectator noted, the Asian Ballers League based membership on a mixture of particular phenotypes, respective performances, and ancestral lines to Asia. "Phenotype" here is the outward manifestation of the human being, such as physical parts, tissues, and hair, as well as material adornments like clothing. In the exchange above, the white spectator and his desi friends used Russians as examples of phenotypic whiteness and white masculinity. The white spectator fell out of the racialized category of Asian America. Mustafa, however, could play even though Pakistan is adjacent to Russia and in South Asia—not East Asia. The spectator appraised Mustafa as at least being "from the subcontinent," indicating that Asian-ness for South Asian Americans was not as easily in doubt as his Russian-ness. However, the relationship of South Asian Americans to Asian America is much more complicated, fraught with various tensions on the playing court and beyond.[14]

At various moments in U.S. history, Asians and South Asians have been lumped into the category of "foreigner." The "foreigner" category, however, is differentiated and not based on equivalence. In early U.S. history European immigrants received citizenship through the 1790 Naturalization Law, but Asians were deemed impossible to assimilate (Ngai 2005).[15] Immigration laws and legal cases in the late 19th-century and early 20th-century United States cemented whiteness with citizenship by offering second-class citizenship to blacks and barring Asians from entry into the legal or cultural fabric of the United States.[16] Legal precedence and popular culture further perpetuated the questionable relationships among citizenship, race, and gender.[17] The Asians and South Asians already in the United States could not vote, could not serve on juries, could not own land, and could not marry white women to attain citizenship.[18] The cases of Takeo Ozawa v. U.S. (1922) and Bhagat Singh Thind v. U.S. (1923) illuminate this consolidation of whiteness and citizenship. Each case pictures the "foreign" body in specific ways that deny citizenship, through different means, to East Asians and South Asians.

In 1922, Japanese-born Takeo Ozawa petitioned the court for citizenship on the basis of his cultural upbringing, since he spent the majority of his life in the United States. Ozawa argued that cultural assimilation is proof of American-ness, an argument further developed by the long extended histories from the early 20th century onward of Asian American engagement with American sport. Although the historian Ryan Reft, sociologist Kathleen Yep, sociologist Christina Chin, and historian Samuel Regalado show the affinity between Asian American communities and American sports of basketball and baseball,[19] performing American-ness through sport does not provide enough substance for their bodies to be read as American. The same proved to be the case for Takeo Ozawa in court: The court denied Ozawa citizenship on the basis of racial science. In a historical moment when race was considered a genetic trait, embedded in genotype, the courts invoked racial scientific evidence that classified Japanese as "Mongoloid." Only Caucasians and blacks could be naturalized through the racial criteria of citizenship in 1922.

Bhagat Singh Thind, a turban-wearing Sikh, subsequently petitioned the court in 1923 for citizenship. Thind appeared in court with scientific evidence demonstrating his Caucasian genealogy (genotype), but the court denied him citizenship on different grounds. The court deemed that whiteness (citizenship) was what the "common white man" understands it to be.[20] The denial illuminates the shifting nature of race and corresponding exclusions from the national fabric. Instead of relegating whiteness to Caucasian genotype as determined by racial science in the earlier Ozawa case, Thind's bodily comportment, his cultural disposition, and his way of being, the court decided, fell outside the boundaries of U.S. citizenship. Furthermore, the court affirmed white men as the evaluators of citizenship, thereby reinforcing white homosociality as the basis of racial citizenship. White men judge the masculinity of other men with regard to racial legibility and racial belonging.[21] Thind did not perform a masculinity that white men racially recognized.

Regardless of how the Japanese or South Asian body was read by the legal institutions, communities of Asians and South Asians in the United States, as a whole, shared experiences of marginalization in the early 20th century. Neither community could acquire citizenship. With the 1924 immigration act and the prior 1917 "Barred Zones" act, South Asian and Asian immigration was severely curtailed, and South Asians and Asians were depicted as "always foreign." Over time, the schema of marginalization changed from genotypic evaluations and phenotypic proclamations to the present-day representation of Asian Americans and South Asian Americans through "racial formations" (Omi and Winant 1994), such as the "model minority." In the Asian Ballers League, players of various backgrounds challenged the essentialization of their communities and performed the "heterogeneity" and "multiplicity" of Asian America.[22] Participants knew that, regardless of racial or ethnic origin, they were seen as nerds and geeks. My Asian American respondents affirmed how this stereotype gets mapped onto their bodies:

PLAYER A: "[There is a] perception of being only 'geeky' NOT athletic enough to compete in sports."

PLAYER B: "This league has shown me that South Asian Americans are not just about education. [Their] love for sports grow [sic] with the league."

Asian Americans demonstrate a common understanding that the nerd stereotype attaches onto yellow and brown bodies. But this shared experience of racial essentialization does not guarantee full membership within Asian America, either. While the white spectator does not gain entry into Asian America, white communities (Russians) do not endure the essentialization of their communities as nerds even as they encounter other monolithic representations in U.S. history. South Asian Americans are not always positioned as full members within Asian America. The fact that South Asian Americans and Asian Americans share the ancestral homeland of "Asia" opens up space to negotiate place within Asian America but does not necessarily translate into unchallenged membership. I asked various Asian American players whether or not South Asian Americans were Asian American:

> PLAYER 1: Since they are part of Asia, they should be consider[ed] as "Asian American." No need to define "South Asian American."

> PLAYER 2: They are because of location. Are not because of physical appearance.

> PLAYER 3: Asians normally has [sic] the image of oriental ppl [people] (i.e., China, Japan, Vietnam, Thailand).

> PLAYER 4: If Asian Americans do American type things (clubs, drinks—if they do "American like" stuff) then they are AA[Asian American]. Citizenship also makes you an AA.

> PLAYER 5: Because of the ethnicity language and the cultural background and like.

The players' thoughts resonated with the multiple reasons that Asians and South Asians were not granted U.S. citizenship in early 20th-century America. Some players discussed pseudoscientific racial differences: "physical appearance" and "the image of oriental" people.[23] Examples like these are problematic on many levels as they fail to accommodate the constant movement of people across spaces through time, which challenges the notion of "closed communities" (Wolf 1962). Indeed, "the image of oriental people" fails to account for the phenotypic diversity in South Asia. The Indian states of Nagaland and Assam have populations with "Asian" features who identify as Indian. In addition, the broad category of "South Asia" includes Nepal and Bhutan. People from these regions may be phenotypically understood as "Asian" but are categorized, geographically, as South Asian.[24]

Alongside the biological (both genotypic and phenotypic) considerations of membership, some Asian American players discussed "cultural citizenship."[25] Cultural citizenship is performed by people and communities through a variety of bodily adornments, symbolic constructions, and consumptive patterns. One of the Asian American players described activities such as "clubbing" and "drinking" (alcohol) as American. Desis who go "clubbing," according to this player, share an American-ness in common with their Asian American counterparts. Similarly, playing basketball, a sport imagined as "American," is an expression of one's American-ness and Asian American–ness.[26]

Scoring for Normativity

To challenge the racial stereotype that they are petite, fragile, and unmanly, South Asian American players deployed a variety of highly technical movements.[27] Even the common basketball practice of jumping inverts the dominant stereotypes given to South Asian and Asian physical abilities. Jumping itself does not garner praise, but in the midst of a game, the correct timing of a jump can be the difference between blocking a shot and getting blocked. When players used their jumping talents to alter the course of a game or dominate the spotlight, they received praise from their peers. Atlanta Rat Pack players showcased their verticality when competing against the Supreme Court, a team composed of mostly Southeast Asian Americans:

> Supreme Court's Jimmy, a 6'7" lanky, white-Asian mixed-race player, caught people's attention with his many successful dunks during lay-up lines. Jimmy did not have any other substantial basketball skills that garnered the same kind of attention as his jumping ability. Amir, Imran, Mohammed, and Mustafa, of the Atlanta Rat Pack, sneaked glances almost every time Jimmy went

up to dunk. Amir also tried to dunk during the lay-up lines. Standing at 5'11", he elevated himself as high as he could to dunk, but he missed on his attempts. Once the game began, Mohammed and I, as the two tallest men on the team, took turns guarding Jimmy. When Mohammed guarded Jimmy, he used his girth to knock him outside of the "paint" (the rectangular area underneath the basketball hoop) as well. Jimmy would not get a dunk on Rat Pack players. To be dunked on was emasculating.

When Amir and Jimmy competed against each other during lay-up lines, each took pleasure in showcasing what their bodies could do. Their acts of competition caught the attention of the other members of the Rat Pack and Supreme Court teams. Amir did not successfully dunk the ball, but he went beyond the expectations of what his body could do by jumping high enough to grab a 10-foot high basketball rim. These are the kinds of ostentatious acts players use to perform a tough, creative, athletic masculinity. While Mohammed, Mustafa, and Imran were starters on the team, Amir did not start games and played infrequently. The lay-up lines provided one of the few opportunities for Amir to showcase his basketball repertoire. By demonstrating his physical abilities during lay-up lines, his status as a bench player elevated the praise given to team Rat Pack. Opposing players witnessed Amir's athletic prowess during lay-up lines and could surmise that the Atlanta Rat Pack must have elite players if Amir sat on the bench.

Players jumped, dribbled, and passed to win approval from others at the gym. These skills positioned desi players against each other as well as in opposition to Asian American players. Dribbling and passing show players' creativity. Mustafa dribbled in ways that eluded the opposing team's defensive schemes. Each time he dribbled past his defender to the goal, Jimmy was forced to leave the person he was guarding in order to prevent him from scoring. Mustafa passed the ball to Mohammed for an easy basket. Acts of dribbling and passing involved using one's body to destabilize the balance of opponents, required speed and agility to get through small openings between players on the court, and necessitated a commanding view of the court to find teammates to pass for baskets. These traits are not readily ascribed to South Asian American men like Mustafa.

At the Asian Ballers games, Asian American and South Asian American men competed against each other to showcase their embodiment of basketball knowledge and physical abilities. Ali, in particular, was known in Atlanta's ethnic basketball circles as one of the more talented, innovative passers. Although Ali was a foundational player on the Atlanta Outkasts, they did not have a team in the Asian Ballers League during Summer 2009. Despite being recognized as one of the best South Asian American players in Atlanta, Ali was not picked up by the Rat Pack, even though his brother Mustafa received an invitation to play. Ali's intensity, recreational drug use, and aggressive treatment of players did not fit in with the middle-class Muslim respectability that Mohammed, Amir, and their peers demand. Mohammed and Imran could make exceptions for Mustafa, but Ali, they believed, could not be incorporated into their version of respectable masculinity. Their own subject position as middle-class pious Muslims played out in how they constructed their team and their politics of exclusion. However, other desi players on other teams did not feel that their religious sensibilities required them to refuse Ali's presence on their team. Sanjeet requested that Ali play with his mostly Punjabi Sikh team known as "Hit Squad" instead. Sanjeet captained this team when it was previously named "Air Punjab," but it had fared poorly the previous season. Sanjeet made key changes and additions: One addition was Muslim South Asian American Salim, who provided height and a steady shot; the other was Ali. Sanjeet met Ali during Monday night pickup basketball. During those pickup games, Ali made cross-court passes, dribbled past defenders, and found teammates for easier shots. Sanjeet immediately asked Ali to play with the team.

Ali facilitated the offense for the Hit Squad with his ability to elude defenders and make intricate passes. In addition, Ali had the means to create his own shot and was a prolific scorer with a high arcing 3-point shot (known in basketball vernacular as a "teardrop" or "rainbow" shot). The precision and pace of Ali's passes baffled the other Asian Ballers players. The deliberation of these passes even sometimes caught Sanjeet off-balance—on one occasion I saw him miss it completely. On another occasion, Sanjeet fumbled the pass from Ali and missed an easy layup. Spectators teased Sanjeet for his blunders, but the Hit Squad won the game, and Sanjeet beamed with pride. Ali's presence and basketball abilities brought Sanjeet's team success as well as individual recognition. After the game, Sanjeet and I talked:

STAN: You and Ali had a great game. You scored a lot. Ali can play. Man, he can find you anywhere on the court.

SANJEET: I agree. He can play. Our team is much better now.

STAN: Well, how come you missed some of those passes? Did his passes surprise you?

SANJEET: I missed some passes. . . . I used to make those catches. I got a girl [daughter] now. You know, I have a baby girl. Being a father changed everything. I got a little girl to take care of.

Missing those passes had a direct influence on how others perceive Sanjeet. However, instead of placing blame on his athletic abilities (limitations), Sanjeet displaced it upon "fatherhood," contending that parenting a daughter diminished some of the masculine traits needed for basketball success. He could just as easily have contended the opposite: As the father of a daughter, Sanjeet could have said that parenting enhances his basketball capacities with "grace" and a "delicate touch." Instead, he retreated to an ideological space in which toughness and strength are the only acceptable traits for basketball players. If he was to fail, the problem must then be "feminine." Femininity and basketball are considered diametrically opposed. Even Mustafa alluded to this understanding when talking about his own daughter and son: "You got to be gentle with the girl. My boy, Sura, I can throw him around. I can be rough with him. He's rough, too. Sheila [his daughter] is gentle." Sanjeet and Mustafa fashioned masculinity through relation to one's biological expression as male and the corresponding practices of toughness.[28] For Sanjeet, his masculinity was enhanced as a father and as someone with the ability to produce children heterosexually, but it was simultaneously compromised in the athletic realm because he has to care for a daughter. The idea here was that he would be tough and rough with a boy and pass the traits of sport down from the father to the son.[29]

Sanjeet used his parenting experience to assert that he was still a man even when he missed passes. Although he could not safely secure all the passes from Ali, Sanjeet's physical play assured him respect in the league. He even won "player of the week" honors. Sanjeet mobilized his 6'2" and 220-pound juggernaut frame to physically dominate other players. When the ball was shot, he leveraged his wide body like a wrecking ball to create space between the ball, himself, and his opponents. Other players who guarded him struggled to escape his ownership of the space and could not bypass his large body to steal the ball or block his shot. In addition, Sanjeet pushed deep into the area underneath the basket like a truck backing in. When he got the ball, the opponent was left defenseless, and he had an easy shot with the defender too far underneath the basket to block the ball. Although a few Asian American players, like Jimmy and Mark (a white-Thai-heritage player on the mostly Korean American team Teddy Bears), had the height and girth to compete with Sanjeet, most failed to match his strength.

Ali, at 5'11" and over 230 pounds, also used his body to pin opponents in uneasy positions. Unlike Sanjeet, Ali did not rely solely on his size to overwhelm his opponents; he also executed various successful, intricate, and difficult basketball maneuvers. One such maneuver was a "no-look" pass, which involved players using their bodies and faces to position their gaze in one direction while passing to a teammate elsewhere, not looking at the teammate while passing the ball. This trickery is a sign of cool and basketball confidence. The entire audience could see the opposing team get tricked for an easy shot and immediately respond with affirming shouts. In the case of these successful passes, Ali walked back to the defensive side of the court at a slower pace as an acknowledgment of his excellence. His well-executed passes set him apart from his Asian American and South Asian American peers. After an assist (a successful pass that leads to a made basket), Ali would hold his right index finger up in the air as he walked by the scorer's table. This gesture was simultaneously a self-acknowledgment as a "number 1" player and a request for the scorer's table to account for his basketball statistics.

While Ali's actions helped to distance him from stereotypes, they also subjected Sanjeet to a lower status. Ali's skills at passing and shooting gave him superiority over other Asian American ballers, including Sanjeet. Ali could very easily limit the difficulty of his passes, but his ability to pull off difficult passing and dribbling feats brought him greater attention. The spectacular nature of his play put even his own compatriots in danger of emasculation as they missed his passes and subsequent easy shots. Each pass, regardless of outcome, ensured positive appraisal for Ali at a cost for Sanjeet and the team. Ali's masculine integrity was thereby kept intact. He continued to excite the crowd of fellow players and spectators with the complex precision of his passes. On one occasion, he threw the ball from the free throw line on one side of the court all the way across the court to his teammate underneath the basket for an easy shot. It was an intricately and powerfully thrown pass.

While Ali's basketball skills identified him as a higher-level player than Sanjeet, his engagement with the larger audience represented the means by which he differentiated himself from his Asian American peers and all the other men in the athletic venue. Although ethnic and racial heterogeneity exists in the Asian Ballers League, when Ali asked for his feats to be recorded on the statistics list, he simultaneously set himself apart from Asian American men and also elevated the category of South Asian American masculinity. In this multiracial venue, he could enjoy the possibility of representing his own ethnic group. However, bodily actions were not the only means for players to assert their difference from each other. South Asian American players regularly employed South Asian idioms to evaluate the Asian American body. By using these idioms, desi players situated themselves in racial categories they felt comfortable with while creating a buffer from other racialized bodies and masculinities. Their self-fashioning of masculine identities was over and against (East) Asian Americans.

From Bodily Actions to Racializing Idioms

While basketball skill constitutes one aspect of difference making, another consists of ideology and representation. Some desi players did not rely on English terms to classify Asian American bodies. Instead of using the English and U.S.-centric term "Asian America," they turned to Urdu and Hindi to reinvigorate racial classifications. Mustafa and other desi ballers used the term "Chapte" in reference to Asian Americans. Before one game against the Practice Squad team, Mustafa and I sat down to scout the other team. He looked at me to make sure I knew he was serious and then warned me, "Those Chaptes can play. Those guys are short but they can jump and blow past you. One of 'em jumped so high. They can just jump like that." I inquired, "What does 'Chapte' mean?" Mustafa answered casually, "It means Asian." However, his initial tone did not match this definition. I asked with doubt, "Really? That is not what it sounds like when you use it." He chuckled as he thought deeper, "You're right. I think it means slanty-eyed."

Such racialized idioms are not simply products of South Asian experiences in the United States. Rather, Mustafa's use of "Chapte" wove together perceptions of "Asians" in South Asia alongside U.S. racial classification systems to project tenets of racial difference in the Asian Ballers League. The desi man is differentiated from the yellow—Asian—man in this heterogeneous social milieu. Like the complicated trajectories through which the term "Kallu" travels in browned-out basketball spaces, the etymology of "Chapte" is never a simple linear path. The definition "slanty eyed" evokes American racializations of Asians but travels across space and time. "Chapte," as a racialized classification, is shaped by epistemologies in South Asia and not the United States alone. For example, the dialogue in the Bollywood film Badmaash Company[30] relies on the stereotypes of the "Chapte" as the key comedic trigger. The comedic effect of the "Chapte" depends upon relational acts that serve to make desi men seem normal in relation to the non-normative Asian. Mustafa's reference, then, consolidated colonial and post-colonial South Asian epistemologies with U.S. racial lexicons.[31]

Players used "Chapte" to ascribe pseudobiological difference to Asian American bodies. Asian men in late-19th-century and early-20th-century America were considered feminine in relation to white men. U.S. society at that time considered Asian men to be both "shorter" than white males and more fit for feminine labor practices such as dry cleaning, cooking, and domestic care.[32] Mustafa expressed his surprise that these "short" men could jump. He manufactured the "short stature" of Asian Americans as an essential character of Asian American–ness that could be antithetical to basketball excellence. Such an idea overlooks the biological diversity in Asia and Asian America by neglecting figures like Chinese basketball great Yao Ming, who stands at 7'4", and Taiwanese American NBA player Jeremy Lin, who stands at 6'3". Yet when Mustafa acknowledged the shortness of the men on the Practice Squad team, he celebrated their (assumed to be innate) exceptional jumping ability regardless of height. Linking the jumping abilities to innate qualities, he validated South Asian American basketball excellence as products of hard work and training in opposition to the innately gifted Asian American athlete. Such an ideological gesture overdetermined the athletic worth of Asians while simultaneously underdetermining their basketball skill set.

The focus on shortness as a biological evaluation projects an ideological sense of Asian-ness as "matter out of place" (Douglas 1978). The idea of "matter out of place" contains cultural values that position South Asian American masculinity in relation to Asian American masculinity. For some of my Muslim interlocutors, Asian American–ness and Muslim respectability were polar opposites, even though there are large Muslim populations in many parts of East Asia.[33] The symbolic difference between Asian and South Asian Americans became evident at unexpected moments during the 2007 Asian Ballers National Tournament.[34] Kdol and his volunteers assembled a food stand for players. The members of the Atlanta Outkasts were resting between games when Mohammed and Imran, who play with Outkasts for this tournament, noticed Asian American players coming back into the gym with plates of rice, a curry sauce, and an eggroll. Both Mohammed and Imran looked on with envy, the tiring day of play only intensifying their hunger. They wanted some food from the food stall but had reservations. Mohammed expressed his ambivalence: "I want to eat but I don't think its halal. Stan, what do you think? Can you check it for us?" As a Christian, I had no such dietary restrictions; I sampled the food and told them that the egg rolls looked like they contained pork, which would violate halal. Mohammed and Imran gave me looks of disgust as if to convey both their contempt for my eating choices as well as the use of dietary patterns to assemble Muslim-ness and South Asian American–ness in opposition to Asian American–ness. Their facial expressions indicated my placement (as well as that of the other Asian Americans) on a lower rung of masculinity. How one looks, but also what one eats, presents a marker of difference. "Chapte" is not an ideologically neutral marker of phenotype (i.e., the shape of eyes); it is embedded in a range of discursive regimes of subject making among Asian Americans.

Such value judgments and identity formations surfaced much more explicitly when I interviewed Amin uncle, Mustafa's father.

On a chilly Sunday in January, I drove from Mustafa's home in Duluth, Georgia (north of Atlanta), to his parents' home in Stone Mountain, Georgia (northeast of Atlanta). Amin uncle lived in a neighborhood with predominantly black Caribbean Americans and Southeast Asian Americans. I had just had dinner with Mustafa and his parents. Asma auntie brought us a savory meal of roti (a variety of bread) and meat curries, and after eating Amin uncle and I sat down to talk about their family history. With the flavor of the food resonating through my body and on my mind, I inquired about the various places that uncle and auntie went to eat. I had loved the local Caribbean and Vietnamese food in this area of Atlanta. I asked Amin uncle, "Uncle, have you tried Jamaican food here? How about the Vietnamese food?" He responded curtly, "Stan, beta [an affectionate term for a young man, which is close in definition to 'son'], we won't eat at those places. Those people [both Jamaicans and Vietnamese] are dirty. They are not halal. I wouldn't eat a damn thing there."

Amin uncle asserted his belief regarding racial-cultural difference by labeling other communities of color as "dirty"—as bodies or "matter out of place." In the process he, as Mohammed and Imran had, positioned Muslim South Asian bodies as pure in relation to *dirty* Asian American and black bodies. A juxtaposing of this sort implicated cultural choices by giving meanings to the racialized bodies. Even though desi, Vietnamese, and Jamaican bodies are all commonly understood as non-normative in mainstream U.S. society, players used their cultural food choices to place themselves higher in this racialized, gendered hierarchy.

Similarly, the use of "Chapte" shares racializing similarities with the term "Kallu." Mustafa seemed to intimate that jumping was an innate skill for members of the Practice Squad. Ali also mentioned the jumping ability and quickness of Asian Americans as something innate to Asian Americans. Were Asian Americans and African Americans racialized equivalently? Did "Chapte" and "Kallu" have the same meanings? No and no. Asian Americans are not understood in the mainstream public as having innate physical gifts such as strength, jumping ability, and athletic success. Are the categories of "Chapte" and "Kallu" equivalent? If they were, then those persons who participated in the Asian Ballers League and in Atlanta's city-wide leagues would regard both leagues as having the same type of play. The African American officials at the Asian Ballers tournaments refereed both Atlanta multiracial city-wide leagues and the Asian Ballers games. They saw dissimilarity between these leagues. During the 2008 Asian Ballers National Tournament in

Atlanta, I asked the lead referee about his perception of Asian American basketball circuits in relation to the other leagues: "Are these leagues all the same?" The African American referee quickly replied, "This is not the same as the other [multiracial city-wide] leagues." I prodded further. "What do you mean?" He responded, "They play a different type of ball here. They [Asian Americans] are not as aggressive or tough. They shoot a lot and don't get much contact. They shoot a lot of threes." The emphasis on "threes" and the note that they "shoot a lot" focuses on certain skills but at the cost of devaluing the players in the Asian Ballers League. Instead of seeing Asian Ballers players working hard and battling over tightly contested shots, the referee perceived physicality and tough play as outside of the Asian American game. This representation of Asian American players by the referees portrayed Asian Americans—and South Asian Americans—as lacking aggression and toughness. Yet, to the contrary, the Asian American national tournaments and leagues are tightly contested spaces where sporting intensity sometimes spilled over into serious conflict. There were a few near-fights at the 2008 Asian Ballers tournament as well as in the 2006 tournament. Aggressiveness and toughness were as commonplace in the Asian Ballers League as elsewhere, but the continual racializing of Asian Americans as weak and effeminate blinded the referees from seeing the play on the court.

The referee's conference of effeminacy upon Asian Americans and South Asian Americans was not an isolated event. The supposed shyness from contact and physicality was central to the construction of the weak, feminine Asian (American) man in other basketball settings. Grant Farred, in his book *Phantom Calls*, uses the case of China-born NBA player Yao Ming to demonstrate how a yellow body conjures up the racialization of black bodies in basketball.[35] In opposition to black basketball players, Yao Ming is seen as fragile, soft, and shying away from physicality. Yao Ming does not get calls from referees when fouled and often gets called for fouls immediately when he plays defense. Officials, according to Farred, visualize Yao's yellow body as frail and most likely to wilt with minimal contact. At the Asian Ballers tournament, the lead referee seemed to follow this logic and was blinded to ways in which the games unravel. In contrast, the game is best understood by the players who feel the physicality, are tuned into the heightened competition, and know that their status is at stake. They understand the intricacies of play and evaluate each other outside the referees' judgments. Even though the referees followed an already-defined protocol of rules, it was the players whose appraisal of masculinity carried the most value for other players. The Asian Ballers community embraced certain players as emblematic of Asian American masculinity. Kdol and other participants created a forum to celebrate and recognize Asian American players; this is a site for hero making.

Hero Making: Manufacturing Exclusion

Each week, Kdol listed one player in the Asian Ballers League as the "player of the week." He additionally posted a list on the Asian Ballers website of the top Asian American teams and players nationally. Kdol listed Mustafa as one of the top 10 Asian American basketball players in Atlanta, but Mustafa did not make the national cut. The Atlanta Outkasts and the Atlanta Rat Pack were listed in the top 30 and top 40 Asian American teams, respectively. Regardless of Mustafa's excellence in the Asian Ballers League, neither he nor any other South Asian Americans infiltrated Kdol's list of the top 10 Asian American basketball players in the nation. Yet there were Asian American players from Atlanta on the list whose skill sets did not warrant such high rankings.

Both the rankings in Indo-Pak Basketball and the Asian Ballers list provided an opportunity for South Asian American and Asian Americans to celebrate their own co-ethnic peers as heroes. In the Asian Ballers list, the rankings centered on localized Asian American players instead of on traditional collegiate and NBA players. The "player of the week" award, in this case, recognized Asian Americans in Atlanta. After each game, members of the Rat Pack would go to the scorekeeper's table to check out their own individual stats. With such importance placed on this ranking system, players made it a point to engage in feats of athletic spectacularity that were also quantifiable on the scorer's sheet—acts such as scoring points, passing (assists), and defense (steals, rebounds, and blocks). The statistical evaluation of players offered explicit and visible recognition that could enhance their basketball status. In fact, Ali's conversations with the scorer's table in the middle of games engendered immediate recognition from the persons on the court but also set the stage for possible recognition as the "player of the week."

The "player of the week" and "top 10" lists ascribed alternate meanings to Asian American bodies by creating a new template of sports heroes. This template did not demand that localized recognition be commonplace in mainstream cultures, even though there was a desire for greater societal appeal. Kdol's list came about as a result of his familiarity with Asian American communities (mostly Southeast Asian, Chinese, Japanese, Korean, and Filipino Americans) throughout the United States. He did not know the Indo-Pak circuit as intimately. Thus, during one of our conversations, he asked me for contact information for desi tournament organizers in order to collaborate with them to expand the Asian Ballers brand. His request illustrated the particularity of his own social network, which constituted a contained, constrained idea of Asian America. The lack of desi ballers on his list demonstrated fissures in the conception of Asian American–ness that accommodated "brown" Filipino American bodies[36] but did not always accommodate South Asian Americans as full members. The list of top 10 players and the weekly awards were products of personal affiliations. Ali did not receive recognition as a "player of the week," even though players informally recognized him. When I asked Ali about it, he asserted his discontent: "I never got ranked in the Asian Ballers league. I never got ranked no matter what I did. You know, I can't stand Kdol, bro. That guy's got ego." He paused and then continued, "Maybe I should have gone to more games." Ali had not invested enough basketball labor and symbolic attachment to the Asian Ballers League for him to receive recognition within this intimate sphere.

There are few Asian American players in Atlanta with comparable skill sets to Ali, but he did not always commit himself to playing in the Asian Ballers circuit. Therefore other players received recognition before he did. One such player was Tran of the team NS2Faded—a Laotian American team from Minnesota—who played in the 2006, 2007, and 2008 Asian Ballers National Tournaments. Tran was ranked nationally by Kdol as the number 3 Asian American baller. He had a swagger that was evident from my very first encounter with him in 2006. Tran wore the NBA's Allen Iverson's jersey number 3 with similar tattoos, performed a slow stylistic walk that is the common symbol of basketball swaggar, and donned Iverson's NBA jerseys and ball caps. Iverson is the embodiment of cool who challenged the apolitical and contained blackness of Michael Jordan.[37] His flashy style of play brings about a different version of "basketball cool" that combines working-class black aesthetics with global appeal. One of the early moments in Allen Iverson's rise to fame was his first encounter with Michael Jordan. He *crossed over* Jordan! Tran embodies an Iverson basketball aesthetic with difficult plays, an uncanny dribbling ability, and a long-range 3-point shot. People on the Asian Ballers court continue to recognize him and offer greater coverage of him than other players. He moves around the court with confidence and a "basketball cool."

The Atlanta Outkasts beat Tran's team NS2Faded in the 2007 Asian Ballers National tournament, but no desi player climbed into the top 10 national rankings, while Tran continued to dominate the ranking at number 3. During the 2008 Asian Ballers Tournament, the Atlanta Outkasts played Team Houston in the championship game. Team Houston was favored to win since it had Brian, a Filipino American ranked fifth on the Asian Ballers list. The ebbs and flows of scoring led to several lead changes, and the fate of the teams was determined only in the final minutes. Bobby, an Afro-Korean American who played with the Outkasts in this tournament, took over in the final minutes.

In between his overseas professional basketball seasons, Bobby was in Atlanta to see friends and family. He grew up playing with Ali and Mustafa. Bobby provided the critical final push. Ali fouled out with two minutes remaining, and the team was down by a few points. With his lightning-fast first step, his deft dribbling skills, and his shooting range, Bobby willed the Outkasts to victory. Riad, Ali, and Mustafa were other key contributors, but Bobby, justifiably, received the most valuable player (MVP) trophy from Kdol. There was a certain tension in the presentation of the MVP trophy. Bobby was ranked as the sixth-best Asian American player in the United States. Once Kdol left, Mustafa griped that Bobby should be ranked higher than Brian of Team Houston. Brian did not have the basketball repertoire to match Bobby's. Mustafa told Bobby, "Kdol doesn't want to give you any props." Bobby shook his head with indifference. Mustafa then asked him, "Were you pissed when you read what Kdol wrote about you?" But Bobby replied, "Let's see what he says now." Bobby's ranking did not go up even though he won the national tournament with the Atlanta Outkasts and received the MVP trophy.

The players on the top 10 list, including Tran, did not always play basketball at a premier collegiate program. Brian did not play high-level Division I collegiate basketball; his recognition was only within the Asian American basketball venues. Other than Bobby, only Jeremy Lin, ranked number 4, played at a recognizable Division I collegiate basketball at Harvard University and was a starter on the team. However, Lin, a Taiwanese American player, received his first mainstream recognition only when his Harvard University team upset Boston College of the powerhouse Atlantic Coast Conference (ACC). Bobby, in contrast, played four years as a starting guard for a premier ACC team. Like Jeremy Lin, who was California player of the year, Bobby was Georgia high school player of the year and a McDonald's All-American. When I met Bobby in 2008, he was playing professional basketball overseas in Turkey. At that time, he alluded to his desire to play in the Korean professional basketball league. In 2009, Bobby was drafted first in the Korean professional league.

With such a strong basketball pedigree, why did Bobby not get rated any higher in the local Asian American community? Why was Jeremy Lin listed at number four when he received national attention while the other players were generally unknown by the larger U.S. basketball public? The people on the Asian Ballers top 10 list are recognized *within* their respective Asian American communities. Jeremy Lin played in California with larger Asian American communities and had been known in those circles for much longer than he had been known in the Atlanta Asian Ballers League. He also did not play at a premier collegiate basketball program that would have garnered him greater immediate national coverage and respect. Thus Asian Ballers League websites and discussion boards did not follow his career path until the Harvard University upset of Boston College. Lin was drafted by his hometown NBA's Golden State Warriors but played very little with them. In 2011, he was picked up by the New York Knicks as a temporary fill-in for the injured African American guards Baron Davis and Iman Shumpert. Lin took a struggling Knicks team on an impressive winning streak with his shooting, passing, and athleticism.[38] As the point guard leading the Knicks on this successful run, Lin captured the American and international basketball imagination.[39] He entered a stratum of basketball at the professional level that is not easily accessible to other players in the Asian Ballers network. Lin embodies style and swagger but was not intimately available in the ways other members of the list were. Other Asian Ballers players would not find themselves playing with or against Jeremy Lin, but they would find themselves playing Brian and Tran. Jeremy Lin is not the same kind of accessible hero as Brian and Tran. However, even this accessibility comes with racial and gendered overtones.

African American players cannot easily play in the Asian Ballers League or in Indo-Pak Basketball. Black bodies are read as innately athletic, dangerous, aggressive, and a threat to the game. Black men cannot (racially) pass through ethnic leagues. Early in U.S. history, the entry of African Americans into professional basketball, baseball, and football were markers of racial progress because the blackness of the athletes is seen as innate. On the other end of the spectrum, Asian American athletes have been routinely cut from the narrative of American sports and racial transgression. As a result of their racialization as feminine and non-white, their entry into professional basketball is rarely accounted for. For example, Wataru "Kilo Wat" Misaka joined the Knicks team in 1947, providing evidence of a racial ambiguity that has clear racial, gendered, and sexualized tones.[40] By being racially ambiguous in a space largely determined by a black-white racial binary, he could not perform a normative masculinity. Without recognizable racial standing, he was invisible and outside the bounds of manhood. In fact, he became the always invisible and yet instrumentally important subject that plays in the realms of hypo-masculinity to stand in opposition to hyper-masculinity (black masculinity), while making white masculinity normative. Misaka entered mainstream professional basketball before African American athletes Earl Lloyd and Nate Clifton.[41] He began in the professional leagues in the same year that Jackie Robinson appeared in Major League Baseball. Yet his body was rendered outside the possible spaces of legibility, and thus his entry was not one of triumph or racial transgression or racial overcoming. African American players, in professional, collegiate, high school, and recreational venues are oversaturated with racial constitutions. Even players like Bobby, who are mixed-race with black heritage, face the brunt of racializations.

Players of mixed-racial heritage play in the Asian Ballers, but the composition of the mixed-racial heritage matters. The inclusion but marginalization of certain mixed-race players provides important information about membership, race, and gender (Ifekwunigwe 2004; Beltran and Fojas 2008). Bobby's blackness destabilized the racial uniformity of Asian American–ness and gave new meanings to his Korean heritage. His mixed-race body was read differently by Kdol and some other members of this basketball community. As Kdol described all players in the top 10, he said: "Bobby lacks the desire to be the best. He has shown many times especially in high school that he was an NBA talent. He should definitely be the top Asian baller in the country, but doesn't want it as bad. . . . If his desire and work ethic changes, so will his game. Because he should be the number 1 player in the country." The phrases "lacks the desire" and if his "work ethic changes" betrayed a personal connection Kdol had with Bobby and a subsequent racial reading of his abilities. Bobby was seen as not having the desire because his accolades in high school and college did not translate into a career in the NBA. Thus he was seen as a failure who did not utilize all the *physical gifts* already available to him. Kdol, unknowingly or knowingly, utilized the "one-drop"[42] rule to map out a blackness that enveloped the mixed-race body of Bobby. While Bobby's blackness should have guaranteed him an NBA career, the same blackness was the site of masculine failure. In this sense, "desire" and "work ethic" are racially coded terms that fall into the long historical discourse that posits that whites (as well as Asian Americans) embody these traits, in opposition to African Americans, who are seen as "lazy" and having a pathological culture.[43]

Such pontifications cemented failure in Bobby's blackness. This discourse did not account for other institutional factors that shaped Bobby's basketball trajectory. Furthermore, one must account for the competition at the professional level of NBA basketball; not all persons can reach that stage regardless of their talent. In addition, Bobby's professional endeavors in overseas basketball affirmed his "desire" and "work ethic." Professional teams would not recruit Bobby if he did not have the exceptional skill set and drive. Bobby's moves and plays on the court made evident his remarkable training. Yet his blackness limited the possible readings of his body by some in the Asian Ballers network who positioned him as a site for oppositional reading of Asian American-ness. In the process, his Korean-ness was erased through his blackness.

In contrast to Bobby, other mixed-race persons on the Asian Ballers list did receive positive affirmations. Mark, a white and Thai mixed-race person on team the Teddy Bears, stood over 6'7" and weighed over 230 pounds. He was quite a formidable force on the basketball court, but

Mark's stamina did not compare to Bobby's. Mark tired during games. Most important, Mark had a limited basketball repertoire; only his physicality and jumping ability prove advantageous for him. Although these traits are markers of manliness on the court, his weaknesses on the court put him in a different class from Bobby. Basketball players with high levels of skill tend to have ambidexterity, which Mark did not have. In order to effectively use both hands, Mark would have had to commit himself to training from an early age. Bobby could handle the ball with either hand and had a wide range of offensive moves. Mark did not have any marquee moves of his own other than his sheer size. Yet Kdol ranked Mark in the top 10, and other Asian American players did not object to his placement on the list. He described Mark this way: "[Mark] at 6'7" can shoot from the outside and has great footwork on the inside. [Mark] is one of the few players in Asian basketball that can consistently play above the rim. [Mark] is known for throwing down some nasty facials [dunking on opponents] in games. So be careful near the rim if you plan on playing against the Jett [a play on his last name] Man." These accolades fell short as Mark actually did not have great footwork and could not shoot well from the outside. Mark's physicality was what mainly garnered him respect. It was his height and girth that stood in contrast to racialized depictions of Asian Americans. Yet, at the same time, Kdol and others did not evaluate Mark's success as part of his whiteness. In a way, his whiteness and respective failures became invisible while his physical stature was hyper-visible as an emblem of Asian American-ness.[44] His Thai-white racial heritage made such acts of toughness and physicality acceptable, and these traits earned him a high ranking. The same attributes of toughness in a person of black heritage might have brought about negative evaluations as "thuggish" and "uncontrollable."

The meanings given to blackness locate mixed-race subjects with black heritage in an ambivalent position in ethnic leagues. Their blackness negates any racial ambiguity, the same hyper-visibility that makes possible the racial ambiguity and invisibility of desis in the various ethnic basketball leagues in Atlanta. Take, for instance, the April 4, 2009, Asian Tournament at the Georgia Institute of Technology. Mohammed and Mustafa took note of the black bodies present as "matter out of place." Instead of a full survey of all players, Mohammed streamlined his vision to players with black heritage. Mohammed pointed to a player with black heritage on the Atlanta Franchise team and one on the opposing team. He smirked, "I guess it must be alright to bring Kallus." Mustafa nodded in agreement. At this point, I motioned to Mohammed and asked him to look at the team on the other court, "Hey, how about those white guys on Ballz of Fury?" Mohammed's voice lowered with an indifferent tone: "Oh yeah, those guys shouldn't be here as well." The presence of players with white or mixed white-Asian heritage did not trouble Mohammed equivalently. Lacking equivalence in a supposedly merit-based space, racial ideologies played out in adding differential values to racialized bodies. Black bodies were the immediate threat for Mohammed. He was somewhat racially blinded to the actual skill level, ability, and training of these white and white-Asian men. In fact, white players on team Ballz of Fury were far more skilled and more athletic than the players with black heritage on the Atlanta Franchise team. Ballz of Fury beat the Atlanta Rat Pack in the first round; the white men dominated that game. These white men and persons of white-Asian heritage could maneuver through ethnic leagues without much protest. Lacking such surveillance of white players, Asian American athletes code whiteness as normative based on the exclusion of the non-normative black athlete. Similarly, Mustafa and his peers could play in various ethnic leagues in addition to the Asian Ballers League.

"Do You Speak a Little Spanish? You'll Pass"

Atlanta has an expanding Latina/o population as a result of the growing economy, industrial jobs, minimal unionization, and the rise in service-sector jobs.[45] This population, often solely associated with soccer, has established its own co-ethnic basketball league. The Atlanta Latino League features players from various Latina/o and Latin American backgrounds. Mustafa capitalized on any opportunity to talk to me about the Latino League games. He frequently started conversations by bragging about his scoring in the Atlanta Latino League: "Man, I scored 30 the other day." "We were down by 20 at halftime but me and Dick [a white player] brought us back. Man, I lit it up [prolific scoring]. We almost won it. We got tired just fighting to get back in the game." Mustafa is racially ambiguous enough, within the dictates of black-white, to slip into this league and take advantage of the intense competition.

During the course of Atlanta Latino League games, spectators, announcers, and players conversed in Spanish with the exception of Mustafa and his white and African American friends. The stands were filled with community members: friends, neighbors, and family. The entire gym was transformed into a Latina/o place. I first came to know of the Latino basketball community in summer 2007 when Mustafa told me about how he made money playing pickup ball against "Mexicans." He attested, "I got into playing with these guys [Latinos] because you can make money. They bet money and they play hard. Damn, they foul the hell out of me." Mustafa smiled, "You can make good money, but you got to be ready for the fouls. I like playing in the league better." He went from playing pickup with Latinos to eventually participating in the Atlanta Latino League. None of the members of the Atlanta Rat Pack team, other than Mustafa, ventured to play pickup basketball or organized basketball with Latinos. Members of the Rat Pack led middle-class and upper-class lives that might not easily converge with the class sensibilities in the Latino league.[46] Lower-middle-class and working-class Latinas/os actively participated in the league. Plus, the valences of toughness associated with Latinos, maschismo and Latino masculinity, might have been a deterrent for Rat Pack players.

But Mustafa found competitive joy in playing in the Latino league, which he wanted to share with me. It was also a moment to showcase his basketball mastery in various basketball spaces. Mustafa said, "There is also a league [Atlanta Latino League], some of these guys are good. They're real good; they can play. I could use you. Do you want to play?" I found this question absurd even though I have been mistaken for Latino in various social situations. I responded, "Come on, man! I am not Latino. Shit, I won't pass." He just laughed off my comments. With assurance in his voice, Mustafa asked, "Do you speak a little Spanish? You'll pass. That is all you need, just a little Spanish." He then asked me to list the words I knew in Spanish. Here, my racialized body was differently irrelevant to Mustafa and the organizers of the Atlanta Latino League. The body could pass to a certain extent and little knowledge of Spanish would further consolidate the passing.

Populations outside the black-white racial binary often occupied ambiguous racial positions. Thus, Latinos and South Asian Americans moved through ethnic leagues with the possibility of being mistaken for each other. At the 2009 Asian American Tournament in Chattanooga, Tennessee, a team of mostly Latinos (a few of whom were Muslim converts) played. Latinos are often mistaken for South Asians and Middle Easterners. Shortly after the attacks of September 11, 2001, some Latino migrant workers in Georgia fled across the border back to their home nations because they feared that their skin color and undocumented status would cause them to be mistaken for "terrorists."[47] The anthropologist Junaid Rana (2011), in *Terrifying Muslims*, contends that the categories of "Muslim" and "terrorist" expand to include a wide variety of men, including Latinos and African Americans.[48] Similarly, South Asians and persons of Middle Eastern background are mistakenly identified as Latino. This proved to be the case with Riad, who played on the Atlanta Rat Pack, Sand Brothaz, and Atlanta Outkasts teams a few times. As a Lebanese American, he shared his experiences of playing high school basketball in Atlanta: "I felt like an outcast playing in high school because I was the only Arab. People would be surprised; some said 'what are you doing on the court, you Arab, you Mexican.'" Since Riad could not be easily classified as white or black, even if persons of Middle Eastern descent are rendered by the census as white,[49] he was in a racially ambiguous position outside the dichotomous racial logic. Thus, in Atlanta with a growing Latino population, white persons and African Americans put him into the only ethno-racial category they had to understand racial outsiders: "Mexican." As a result, even the Atlanta Latino League was open to racially ambiguous subjects like South Asian American men. Mustafa, Riad, and I could enter the Latino league; I even played in a couple of games.

Similarly, the racial ambiguity of South Asian Americans meant that their masculine identities existed outside of the confined racial meanings of whiteness and blackness, but always in relation to them. Because of this, South Asian Americans could enter the Latino league and not threaten to disrupt the ethno-racial character of the league. Mustafa characterized the players in the Latino league as tougher and better players than those in the Asian American leagues. Succeeding in a realm in which he already racializes Latinos as tougher garnered symbolic capital for Mustafa. He played in the "A" division of this league and thus competed against some of the best Latino basketball players in Atlanta, some of whom played professional overseas basketball.

Although Mustafa and I could play in the Atlanta Latino League, there were some moments in 2009 in which our racial ambiguity clearly did not give us full membership within the category of Latino. The representation of ideal Latino masculinity, as well as those outside it, became evident during the post-championship awards ceremony. Neither Mustafa nor his African American peers received any awards, even though other players ranked them highly. Mustafa and Ben (an African American player on the other team) vented about the awards ceremony. Ben said, "That MVP award is a joke. Only Mexicans win it, no non-Mexicans. Blacks are not given the MVP award." He essentialized and racialized Latinos as *Mexicans*. Mustafa interjected, "Who gets to decide who gets MVP?" He could enter the league, but his brown body does not fit in with the racialized, celebrated ethnic contours of Latino masculinity. Even in this space, race and culture worked to create exclusions at various moments. Ben and his African American peers were scrutinized to an even greater degree than Mustafa.

Mustafa could slip into an ambiguous category of Latino-ness but always as a partial member. He might be thought to look "Latino" in mainstream U.S. society, but his way of being and phenotype did not pass so easily in the Latino space. He could never win the awards that were for members (Latinos) only. Mustafa was allowed entry into this space as not "Latino" but as "almost-Latino." This "almost-Latino" category was situated in opposition to blackness. Mustafa played for team Mayas and brought his white and black peers to play on the team. There was a different kind of surveillance of white bodies in relation to black bodies. Dave, an African American player with strong basketball skills and a physical presence, was no longer allowed to play. Likewise, another black player had to produce documentation, including a passport and confirmation of family heritage, to ensure that he was "Afro-Latino" and not "African American."

Mustafa and his peers played and maneuvered in ethnic basketball leagues but could not move into white spaces as white men. South Asian Americans might have been considered "Caucasian" at one historical moment, but they have not been able to claim whiteness (or white masculinity) in full. In fact, during the time of my research in Atlanta, a white-only basketball league emerged out of Augusta, Georgia, in 2009. The creators of the league expressed a sense of discontent with the black dominance of professional basketball (both stylistically and corporeally) and wanted to restore a "pristine" form of basketball. "Pristine" is a racially coded work that further deflects "dirt" and "matter out of place" to black and blackened bodies. With bylaws and promotional materials that emphasizes a racial whiteness not available to South Asians, Ali, Mustafa, Mohammed, and other racial minority players would not be allowed to play in this league. By contrast, South Asian American men played in both the Asian Ballers League and the Atlanta Latino League. Part of this allowance was based on the racial ambiguity of South Asian American men as neither possessing normative white masculinity nor hyper-masculine black masculinity. Desi men could pass in other ethnic leagues as a result of their racial illegibility in the black-white racialized system of belonging.[50] Mustafa played in both Asian American and Latino leagues, but there was always an understanding that he was a different sort of man—different but not threatening. He might be seen as "threatening" and "terroristic" in the U.S. public sphere as a result of his ethnic heritage, but in basketball spaces he enjoyed the racialization of "nerd" and subsequent racial passing. Mustafa derived pleasure from winning in a league where men are seen as tougher, more threatening than Asian American men.[51] Yet even when he excels against and over some Latino men, he never garnered the same accolades as the men who fit the image of "Latino."

South Asian American men found their own pleasures in these leagues despite their cultural and racial membership being in flux.[52] The Asian Ballers League became the key site for South Asian American competitive basketball in Atlanta. The Hit Squad/Air Punjab, Atlanta Rat Pack, Atlanta Outkasts, and Sand Brothaz (a team of Muslims, Sikhs, and Hindus) teams used their participation in the Asian Ballers as a way to perform their masculinity both in relation to their co-ethnic peers and Asian Americans. The racial ambiguity of being South Asian American allowed them to maneuver through various ethnic-only leagues, but such maneuverability was possible only because South Asian American men were *not* read as either threatening or disrupting masculinities with the potential to unravel the ethnic categories of "Asian America" and "Latino." By embracing their racially ambiguous position, South Asian American men comported their bodies to assign normative judgments to themselves in relation to other men of color. Blackness, in the

Asian Ballers League and Atlanta Latino League, sets the boundaries of exclusion that allow South Asian American men, as non-black subjects, to move through various ethnic leagues.

Mustafa traveled across Atlanta to play in the various ethnic and multiracial leagues. He did not move across the city just for the purposes of basketball but also for other leisure pursuits. Basketball players inhabit various parts of city life in addition to their homes, their jobs, and the courts. They congregate and create their own sets of desi spaces in post-game party venues. The next chapter examines the leisure dance party scene in Atlanta and South Asian American participation in it. In gender-integrated spaces, femininity and masculinity take shape in relation to each other. At these parties, much more explicit social interactions between men and women take place than those possible at games. Heterosexual desires are stated explicitly on the court and at the party scene, attesting to the relationship between the contours of masculinity on the court and at subsequent leisure spaces.

4

Getting "Digits"

Playing with Heterosexuality and Other Sites of Leisure

Welcome to Atlanta where the players play
And we ride on dem thangs like every day
Big beats, hit streets, see gansters roamin
And parties don't stop 'til eight in the mo'nin
—Jermaine Dupri, "Welcome to Atlanta" (2002)

The team name "Atlanta Outkasts" was a product of Mustafa's and Qamar's engagement with a Southern brand of hip-hop known as "Dirty South." Jermaine Dupri, whose lyrics are featured above, is one of the central figures of this brand. The term "dirty" refers to the style of beats, slow and extended with deep bass tones. With these deep bass tones comes a variety of dance movements where the bodies in gender-integrated spaces come into contact and get "dirty." The moments of contact synchronize with the rhythmic flow to highlight sexual tones. The Southern flavor of hip-hop stretches across New Orleans, Houston, Nashville, Memphis, Charlotte, Miami, and Atlanta, with lyrical and technological nuances in each location. As a whole, Southern hip-hop is a reaction to the dominance of the New York and California genres, and Atlanta is the central hub of this genre.[1] This struggle for legitimacy and recognition in hip-hop parallels the hegemony of New York City, San Francisco, and Chicago in South Asian American history. Scholars and lay audiences pay little attention to Southern cities as major destination cities for South Asians. Yet Metro Atlanta, and in particular Gwinnett County, has one of the fastest growing South Asian communities in the United States. How Atlanta's South Asian Americans constructed their identity was a product of their engagement with their local environment, local histories, and local sites of pleasure. Thus, when Mustafa and his friends came up with the name "Atlanta Outkasts," they signaled their active participation in the local hip-hop/dance club scene. When they hit the party scene, they got down and *dirty* with Southern hip-hop.

For various members of Outkasts and other South Asian American basketball teams, Dupri's lyrics resonated intimately with their own ideological formations of manhood. Young men saw courtship as a game and embraced the title of "player" to emphasize the idea that they "played" multiple women. Thus, they saw themselves as "players" (or "Playaz," like the Virginia Indo-Pak team we met earlier) and used their numerous encounters with women in leisure spaces to present themselves as masculine. When frequenting dance clubs, Mustafa and his friends carried over some concepts of "playing" and "scoring" from the court. They did so while taking part in a different set of kinetic expressions, symbols, and consumptive practices. The parallels between the basketball court and the club scene are often remarked on in contemporary U.S. society. One link between the court and the dance floor can be seen in the intimate tie between hip-hop and basketball.[2] The players' consumptive practices of hip-hop and black stylistics might seem like a racial engagement. However, such an analysis of these social practices does not get at the complexity of masculinity making and the intersections along the other axes of race, class, and sexuality.

Black cultural forms present one venue through which to navigate the terrain of heterosexual masculinity for these South Asian American men. The "model minority" moniker and corresponding nerd stereotype project an asexual or failing sexuality onto South Asian American and Asian American bodies. South Asian American men practice toughness and explicitly express heterosexual desires in order to shed the nerd identity. They have to be "players," in the sense of a heterosexually active man, to recover from such emasculation. South Asian American men interact with women and other racialized men in order to successfully manage their heterosexuality. Thus, in one instance, these men turned toward black cultural forms and simplistic depictions of black masculinity as both "cool" and "hyper-masculine."[3] They consume representations of black masculinity as hyper-sexual and tough in order to salvage and resuscitate South Asian American heterosexual masculinity.[4] South Asian American men cannot, as a result of their social location, claim normative white masculinity, but they can use cultural blackness to climb up the gendered hierarchy of American-ness. They utilize the valences that associate black masculinity and "cool pose" (Majors 2001) with heterosexuality, without the burden of carrying the "threat" (to white women) that is projected upon black masculinity. Even the historian Vijay Prashad (2001), in his seminal piece *Everybody was Kung Fu Fighting*, envisions resistance to white supremacy and global capitalism through strong heterosexual, masculinist racialized figures such as Jim Kelly and Bruce Lee. In this worldview, the means for entry into normative masculinity and the construction of South Asian American–ness is through sexual conquest, sexual domination, and a physical toughness.

Since the club scene contains many gender-integrated interactions, desi basketball players performed a toughness and aggression that works in a space inhabited by both men and women. As we will see, fighting with other men and aggressively courting women constituted a few aspects of toughness on the dance floor. By expressing this toughness, desi athletes marked their homosocial, homoerotic interactions on the basketball court as heterosexual, and this marking then bled into other social spaces. In the process, the men performed masculinity and represented themselves as "players" by perpetuating gender and sex binaries. By courting women and fighting other men, desi men assembled the symbolic order of masculine-feminine and straight-queer.

When Jermaine Dupri, in the epigraph, locates Atlanta as "where the players play," he paints a picture of the party scene through the metaphor of sport/game. Here Dupri marks "players" as young men with abilities to play the game of sexual courtship. Competition among the men for women, aggression towards both women and men, and "scoring" (successful sexual conquest) are attributes given to a "player." Young desi men repeatedly express pleasure in competing over anything and everything. For example, Mustafa and Ahmed, his younger protégé who is a member of the Atlanta Franchise team, started trash talking after an Asian American tournament. Ahmed began by asserting his superiority over Mustafa at pool. The two then started listing off other activities in which they could defeat each other. As we walked out of the gym, we noticed table tennis tables. I joined the conversation and told Mustafa I could beat him at table tennis.

MUSTAFA: I would easily beat you in ping pong. I played it at a high
   level when I was a kid.

STAN: You can't beat me if you still call it ping pong; it's called table tennis.

AHMED [laughing]: I'll beat him at that [table tennis]. I can beat Mustafa at anything.

MUSTAFA [to Ahmed]: I could write better essays than you.

AHMED: I got you. I can beat you at essays.

MUSTAFA [flaring his chest and swatting at the air in a manner to convey his dismissal of Ahmed's statement]: There is no way you can beat me. Nobody can beat me in an essay contest.

MUSTAFA [looking over and realizing that I, the researcher and scholar, was still there, then smiling]: I can't beat Stan, but I will beat you [Ahmed].

Just talking trash does not suffice, although it is one element of performing a tough masculinity.[5] One primarily has to show evidence of successful domination over others by winning sporting contests, by having successful sexual liaisons with young women, and through fisticuffs with other men. When they call themselves "player," young men align themselves with heterosexual masculinity through their performance of toughness and creativity in seducing women.[6] In mainstream stereotypes, South Asian American men are constantly projected outside the boundaries of normative masculinity: They are either sexually defunct nerds or sexually promiscuous harem overlords whose libidinous desires exceed the heteronormative foundations of the nuclear family. But courting many women on the leisure circuit does not threaten to project desi men as licentious "terrorists" and "Muslims." To overcome the nerd stereotype, desis can assert heterosexuality by browning-out dance clubs, parties, and strip clubs.

Although desi men can manufacture a desi-only cultural and racial milieu on the basketball court, the young men cannot do the same at a mainstream club, since that would require considerable capital and would exclude white women and Latinas.[7] Part of the process of creating distance from the common stereotype involves these young men courting women who fit mainstream definitions of beauty. Latinas are represented as an exotic Other while white women represent the epitome of American femininity. Some desi men seek encounters with white women and Latinas at multiracial clubs where racialized desires are woven through with hip-hop at mostly non-white clubs. Atlanta's leisure spaces are seg-regated as black and white, with the exception of dance clubs in Midtown Atlanta and Buckhead. As a result, Mustafa and his peers took part in browning-out dance clubs in Midtown Atlanta with their numbers in order to make these mainstream leisure spaces seem like desi places.

Browning-out leisure spaces allowed these young men to partake in desires and pleasures not always available or allowable in the larger South Asian American community. They found opportunities to express a wide assortment of practices of heterosexual desire. The historians Kevin Mumford and Fiona Ngo, in their respective books, emphasize how leisure spaces contain an unusual mix of desire, pleasure, and vice.[8] At the "black and tan" clubs and jazz clubs, Mumford and Ngo detail how Prohibition-era America created multiracial social interactions through (underground) places of leisure, where multiple ideas of sub-jectivity, race, sexuality, class, and gender were appropriated across local and national terrains. These clubs offered patrons spaces where various racial communities could engage in desires, such as heterosexual misce-genation, that were coded as vice in other spaces.[9]

In a similar fashion, by browning-out mainstream dance clubs, South Asian Americans have the ability to embody desires and pleasures that might be read as "taboo" (non-normative and inappropriate) in the larger South Asian American community. Community elders police spaces at community-wide events and often enforce gender segregation. However, both basketball brown outs and the browning out of clubs are similar in that they are peer-group structured spaces with possibilities for enacting heterosexual decadences. The projection of heterosexual desires is part and parcel of the male-on-male space of basketball. Vari-ous players express joy in being able to check out the party scene in host cities and meet young women. With a smile on his face, K-Rock of the Philly Fay team elaborated, "You get to travel to new cities. You meet new girls." Indo-Pak tournaments institutionalize heterosexual desire into the very experience of the weekend-long athletic excursion. Tour-naments are planned with the opportunity for the participants to attend private parties and frequent the local city's night scene.

Even my first encounter with Indo-Pak Basketball at the 1994 Green-ville tournament was accompanied by an after-party, where Mustafa and his older brother Qamar danced and flirted with some of Greenville's young South Asian American women. This relationship between basketball and the party scene is critical to understanding South Asian American masculinity formation. In the cases I introduce below, "It is through masculinity that men construct their sexuality, and, through that sexuality, confirm their gender identity" (Fracher and Kimmel 1998). South Asian American men's identities take form in relation to other men and in relation to sexual desires for the category of femininity and other racialized women. Each racialized woman is given different worth and bodily capital (Hoang 2011). Young men then compete to accrue symbolic status based on sexual relations with certain racialized female bodies. These explicit acts of heterosexual conquest do not suffice in other places such as work, home, or community gatherings, where such acts would be read as unacceptable.

When at community-wide functions, these young people do not have the chance to express certain forms of heterosexual masculinity. Even though community-wide events are read as heterosexual, these men perform renditions of masculinity that are in line with respectability. They defer to elders with their voice and body, do not try to forcefully invade women's spaces, and routinely maintain gender segregation. Through participation in the browning out of co-peer leisure activities, the desires denied in everyday lives are performed, normalized, and legitimated.[10] By attending in groups, these young men also brown out multiracial club spaces and make themselves the "insiders" in this social setting. They create a certain racial milieu to diminish the threat of black or white masculinities.

Competing for Women

Mustafa arrived at my residence in his black SUV with bright shiny rims, tinted windows, and hip-hop blasting through the speakers. He had shaved his face except for a jazz tee (a triangle-shaped hair trim underneath one's bottom lip). His neatly pressed beige pants matched his polo shirt and light-brown leather shoes, and he had gelled his hair. He had a "blinged"-out watch, oversized with multiple gem stones and shiny chrome. Our first stop on this night out was a strip club on Buford Highway. Shooter's Alley stood in front of a Korean restaurant and Mexican restaurant. Upon our entrance, hip-hop music resonated through dimly lit rooms. Exotic dancers were mainly African American, with a few Latinas. African American men and Latinos frequented this club along with an occasional white man. One African American dancer caught Mustafa's eye, so he went over and flirted with her. Mustafa put dollar bills in her g-string and asked for a lap dance. When the dance was over, Mustafa looked at me and said with pride, "Back in the day, me, Qamar, and Ehsanul [Qamar's friend] would've taken these girls home."

We left Shooter's Alley and picked up Mahmoud. We then met Mahmoud's Hindu finance professional friends and drove to Midtown Atlanta. The place of choice, Club Opera, was one of the trendy dance clubs with a large South Asian American, Asian American, Latina/o, white, and African American contingent. The main floor blasted hip-hop music and catered to a multiracial crowd. There was also a salsa room with more Latinas/os. During the course of the night, Mahmoud focused his gaze on Latinas and white women. Yet he did not readily approach these women. Mahmoud explained, "I got no game." He paused for a second. "But if I break the ice then I'll fuck them!" There were several young South Asian American women at the club. Several walked by, but Mahmoud did not look at them. I asked Mahmoud, "What do you think about those girls?" He shook his head. I prodded, "Don't you want to talk to them?" Mahmoud replied firmly with disinterest, "It is too easy to fuck desi girls." At closing time, Mahmoud came back to Mustafa with pride in his voice, "I got some digits [phone numbers]. I am going to get them [two Latinas] to meet up with us later."

Once South Asian American basketball players finish playing basketball, they do not retreat from other forms of U.S. popular culture. Their spaces of leisure, outside of basketball, are not limited to "South Asian cultural forms" such as bhangra, raas garba (a popular Gujarati stick dance), and Bollywood. Rather than attending only community-wide cultural events in their spare time, Mustafa and his peers brought their community of men with them to mainstream spaces of leisure, dance clubs and strip clubs. Through such group participation, the young men performed contours of masculinity that always involves race, class, and sexuality.

Mustafa and Mahmoud changed their garb and disposition when they went from community events and the basketball courts to the clubs.

Instead of wearing jerseys and sports gear, they donned clothing that was business casual but urban cool. Mustafa meticulously combed his hair and applied the right amount of gel to create sheen. These were conscious acts to fit the part of the urban denizen and modern consumer. Mustafa was claiming a sense of belonging with his presence at the multiracial clubs. Participation in Atlanta's leisure spaces made these men legitimate metropolitan city dwellers. In *Desis in the House*, the anthropologist Sunaina Maira describes this relationship: "Desi youth turn to hip-hop because it is key to marking their belonging in the multi-ethnic urban landscape of New York City" (2002: 58–59). Part of belonging to the city and performing normative masculinity consists of wearing certain styles and patronizing certain clubs. With expressions of a certain urban cool based on clothes, cologne, and comportment, Mustafa differentiated himself and his peers from racialized masculinities, including newly arriving South Asian immigrants who they discursively represented as not American enough and not man enough. During my stay with Mustafa in January 2009, there were several nights when I cooked South Asian meals that infiltrated his home with a certain aroma. After a day at work, he arrived at home and laughed at the particularity of the smell. "What are you cooking? My house smells FOBBY. I smell like a FOB now." The FOB, a stigmatizing term for new immigrants labeled as "fresh off the boat," represents a failed masculinity in relation to his embodiment of urban cool with his cologne. Thus, when Mustafa went out with his friends, they were South Asian Americans who formed a sense of community through distance from newly arrived immigrants (or at least those perceived as such) and other racialized men.

At Club Opera, Mustafa performed sexual aggressiveness and a sense of competition that is read as part of the terrain of normative masculinity. He contrasted such aggressiveness with his imagination of the FOB. For him, the FOB is a weak and effeminate subject. During the course of my ethnographic research in 2009, Mustafa and his wife, Fatima, separated. Mustafa reasoned that she demanded too much of him: "Fatima is asking for too much. She can just go and get one of those FOBs. Those guys will treat her nice and do whatever she asks. They got no balls." Mustafa affirmed his masculinity through a certain type of aggression, toughness, and corporeal constitution (balls) that he believed the FOB did not have. In addition to such toughness, he placed value on the ability to court women and produce opportunities for sexual intercourse. Mahmoud, as well as Mustafa, took full advantage of opportunities to brag to each other about the women they have "fucked" or "hooked up" with.[11]

If the young men had partaken only of the community-wide cultural festivities, then they would have reified the stereotype of the unassimilable, effeminate foreigner. At the club scene, they engaged in acts of one-upmanship by competing for women. This type of competition provided a forum for pleasure while confirming their place within the fold of heterosexual masculinity. Their renditions of masculinity came with demands for what the queer theorist Adrienne Rich (1994) calls "compulsory heterosexuality." But in order to perform such "compulsory heterosexuality," they must procure safety in numbers, creating desi spaces in multiracial social environments. In this racial fold, their bodies were valued much more highly than they would be at white or black clubs.

South Asian American young people form a formidable force in negotiating identity formation.[12] At dance clubs and strip clubs, young men act out bravado and toughness directly with racialized women and other men. Toughness and bravado can be established through either the sexual conquest of women or through the physical domination of other men. Mahmoud did not think he could match the virile masculinity embodied by Mustafa, but he found ways to position himself as a man: "If I break the ice then I'll fuck them!" Mahmoud explicitly bragged to Mustafa about the "digits" he procured in the midst of hundreds of other men at the club. These phone numbers, and attempts to get them, constituted practices of heterosexual conquest. Through such practices as "getting digits," players draw straight lines to heterosexuality through their talk and their movements.[13] The digits are translated into literal numbers of the women in their sexual universe. Each phone number is another badge on the mantle of heterosexual masculinity.

Explicit competition in courting women receives approval from other men.[14] Mustafa similarly bragged about how he took "girls" from strip clubs home. He used instances like these to distance himself from some of his co-ethnic peers. For instance, Mustafa referred to Mohammed, Imran, and Amir as "boys" since they have "no game" and "are scared of girls." In a separate interview, Mustafa's brother Ali boasted, "Malik, Imran, and those guys [mostly young men with ties to the post-1965 wave of professionals] are sheltered. We [Mustafa, Ali, and Qamar] could bring girls home." Facing demands to fit the "model minority" moniker, the supposed sheltered lives of the young professionals limit their engagement with other aspects of social life. Here both Ali and Mustafa distinguished between themselves and other men by their own ability to court women.

At the clubs in Midtown, Mustafa articulated his "game" through his ability to approach women and begin conversations. Young men at the clubs interacted with women through "forceful and space-occupying ways" (Wenner 1998: 310). Mustafa and Mahmoud did not need to defer to anyone at the dance clubs as they had to do at South Asian American community-wide events. Furthermore, the ways of occupying space at the clubs are both similar and dissimilar to the activities on the basketball court: In both cases men act in "forceful and space-occupying ways," but on the basketball court men are aggressively approaching other men, not the women they approach in clubs. On the court, defenders attempt to minimize the distance between themselves and their male opponents. Delimiting space is a way of showing physical domination since the offensive player does not have the capability to escape the defensive pressure, even though he needs to create distance in order to score. Without space, one could fall prey to a block or a steal. Invading other men's space is foundational to basketball play. Constant body contact, the tussling for space, and the interplay between offensive and defensive players are considered normal basketball practices with no sexual connotations. They desire male bodies through their athletic interactions, as well as through their consumption and production of basketball heroes. Straight men do not consider these sporting actions homoerotic. While such physical intimacy, close quarters, frequent bodily contact, and the pleasures in physical play can be considered homoerotic with many queer possibilities, the basketball players consider them just basketball play and never extend them into the realm of the sexual. But the desi men also find ways to constantly perform heterosexuality in mostly male settings. In fact, the superfluous conversations on the court about women as sexual objects mark the male-on-male space as heterosexual.

The talk about women on the court leads to intentional efforts to seek encounters with women and to talk to women off the court. Players can engage with women directly at the club scenes, strip clubs, and parties. Checking out "girls," as the sociologist Beth Quinn (2002:

387) argues, "functions as a game men play to build shared masculine identities and social relations." Perusing women in the club established male bonds between Mustafa and Mahmoud. During such encounters, women were rated along a racial-gendered-sexualized spectrum. Mahmoud specifically boasted about intimate encounters with white women and Latinas, and, accordingly, he sought out white women and Latinas at Club Opera. Similarly, Ahmed invited Mustafa out to Club Pure on "salsa night." The Latina body has a special place in the sexual landscape, where it is exotic, in excess, but within the confines of heterosexual desire.[15] Other women, such as desis and African Americans, attended Club Opera, but neither Mahmoud nor his friends sought them out. As we have seen, Mahmoud's gaze was focused. When South Asian American women passed by, he dismissed them. He described desi women as "easy to fuck," thus locating them as low on the sexual totem pole. As co-ethnic women, desi women may not necessarily be "easy to fuck," but sexual encounters with them would be seen as normal practice of co-ethnic socialization. Sexual relations with desi women would not counter the mainstream gendered, raced, and sexualized stereotypes of desi men.

The attraction to non-desi women is a product of trying to reconfirm a normative masculinity by "hooking up" with women considered to be symbols of mainstream beauty. Even these sexual desires were racialized. White men and the mainstream media racialize, sensationalize, exoticize, and sexualize the female South Asian American body, but this body does not have the same value when penetrated by co-ethnic men.[16] Thus Mahmoud searched the club for attractive Latinas and white women. Each successful sexual encounter with white women and Latinas pushed the stereotype of South Asian American men from the asexual nerd into the domain of virility. Both before and after our visit to Club Opera, Mustafa and Mahmoud listed to each other the women with whom they have had sex. Mustafa pointed out the women who are currently "trying to get with me." He stressed his virility and prowess in the past, present, and future tense to make sure that no one assumed that his marriage diminished his virility. Mahmoud subsequently listed the various Latinas with whom he had hooked up by detailing their Latin American country of origin. He simultaneously mapped his sexual prowess across bodies and countries, each serving as a badge of masculine affirmation.

Having recognized a particular pattern of sexual desires, Mustafa asked Mahmoud, "Have you hooked up with a black girl?" Mahmoud scrunched his face in a show of disgust. "Kallus? No. I don't have a taste for that. Man, I wouldn't ever touch a Kallu." Sexual acts with white women and Latinas earn these men accolades. Mahmoud's statement located black women outside the realm of sexual desires. By referencing black women as "that," he denigrated their bodies.[17] There were numerous African American women at Club Opera. Mahmoud moved intentionally through the club space to end up in the salsa room and in the clusters of white women near the large hip-hop section. He did not frequent Shooter's Alley, where the majority of exotic dancers are African American. Even when young South Asian American men initiate intimate contacts with African American women, the meanings produced through such corporeal intimacy are not the same. For example, Ahmed called Mustafa to chat about playing pool. He also told Mustafa about a black woman he was "hooking up with." Before he got off the phone, he begged Mustafa, "Don't tell Fatima [Mustafa's wife], she'll get mad at me for having sex with Kallus." The competition for women means that these young men pin their hopes of sexual appraisal on perpetuating sexualized racial hierarchies and penetrating certain bodies.

Although Mahmoud placed South Asian American women low on his sexual rating system, other South Asian American men appraised South Asian American women differently in ways that interject variant sexual values in relation to white and Latina women. Under some rubrics, South Asian American women received contradictory valences of promiscuity and purity, an attempt to control women's morality that constituted one expression of masculinity.[18] Some desi basketball players and their peers discursively and performatively constrained the representation of South Asian American femininity. Jahm, an Ismaili South Asian American male, had a social life that embodied this contradictory impulse to sexually conquer women but yet control certain women's morality. He exercised at LA Fitness gyms and met Mustafa and me on a few occasions. Jahm is nearly 6-feet tall, over 200 pounds, and has an immense, chiseled upper body. He wore a tank top—known as a "wife beater" (an irony, considering his statements about his wife)—to showcase his muscular arms, shoulders, and chest. While working out, Jahm shared stories of his arranged marriage as well as his sexual conquests in Midtown Atlanta.

Jahm explained why he continues to go out clubbing to meet other women even though he had just gotten married. He elaborated with softness in his voice, "You got to be gentle with the wife and respect her." His voice rose, "You can't do things with your wife that you do with hoes. . . . You need hoes [whores] to do other things *you* need."[19] The heterosexual family as a cultural domain is discursively modeled, through the figure of his wife, to represent "tradition" and "purity." Although South Asian American women embody many positions along the spectrum from "pure" to "whore," Jahm's insistence on the purity of his wife showed how women who represent the home, diaspora, or nation must be kept "pure." Jahm would not let the possibility of "whore" to enter the lexicon of wife, and thus "purity" is denied to the women he met in Midtown Atlanta. The sociologist Margaret Abraham, in her study of domestic abuse in South Asian American families, elaborates upon the connection between masculinity, femininity, and morality: "Masculinity in mainstream South Asian culture is defined to a large degree in terms of men's power, visibility, and ability to control women's morality and sexuality" (2000: 90). Whereas young men and community elders maintain the morality and purity of South Asian American women at large cultural functions, the young men actively police the morality of their spouses in the family unit. While maintaining the heteronormativity of the family unit, they contradictorily partake in sexual escapades in the leisure circuit in order to accentuate normative masculinity.

During one conversation with Jahm, his muscles tensed up as one hand mimicked choking someone while the other hand mimed slapping someone's buttocks. Jahm said with seriousness, pride, and laughter mixed together: "The hoes at the club, I can choke the bitch when I fuck her! I can fuck her up the ass and cum in her ass. . . . I can't do this with the wife." Each description of sexual intercourse is an allusion to manning up. Jahm's machismo does not seem out of place with such violent language. The violence exists alongside heterosexual pleasure. Such a coupling makes the violence invisible as the pleasure principle takes center stage in his recounting of sexual encounters: if "choking" is part of sexual pleasure, the violent, misogynistic overtones become harder to see. As long as the two referents are a man and a woman, the acts are seen as conventional heterosexual practices. However, these same men, along with mainstream U.S. society, read the acts of violence and rape in the biblical telling of Sodom and Gomorrah as sexual in ways that pathologize LGBTQI (lesbian, gay, bisexual, transgender, queer, questioning and intersex) communities.[20] The acts of violence and rape in the Bible and Quran are substituted for acts of same-sex desire. Heterosexual acts, like the ones above, are not coded as violent in the same way as same-sex acts are. Rather, the acts of slapping a woman's buttocks, climaxing in her buttocks, and choking her constitute signposts on the terrain of heterosexuality.

"Freakin'": Getting One's Groove On

At the club scene, very specific signposts exist in dance clubs and strip clubs that delineate "femininity" and "masculinity." The dance act of "freakin'" (also known as the "bump and grind") constitutes one of the common and sexualized bodily movements for young people.[21] Men and women have different bodily expectations in this dance form. Without surveillance and policing by community elders, Mustafa and his friends engaged in certain styles of dancing where a thrusting of the hips and movement of the torso contrasts with basketball movements. That night at Club Opera, Mahmoud made a mad dash to "get digits" when the club's lights flickered to signal its closing. Women at the club did not readily give out phone numbers: Mahmoud had to labor to reach his goal. Dancing with women represented one means to getting digits. Mahmoud searched the dance floor for white women and Latinas. They were the women who could allow him to rebound from "having no game." When he spotted someone suitable, Mahmoud approached the woman's space and started dancing next to her but not in direct physical contact. If the woman conveyed any interest, Mahmoud occupied her physical space and started shaking his hips while moving in closer proximity to her. Mahmoud found two Latinas to dance with. At this time, two inebriated white women made their own rounds in the club and approached Mustafa and me. Mustafa smiled and accepted the white women's invitation. One of them faced away from Mustafa and projected her backside onto his front side. Mustafa had his arms in the air while the woman gyrated her hips with a constant push of her buttocks onto Mustafa's crotch. His response was a smile and a thrust forward with his hips. She then dropped her torso forward (while continuing to thrust her buttocks) and touched the floor in a way that elevated her buttocks. This move accentuated her backside and pressed it more forcefully into Mustafa's crotch. As soon as she rose back up, she quickly left with her friend in the midst of giggles.

Mustafa's own actions of thrusting his pelvis into the backside of the young woman resembled the sexual act of penetration. He referred to these actions as "freakin'." Mustafa mentioned "freakin'" many times when he described Ahmed's 21st birthday party. A young Muslim friend hosted Ahmed's birthday party in Duluth, Georgia (far away from Midtown Atlanta). "At first it was lame. I was about to leave and take Ahmed to Midtown. Man, there were no girls. Just dudes . . . all these young guys," Mustafa complained. Then "these cuties [South Asian American women] got there. We could freak these girls. I started freakin' one of the girls." Freakin' allows for certain pleasures through particular bodily movements. He cannot mimic these movements and thrusts on the basketball court. Rather, on the court players use their hips and backside to propel opponents from their space. One's hips—swung from side to side—give leverage to push opponents out. There is no thrusting forward. At Club Opera, the woman initiated the dance with Mustafa by leading with her hips and her backside; she was pulling Mustafa in. Basketball players do not resort to leading with their buttocks when in the midst of a game, nor do they thrust their crotch forward at their opponents. Such a move would disturb the fragile sporting space where homoerotic movements are constantly read as sexually neutral.

By "freakin'," Mustafa, Mahmoud, and Ahmed oriented their bodies toward feminine subjects. Although same-sex desire incorporates the bump and grind at gay clubs, the young South Asian American basketball players take part in the bump and grind to foreground their heterosexual desires. When doing the bump and grind, Mustafa did not position his back against the front of the female dancer; the female dancers turn their backs and position their buttocks against his crotch. A switch in position would slip into the realm of the effeminate and emasculated, as he would then be the one who is penetrated. Thus, to portray acts of sexual intercourse in the public setting of the club, the young men thrust forward with their crotch. The only moments when heterosexual men would push their buttocks against women or other

heterosexual men are for comic value. With the presence of clothes preventing real intercourse, the bump-and-grind dance form brings about
physical contact and subsequent pleasures. For Mahmoud, the bump
and grind enabled intimacy in the wake of which the Latinas gave him
their phone number. Each phone number he acquired was a sign of his
sexual prowess, with the digits standing in for fantasies of sexual conquests. Getting digits is the reward for competing with other men. Yet
such competition for women does not produce solely male-on-female
social interactions. Rather, men compete against each other and come
into physical contact with each other.

The intensity on the basketball court is transformed into greater
modes of aggression and toughness in the dance club scene. Away from
the basketball court, my interlocutors do not attempt to occupy the
physical spaces of other men except in the case of fisticuffs. "Being in
somebody's face" can be the spark that sets off a fight. Even though the
fights take place with other men, men's heterosexual desires are woven
into them. The fights, in the process of browning out clubs, often take
place with other South Asian American men. Each fight represents an
opportunity to one-up another brown man.

Roughing It Up!

Even in a multiracial club scene, young brown men found each other
to fight. Brown-on-brown physical violence is one means to place oneself literally and figuratively on top of another brown man. Fighting
becomes a way to gain respect and status within the South Asian American community. It is a way to shed "effeminate and possibly homosexual
identities" (Pascoe 2006: 3). By fighting, the young men make a clear
distinction from femininity and queer masculinity, both of which they
see as incapable of embodying "men."

The leisure studies scholar T. F. Burns (1980: 280) notes, "When
young males are together, their conversations are filled with references
to street fighting, acting 'tough,' and 'being rowdy.'" Such was also the
case with Ali, Abdul, and Mustafa. At Ali's bachelor party, Abdul and
Ali reminisced about pranks they had orchestrated and fights they had
had in their younger days with other desis. Abdul related one particular instance in which another South Asian American young man had

postured up to him. "I punched that nigga in the face!" The act of male-on-male violence induced more laughter from Ali, Mustafa, and Bill. In this case, Abdul called other South Asian American males a "nigga." The term "nigga" simultaneously represents co-ethnic intimacy and an abject masculine figure. In this sense, Ali appropriated a racial epithet for black men and converted it to refer to a problematic South Asian American man. Mustafa and Ali laugh not at Abdul's use of the term but rather at Abdul's acts of physical violence. These acts are seen as appropriate, pleasurable yet comical. Young desi men fight each other and use the physical altercations to position themselves within the hierarchy of South Asian American masculinity. Although fighting can fall outside the middle-class notions of respectable masculinity, Mustafa and some of his peers were already lower middle class and have status related to their physicality rather than professional achievement. Therefore, on the streets or in the clubs, one's professional status and educational achievement does not matter as much.

Although the "model minority" moniker implies a certain physical and cultural constitution for desis that provides safe racial distance from black and Latino communities, this racial distance cannot cushion either the physical or symbolic blows in the party scene. A group of young Muslim South Asian American men, known as The Islamic Brotherhood (TIB), proves this. They have been infamous in Buckhead and Midtown for their fights, mostly with affluent Hindu South Asian Americans, since the late 1990s. The Islamic Brotherhood is primarily composed of working-class South Asian American Muslims with ancestral ties to Bangladesh and Pakistan. They fought with various members of Atlanta's South Asian American community in Buckhead, Atlanta's main financial district and historical residence of affluent whites, in the 1990s, when it was known as a party scene. When the prestigious party scene shifted from Buckhead to a gentrified Midtown Atlanta during the late 1990s, TIB and other South Asian American communities followed. At the clubs in Midtown, TIB runs into various members of Atlanta's South Asian American basketball community. The Muslim members of TIB are considered by my informants to be "lower class" and most likely part of the post-1980 Family Preference immigration waves. The fights against the "model minority" leverage working-class TIB members into the arena of tough masculinity. Some members of the Indo-Pak Basketball team the Tennessee Volunteers, most of whom are Hindu and mostly finance professionals, lived in Atlanta but were tired of constantly getting roughed up by TIB.

The Islamic Brotherhood does not single-handedly orchestrate fights. On the contrary, several basketball players, often affiliated with the post-1980 waves, have a history of fights. The fights do not result from a deeply ingrained pathological condition. They are not products of psychopathic constitutions. They do not diffuse into all communities. For the most part, they are intra-ethnic fights, and they are common. Very rarely do they extend into fights with other communities, apart from instances of self-defense against white men. At the April 4, 2009, Asian American Tournament at Georgia Tech, Mustafa and Sanjeet joyfully imparted details about fights and compared notes on the times they had been in jail. Amir sat silently eating his McDonald's fries; he had no such stories. Fights are commonplace in the Atlanta club scene for some South Asian American men. Both Mustafa and Sanjeet had been arrested numerous times for fighting. Sanjeet never served any time in jail even though he was arrested many times. "Been to jail 12 times, my dad [a prominent business man] *knows* people. I never had to serve a sentence," he explained.

During a subsequent interview with Sanjeet, he alluded to the college desi parties, browned-out spaces, where he initially encountered members of TIB. When Sanjeet fought TIB, he was staking a claim to manhood in a brown racial milieu in the presence of other co-ethnic peers. Since Sanjeet is a Sikh American, these fights with Muslim TIB members were also moments in which minority masculinities in Indian politics struggle over positions of dominance and subjugation within South Asian America. Sanjeet said with confidence,

> I would take on these desi guys since I was much bigger. They would start shit and I couldn't walk away, my pride and ego got in the way. . . . These fights kept going since TIB couldn't beat me and my friends. It got us respect with desi crews; it would always get [us] a reward; desi girls wanted to hook up with us. People started to recognize us at desi events. Being Sikh, I didn't back down. You can't back down because you are going against your culture and religion. . . . I had to stop going to clubs because of all the fights. . . . It got worse as guns were brought out.

The act of performing masculinity through physical violence expressed ethnic sensibilities and had sexual consequences for Sanjeet. The ability and willingness to stand up and fight brings respect. He was a physical juggernaut with strength that allowed him to ward off several TIB men who attacked him at once. Sanjeet concluded that desi women were drawn to such attributes. Yet, as we have seen, fighting does not always guarantee respect within the South Asian American community. In fact, certain teams with a history of fights are disallowed from tournament participation. "Black" becomes the marker to label the players on teams with histories of physical violence. Similarly, desis mark other desis as "black" if they have a propensity for fighting. When I asked Ali to provide greater detail on the meanings of "black" when used to reference South Asian Americans, he responded, "Depends on who they are. Lets say TIB, that's a gang of black dudes, that's a gang of black dudes." He added, "They gang banging, they shoot, they fight, they drink. They're just thugs . . . thug mentality, still run illegal businesses . . . don't know any better. . . . I don't think any of them graduated from college or high school or whatever. . . . What they do is run gas stations or any money laundering thing." Fighting, illegality, and other class markers were used by Ali to define the *blackened* South Asian American man in opposition to the image of the "model minority" as passive, non-physical masculinity. The competition on the basketball court set the stage for masculinity that took place in other contests. Teammates frequented the party scene together. Fights, at times, were also fights of one team versus another team. In the first session of the summer Asian Ballers League in 2009, two Sikh brothers on Sanjeet's team, Air Punjab, were in conflict with two other Sikhs on the Sand Brothaz team. The Sikh men on both teams had fought each other the previous night in the club scene. Elders came for the first time to these games to prevent a sequel to the previous night.

Whether the young men take part in dancing, fighting, or both, physical limits are established.[22] Only within a contained set of bodily movements can one ensure that the practices of masculinity are appropriate for each social context. Fighting at a religious event or a cultural festival would not bring the same rewards that it did for Sanjeet at parties. Similarly, men are limited to what types of dances and body positions they could engage in. Extending beyond these limits could produce various queer, effeminate readings.[23] The kinetic performances by Mahmoud and Mustafa at Club Opera symbolized the act of sexual penetration with the man as the penetrator.[24] Reversing such bodily positions and comportment could transform the male into the feminine subject and object of penetration. Yet, the aggressive act of occupying a women's space was not uniform in all leisure settings. When at the strip clubs, the young desi men could not physically approach exotic dancers, as they did the women at the dance clubs. In addition, the men did not become the objects of pleasure for the female strippers as Sanjeet was for the desi women at the parties. At the strip club, female exotic dancers/strippers exaggerate their sexual flirtations while the male clients refrain from occupying the dancer's physical space. Mustafa and his peers actively participated in the strip club scene as another leisure activity that ties up masculinity and heterosexuality, at the same time operating within the confines of sensorial passivity.

"Makin' It Rain!"

Some of the foundational elements of the bump-and-grind dance style take shape at the strip clubs.[25] Unlike at the dance clubs, at strip clubs young men cannot partake equally in the acts of bumping and grinding, "freakin." The exotic dancers gyrate their toned bodies and use their curves to initiate contact with the client. Dancers thrust their hips, their backsides, and their breasts upon the clients. The young men know the social codes of this space and refrain from touching the dancers. There are different levels of power and agency exerted both by the dancers and by the male desi clients.

> After a few hours at Club Karma, Ali's face bore the signs of a busy two weeks of Muslim festivities and preparations for his Christian wedding ceremony on April 18. He went directly home and did not want to take part in the customary bachelor ritual of attending a strip club. Abdul did not want to forgo this opportunity to spend time at a strip club. Mustafa, Bill (Ali's future brother-in-law), Abdul, and I proceeded to a club called "Follies" in a multiethnic, immigrant neighborhood on Buford Highway. Upon entry, Abdul found the only white dancer and spent the rest of the night in a dark corner of the club getting lap dances from this young woman. Bill was noticeably uncomfortable and was planted at our table. He got uneasy

when dancers approached him. In contrast, Mustafa found a young African American dancer to his liking. He paid for several lap dances and flirted with her throughout the course of the night. While Mustafa got his first lap dance, a group of darker South Asian Americans entered the club. They were Bangladeshi Americans of the post-1980 immigration waves and were regulars at Follies. Mustafa and Abdul exchanged greetings with the Bangladeshi Americans; they were acquainted through years of engagement in the local party scene. The Bangladeshi Americans went to the many dancers at the club. One young man with long, black hair in a ponytail went around the club securing dances. With each new dancer, he would take a wad of dollar bills and throw it in the air above the head of the dancer. The bills descended on the dancer like autumn leaves to which the young man shouted, "Makin' it rain! Makin' it rain!"

The Bangladeshi American man with the pony tail approached women for dances. His material capital was the way to engender intimacy with them. He could not initiate physical contact although he could initiate the social interaction. Certain levels of passivity undergird strip clubs. The exotic dancers thrust their own bodies and determine what the men can do in return. Exotic dancers, when giving a lap dance, are the only ones who bump and grind. Only if the client asks to go to the VIP room can the sexual tension escalate to both parties possibly touching the other. Even in the VIP room, clients touch the dancer only at her discretion. When giving a lap dance, the dancer thrusts her body in ways that represent the acts of sexual penetration. At this moment, she only penetrates the realm of sexual desire. The men do not physically become, at any point, the penetrated. Rather than initiating the contact and using body rhythms to convey penetration, male clients continue to find pleasure, but with a certain level of physical immobility. The passing of money sexualizes the interactions. Even though the protocols of strip clubs demand a passive bodily comportment, this interaction based on heterosexual desire (albeit one-sided) affirms the symbolic binary of masculine and feminine.[26]

The strip club is part of the South Asian American cultural sphere for several of my interlocutors. Mustafa attended strip clubs that featured women dancers of color, such as Follies and Shooter's Alley. However, neither Follies nor Shooter's Alley are well-known clubs in

Atlanta's nightclub landscape. Clubs such as Pink Pony, Cheetah Club, Oasis, and Gold Club[27] dominate the Atlanta exotic dancing economy. The female dancers and strip clubs are embedded in a hierarchy structured through race and class. In her fascinating study of sex workers in Ho Chi Minh City, Vietnam, the sociologist Kimberly Hoang (2010, 2015) details three tiers of sex work. Each tier highlights the social location of the sex worker, the class sensibilities of desire, and the status of the client. This sedimentation and social stratification produces different means of subject making between clients and sex workers at each tier. Thus the clubs are differentiated through Hoang's informants' class, race, bodily integrity, bodily capital, and nationality. The high tiers underscore the symbolic and financial capital of both client and sex worker. Similarly, strip clubs in Atlanta exist across various social locations and symbolic capital.

The Pink Pony and the Cheetah Club are clubs that Mustafa labeled as "too white," attracting affluent white men. These clubs are the iconic clubs in the Atlanta cityscape. Daniel and Harpreet, whom we met earlier, patronize the Pink Pony. Both men, who are finance and technology professionals, admitted that they take their clients to the Pink Pony. The Pink Pony features mostly white dancers with toned bodies and augmented breasts, along with a smaller number of African American and Latino dancers. These women represent the pinnacle of exotic dancing in Atlanta. As such, they receive the type of clients who pay well for their services. Even the built environment for the Pink Pony is suited for a large, affluent client base. There are several private rooms along with three different dancing areas. The posh furniture and velvet reflects a different class aesthetic than Follies. Furthermore, the Pink Pony's parking lot is built to accommodate limousines and numerous cars.

Lower-middle-class communities, working-class communities, and communities of color frequent places like Follies, which is located in the multiethnic, working-class neighborhood known as Buford Highway, as is Shooter's Alley. It features African American women of many hues and tones. Most of the dancers at Follies and Shooter's Alley have natural breasts that are small in comparison to those of the dancers at the Pink Pony. These women highlight other curves, such as their toned, firm buttocks. They do not need to augment their breasts, as the enlarged size of those body parts may not be the main sites of desire for their male clients.

At Follies, the Bangladeshi American men could express a sense of higher-class subjectivity with their money. Mustafa informed me that these men operated gas stations and took part in various underground enterprises that were not respectable class markers elsewhere. With their ability to "make it rain," they marketed themselves as desirable men at the strip club. They could visit Follies often but might not have the capital to do so with similar frequency at the Pink Pony.

Men do not always visit the strip clubs alone. Sometimes the young men bring their partners and simultaneously affirm while complicating notions of the heterosexual, nuclear household. Mustafa informed me that even Fatima, his wife through arranged marriage, enjoyed going to strip clubs with him. When she accompanied him, the presence of desire was multiple and not easily containable as Mustafa, Fatima, and the dancer existed in the same space. Mustafa admitted, "She [Fatima] loves it [attending strip clubs with him] but won't tell people about it." Mustafa was explicit about going to strip clubs. This visibility underscores his masculinity. Fatima, however, did not invoke femininity as a static category; rather, she kept it somewhat fluid. She could maintain the line of "purity" by keeping it a secret from the larger community while indulging in the pleasures of sexual voyeurism.

Mustafa and his peers shared with each other the intimate details about the dancers and ethos of the strip clubs they frequented. There is a certain level of passivity at the strip club even when the men take explicit pleasure in gazing at female bodies. The men are commodified as sources of money. They control only their money and cannot play with women's bodies; they cannot occupy space in the same manner as they can at the dance clubs. Even on the basketball court there is a certain level of give and take with the opponent where one can press forward with the action. Such is not the case with the strip club; the men can force the issue only to a certain extent with their bodily ability. They can make a demand for more with their wallets, but even that is limited. This sort of passivity can be read as weak and effeminate. After all, the men at the strip clubs become the playthings of the exotic dancers. Exotic dancers control the realm of fantasy and dictate the terms of sexual arousal.[28] In fact, the dancers occupy and dominate the physical space of the male clients.

Each dancer uses her own version of the bump and grind to stimulate the clients. In a way, Mustafa, Abdul, and Bill were helpless in that they could not readily act upon their sexual urges. Clients are kicked out when they cross boundaries of acceptable behavior and touch the dancers. One of the only times that clients can make contact with dancers is when they place dollars bills in the undergarments of the dancers. At these times, Mustafa took out money and slid it down the contours of the dancer's hip to the only piece of clothing left on the dancer's body—her G-string. He could not do anything more. Even in this heightened sexualized moment, the young men still find various points of agency at the moment of submission to the whims of the dancers.

Through making the scene at strip clubs, desi men countered their representations as embodying always queer masculinities. Even though they did not have much control, these men *straightened* their desires toward female bodies. They expressed their agency by purchasing dances and choosing to be sexually aroused. When the Bangladeshi man shouted, "Makin' it rain!" he was able to own the space of the club and the dancers' bodies in space for a finite period of time. As the dollar bills floated down, the young man indulged in the sexual tease. For the Bangladeshi men who frequent Follies, the sexual teases by the dancers can lead to sexual intercourse. As the club shut down, the Bangladeshi American men asked several dancers to go home with them. In this instance, they subverted the norms and protocol of the strip club by engaging in mutually explicit sexual practices with the exotic dancers. By spilling over these institutionally acceptable boundaries, they were not expressing non-normativity; rather, they were indulging in socially acceptable and celebrated parameters of masculinity. As Mustafa implied in the earlier vignette, the ability to "take these girls home" is an expression of sexual bravado. Engendering short-term or long-term relationships between dancers and clients stands as one field where the young men contest the social protocol but still perform a normative masculinity.[29]

At the strip club, Mustafa delved into his own ideas of strength and control. He conveyed toughness at the moments of passivity. Toughness is coded into "restraint." When the African American dancer at Follies finished giving Mustafa a lap dance and left, he looked over at me with a big smile. "Her hands were down my pants. . . . She . . . grabbed my dick. But I made her stop." He then explained, as if talking to the dancer, "Don't touch my dick unless I am going to fuck you." Showing constraint and restraining the dancer afforded Mustafa some sort of power. He determined how far this sexual tease will go. He was aroused but manned up by stopping the female dancer from further fondling him in certain ways. Although an orgasm is a thing of pleasure, he wanted to control the female dancer and his orgasm. Mustafa did not want to orgasm in his pants, which would have shown clearly the power of the dancer. By simultaneously enduring the pleasures of such sexual flirtation without losing control of his penis, he affirmed his strength by sharing this story with me. Heterosexual desire resonates through these interactions with complicated shifts in agency and passivity.

Be it at the dance clubs or the strip clubs, young South Asian American men respond to mainstream racializations through their own brand of conservative gender politics that celebrates aggression, toughness, physicality, and "compulsory heterosexuality." Affects and displays of toughness are embodied in notions of "blackness" along with corresponding consumptive practices of cultural blackness. However, few South Asian American players physically engage with actual black bodies, male or female. Rather, they seek out white women and Latinas as embodiments of socially valued sexual bodies. Black women, for Mahmoud, were sexual Others who cannot reconfirm his own heterosexuality. Sexual interactions and intercourse with white women and Latinas trigger positive values for these desi men. In addition to courting women, men assert heterosexuality and masculinity through their interactions with other desi men in the club scene. Although embodying their own problematic constructions of blackness as threatening, these men do not frequently fight and try to dominate "Other" racialized masculinities. Rather, they fight among each other to move up in the South Asian American masculine hierarchy.

As these young men used basketball and leisure spaces as platforms to deconstruct, reconfigure, negotiate, and manage South Asian American masculinity, they assembled the parameters of South Asian American identity through conservative gender, sexual, and racial orders. In the process of elevating South Asian American masculinity, the practices of manning up in brown outs exclude women, people of color, and queer subjects. The feminine and queer Others always exist in brown outs. They are the foundational oppositions, in addition to black masculinity, that shape South Asian American masculinity. At Club Opera, Mustafa shared experiences of gay men hitting on him. Midtown Atlanta is known to have a large gay population and gay-friendly leisure activities, so the presence of gay men at the club is not surprising, though Mustafa expressed agitation about their coming on to him. By contrast, gay men were not as visible in brown-out basketball spaces. However, queer and feminine subjects are continually constituted and negated by the basketball players. The following chapter looks at these practices of constitution and negation while centering the voices of women and queer subjects to showcase how they manage the fields of power on and off the basketball court.

5

Breaking the Cycle

The Ballplayer Posture and Performances of Exclusion

After a night out at Club Opera, Mahmoud, Mustafa, and I ended up at the Waffle House, a 24-hour Southern eatery. Shortly after we ordered our food, a group of four or five African American men came in with boisterous laughs. They sat in a corner booth to the left of us. All the other patrons shifted their attention to them, including the three of us. These African American men seemed to me to be gay. A few of them swayed their hips as they walked in, and two of them wore brightly colored bandanas on their heads. One young man in particular caught Mahmoud's attention. This man wore a midriff shirt; a red bandana on his head; makeup on his face, including red lipstick; and skin-tight broken-in denim shorts. He spoke with flair and moved his arms from side to side theatrically. Mahmoud grew a little uneasy and was agitated by the sight of him. His expression morphed into one of distaste. Speaking in Urdu, he called the men "Kallu Chakkas" and "Gandus." Unfamiliar with these Urdu terms, I asked, "What does 'Gandu' mean?" Mahmoud and Mustafa replied that "Chakka" and "Gandu" were terms for gay people. This response had little affective quality and seemed indifferent. Then, after a slight pause, Mahmoud lowered his voice, "It means 'faggot.'" He turned to me and said, "Stan, you know stuff, you have learned all this stuff. Why are they gay?" This was a rhetorical question, and Mahmoud answered it with another forceful question. With heightened disgust in his voice, Mahmoud demanded, "Why can't they just man up?!"[1] As we continued to talk, with Mahmoud controlling the conversation, he turned to Mustafa and told him, with jest and gravity in his voice, "Man, I wouldn't ever let you become a Gandu." The statement was said in a manner that suggested that there was no doubt about Mustafa's heterosexuality. Mahmoud chuckled as he warned Mustafa, "I would have to beat you up if you were a Gandu."

Young desi men turn to consuming and performing elements of black aesthetics as a strategy by which to re-enter the fold of normative masculinity. They appropriate a model of cultural blackness that constructs a tough, aggressive, and heterosexual masculinity as a means to escape their racialization as weak, nerdy, and hypo-sexual. However, as evident in the vignette, heterosexuality and racial identities are not neatly, uniformly inhabited. The black men above challenged the hyper-masculinity and staunch heterosexuality associated with African American men. Whereas South Asian American men might feel less masculine than straight black men, here the presence of gay black men complicates the making of desi masculinity. Mahmoud and Mustafa performed an acceptable heterosexual racial Otherness in relation to the gay blackness. Regardless of their own social location within the nation and diaspora, the stigmatizing of gay subjects provides one possible way to claim a higher social standing.[2] Although homosexuality is invoked to regulate the boundaries of heterosexuality,[3] the presence of the black gay men simultaneously disturbs, complicates, and contradicts South Asian American belonging in the nation, diaspora, and sporting spaces.

While South Asian American men use leisure activities to create their own models of identity and American-ness, their acts cannot be understood simply as resistance. Identity formation involves exclusions, regulations, and foreclosures. Desi men embody and occupy various positions of hegemony, resistance, conformity, and oppression simultaneously.[4] Even acts of resistance and contestation, when structured through racial heteronormativity, serve only to ingrain social hierarchies. Although sport is reflective of greater society and a microcosm of larger social processes, it still imposes limitations on bodily comportment, identity formation, and resistance.[5] The post-colonial scholar C. L. R. James, in his examination of West Indian cricket players, contends that "he [the West Indian cricket player] never forgets that this liberation exists only within the boundaries of the game, and then only for the gamers. . . . Sport is no sanctuary from the real world because sport is part of the real world, and the liberation and the oppression are inextricably bound."[6] Like the cricket players, South Asian American basketball players engage thoroughly in the pleasures of competitive play and subsequently attempt to liberate their brown bodies from mainstream stereotypes. Within their sporting practices, the athletes integrate elements of the social order and its consequent social hierarchies. Players negotiate desi racialized masculinity between (hetero)sexuality and femininity at the expense of marginalizing gay men and women, who are key subjects in the production of masculinity. By centering their racial position, heterosexuality, middle-class sensibilities, and masculinity, South Asian American men, knowingly and unknowingly, confirm the binaries of male-female, masculine-feminine, respectable-unacceptable, straight-queer, and racial binaries. In order for their acts of sporting pleasure to truly foster systemic change, the very system of organization of masculinities, femininities, and non-normative identities must be altered where difference is not built into oppositional exclusion.

Desi basketball players and allies do not dismantle the operation of power; instead, they interweave themselves into the national fabric that continues to uphold whiteness, heterosexuality, masculinity, and middle-class respectabilities. The young men, like Mahmoud, are guilty of consuming what the black feminist Audre Lorde describes in *Sister Outsider* as a "mythical norm": "In america, this norm is usually defined as white, thin, male, young, heterosexual, Christian, and financially secure. It is with this mythical norm that the trappings of power reside within this society" (1984: 116). Lorde specifically refers to the fabric of social life in U.S. society, where power, in the normative representation of the white, middle-class, heterosexual Christian male as the ideal citizen, is taken for granted.[7] Accordingly, gay men and women constitute one key part of the oppositional foundation by which the mythical norm is structured. By striving toward this ideal, by overemphasizing heterosexuality, middle-class respectability, and masculinity, communities take part in stigmatizing and marginalizing Others who cannot aspire to this racial white heteronormative ideal. Mahmoud embodied this mythical norm by positioning himself as heterosexual in racially acceptable terms and in opposition to both blackness and gayness as embodied by the black gay men. Although he could not attain the mythical norm of masculinity as a result of his own racial position and religious identity, his performances pointed toward a desire to achieve a higher social location at the expense of various (queer, racial, and feminine) Others. Accordingly, the young South Asian American basketball players did not understand that their racialized exclusion as "nerds" and "terrorists" is part and parcel of the masculine, heterosexual, white, and middle-class nature of belonging in the United States.

Instead of using their marginalized social location in the United States to work with Other sexualized, racialized, and gendered communities, some resorted to using the lexicon of their exclusion in hopes of exiting the social margins. During our conversation at the Waffle House, Mahmoud followed up his comments with another rhetorical question: "Why if god made *legs* to *walk* then would *gays fight god and nature*?"[8] This kind of discourse invokes "nature" and "god" to legitimate his manliness across the different spheres of science and religion.

This process of "exclusion" (of the black queers) at the moment of inclusion into aspects of normative masculinity (mythical norm) by Mahmoud further resembles Audre Lorde's theory of liberation. Lorde interrogates mainstream feminism, in which white women celebrate their subversive acts against patriarchy and believe that "man" (as a uniform category) is the source of all oppression. She asks them not to seal sexism in a vacuum but rather to see how white supremacy, poverty, homophobia, imperialism, and other struggles could be problematically co-opted in the struggle for women's rights. Lorde explains, "The master's tools will never dismantle the master's house. They may allow us temporarily to beat him at his own game, but they will never enable us to bring about genuine change."[9] Lorde's critique of the feminist agenda and its singular conceptualization of injustice parallel some of the ways in which desi basketball players problematically challenge mainstream racializations. While Mahmoud struggled against mainstream stereotypes of desi men as effeminate nerds or terrorists, he responded by taking the foundations of heterosexuality, racism, and masculinity to express his identity at the cost of excluding gay black men.

Why must gay black men serve as a counteridentification for vice, failure, and need for regulation? Mahmoud's demand for them to *man up* illustrated the fragile realm of heterosexual masculinity, which demands the presence of sexual, gendered, and racial others for its own articulation.[10] When Mahmoud could no longer consume cultural blackness as hyper-masculine, he turned toward forms of regulation by which to construct gayness (coupled with blackness) as opposition. In the process, he feminized the gay black men in contrast to his own performance of heterosexual masculinity. In feminizing the gay men, he made a value judgment: masculinity here has greater power than femininity. Although the use of "Kallu" in basketball circuits and at the clubs signaled a threatening, hyper-masculine black man, at the Waffle House it constituted black men as non-normative in a differently sexualized way. While displacing queerness upon the African American gay men, Mahmoud affirmed the proper type of male homosocial bonding—as friends, teammates, and brothers—that serves to orient the basketball social interactions and subsequent activities as heterosexual.

Racialized masculinities, such as desi masculinity, took shape in relation to gay men and women. While heterosexual black men embodied a desirable sporting masculinity to these desi men, the gay black man embodied something of the opposite. The gay man's purpose there is to allow the straight desi man to construct heterosexual masculinity through opposition. In order for desi sporting masculinity to have substance, gay Others and woman are critical to managing heteronormativity in leisure spaces. In this instance, the straight athletes drew on various forms of homophobia to foreground heterosexuality. By creating homosexuality as opposition, desi players activated the heterosexual components of the mythical norm to enter the fold of normative masculinity. The other strategy of homosociality is compulsory heterosexuality and patriarchy on the court in order to consolidate diasporic and national subjectivities along particular sexual orientations.[11] In this instance, South Asian American men distanced themselves from femininity. In the process, they foregrounded the "patriarchal dividends" (Connell 1995) of being a man according to the mythical norm, which naturalizes sporting cultures as innately masculine. As a result, South Asian American basketball players structured the sporting desi identity by treating various subjects as *outsiders* to desi masculinity: African Americans, gay men, and South Asian American women.

Homosociality and Gay Men

Mahmoud imagined that gay black men have the innate right to claim masculinity, but their performances and desires fail to live up to his expectations. There is a sort of melancholy to his fantasy, a longing for a "true blackness" that is heterosexual. South Asian American consumption of hip-hop and appropriation of cultural blackness is one that structures black masculinity as a repudiation of the gay Other, regardless of the gayness that has always existed within black communities.[12] As a result, the activities of the black gay men at the Waffle House muddled the gendered, raced, and sexualized terrain of desi masculinity.

Mahmoud drew on the gay black men at the Waffle House to perform heterosexual masculinity *through queerness as opposition*, but this is not the only way in which South Asian American basketball players engage with queer masculinity. During my research I frequently saw the players invoke and perform queer masculinity, using *homosexuality and queerness as intimate irony*. Since South Asian American basketball players frequently used basketball and its corresponding activities as signifiers of heterosexual masculinity, gay men do not frequently participate or self-identify as gay in these brown outs. Without an actual gay subject on the court to provide the substance of opposition, the desi players kinetically conjure up queer masculinity that serves to police other men to heterosexual masculinity. Although desi players manufacture distance from queer subjectivity, ironically, they could only do so by intimately knowing the very contours of queerness that they then must repudiate.

Queerness as Opposition

At the Waffle House, Mahmoud resorted to positioning the gay men as a permanent *opposition* to heterosexual masculinity. Striking at homosexuality is one way to entrench claims to normativity within the nation and diaspora.[13] As a convenience mart and gas station owner, he could not accrue the same kind of symbolic capital as finance and medical professionals like Mohammed, Daniel, or Vivek. He is *not* the "model minority." Furthermore, he did not have the kind of basketball acumen that could secure clout like Ali, Mustafa, Imran, or Mohammed. His simultaneous claims to manhood and South Asian American–ness came through the means of locating homosexuality and corresponding meanings of femininity on a lower echelon within the masculinity hierarchy. Mahmoud's use of the terms "Chakka" and "Gandu" was not confined to the dance party scene. South Asian American players use these terms in basketball circuits, including co-religionist settings. Even during their youthful encounters with basketball, South Asian American men routinely conflated the male body, masculinity, and heterosexuality.

Sharif, a self-identifying gay Muslim South Asian American man, interacted with members of the Atlanta Outkasts at their mosque during his formative teenage years. He continued to be a peer and kin in this network of Muslim South Asian Americans. But he was not a frequent presence in Indo-Pak tournaments or corresponding places of heterosexual leisure. Sharif, in this case, became, as a result of his identity and identification, an "outcast" who could not be an Outkast. Yet, in his younger years, he found that sports embodied contradictory liberal and conservative impulses: "We [young Muslim men] were introduced to each other and non-Muslim South Asians at the mosque. I played in the sport gatherings with groups; I played basketball and football. People would make friends through sport. It [sport] got me out of my shell because I was introverted. . . . Sports gave me confidence, I did not feel defiled when I played. Overall, it was good." As young Muslim South Asian American men interacted with each other through sporting activities at Al-Farooq Masjid in Atlanta, they indulged in the heterosexual overtones of American and Muslim masculinity. While sport interactions engendered intimate relationships with other men, the nature of these relationships came with its own brand of compulsory heterosexuality. Sharif added, "Being gay led to minimal conversations other than in sport. There were talks about girls and marriage, these were the salient topics and made me feel isolated. . . . I was not on Atlanta Outkasts because those guys went to more heterosexual places, clubs, with girls." Even the basic moments of male bonding on the court involved a constant iteration of heterosexual desire and progression to the mythical norm with the gay man as opposition to the sporting space.

The talk of heterosexual desire served to cement the relationship between sporting masculinity and heterosexuality.[14] When at gender-integrated events such as dance clubs and strip clubs, Mustafa and Mahmoud took pride in listing their (hetero)sexual conquests. Even within the homosocial two-hour period of pickup basketball, the men spoke in excess about young women they consider sexually attractive. Such talk spilled into heterosexual fantasies that allowed them to be "men" and perform middle-class respectability as hard-working husbands and fathers. After one night of pickup ball, Harpreet, Joe, and Daniel passionately talked about the various action movies of Summer 2009. Harpreet expressed his joy with the movie *Transformers*[15] and its quality of action and special effects. Quickly the discussion turned toward one particular actress in the film. With smiles on their faces and enthusiasm in their voices, they all found pleasure in describing the movie star Megan Fox, her body and her curves. Although the movie contains major male actors, like Shia LeBouf and Tyrese Gibson, who are seen as heartthrobs in their own right, Daniel, Joe, and Harpreet did not mention them in the same discursive space as Megan Fox. Through conversations about their desires for her body, Harpreet, Joe, and Daniel expressed their sexual orientations. The sexual desires symbolically solidified heteronormativity by mapping femininity to female bodies, mapping masculinity to male bodies, and mapping a pattern of desire for the opposite sex.[16] When Harpreet, Joe, and Daniel positioned femininity in opposition to masculinity through their sexual desires, they did so, as the queer theorist Eve Sedgwick argues,[17] by managing the sexual ambiguity within homosociality through enforcing compulsory heterosexuality.

The talk of women as well as the distancing from gay men is part of what former NBA player John Amaechi describes as the "ballplayer posture." In his autobiography *Man in the Middle*, Amaechi discusses the homoerotic actions in the locker room, such as communal showers and sharing of clothes, which have to be continuously articulated as heterosexual.[18] He explains, "Coming out threatens to expose the homoerotic components of what they [basketball players] prefer to think of as simply male bonding. . . . Homosexuality is an obsession among ballplayers, trailing only wealth and women. . . . Over time, I became convinced that anti-gay prejudice is more a convention of a particular brand of masculinity than a genuine prejudice. Homophobia is a ballplayer posture." Amaechi alludes to how sexuality is such a critical part of sporting practices; as a result, homophobia is prevalent in order to create the *outsider* in physically intimate venues of sport. As racializations already posit South Asian American men as non-normative, their participation in American sport requires an oppositional relation structured around the figure of the gay man—the socially constructed antithesis to sporting masculinity.[19]

Mahmoud's heteronormative evaluations of masculinity were part and parcel of playing basketball.[20] Even though he used "god" and "nature" in his devaluation of queer desire, his homophobic rhetoric should not be attributed to his religious identity as a Muslim.[21] Some gay Muslims, like Sharif, argue that Islam is not the main source of their marginalization; rather, they say, certain social venues harness religion as a force of exclusion. The anthropologists David Murray, Don Kulick, and Martin Manalansan, in *Homophobias: Lust and Loathing across Time and Space*, argue for a nuanced understanding of sexual exclusions that is context specific, a rendering of homophobias in the plural, and an emphasis on not essentializing the exclusion felt by white, middle-class gay men across the entire LGBTQI community.[22] During my research, I witnessed Sharif's experience of "home" and "family," an experience that was very different from the violence predicted by the Western narrative of LGBTQI identity formation. Sharif found safety in the sites where he socializes with Ali, Mustafa, Sultan, and their friends: Homophobia on the basketball court does not uniformly spread throughout desi social spaces. Gay men of color, like Sharif, find safety in the private spaces of the home where they can be and do the work of identity on their own terms, as opposed to public settings such as work and play. Sharif did not let people in his professional circles and public settings, such as larger Muslim community, know that he is gay.

Sharif, although close friends with Ali and Mustafa, did not play basketball with them. However, he has "come out" to their families. Accordingly, his family and extended family no longer try to match him up in a heterosexual marriage, although Amin uncle, Mustafa and Ali's father, and Asma auntie had their own strategies for *straightening* Sharif. When sport, seen as the quintessential tool for socialization into heterosexual masculinity, did not suffice in pulling Sharif back to "batting for the right team," uncles and aunties offered their own remedies. Amin uncle attempted to get the "right [female] prostitute" who could bring Sharif into the straight fold. Asma auntie tried to slip meat into his meals as ways to overcome the protein deficiency that had supposedly resulted in his gayness (the protein consumed during fellatio did not count in Asma auntie's food pyramid). Regardless of his sexual desires and sexual orientation, Sharif was a respected and a valued member of their community. Although other Muslims, like Mahmoud, considered homosexuality a sin, Ali and Mustafa were ambivalent about the connection between Islam and homosexuality as a result of the close friendship with Sharif. When I prodded deeper into his own ideological standpoints on Islam and homosexuality, Ali's answers showed his own uneasy position.

STAN: What is the connection between homosexuality and Islam?

ALI [thinking deeply]: You know, the Quran, says it is against it. But [pause], I don't know.

STAN: Tell me more.

ALI [with a forceful tone]: If you're gay, you're gay, who am I to say what's right or wrong. If I live by the religious guidelines then you [gay subjects] are supposed to be stoned in public. That's crazy! As for a personal basis, I have several friends who are gay, I- I- I- I accept them.

That pause and stutter affirms the ambivalence around sexuality in South Asian American communities. Although Ali self-identified as Muslim, his ambivalence demonstrated that regardless of religious dictates, homosexuality does not lead to expulsion from social life.[23] Yet, he still considered same-sex desires to be outside the boundaries of the normal: "The normality in my mind is male and female, outside of that is abnormal . . . whether you are born with it or not, I don't know." By producing the normal, Ali further ingrained himself into the narrative of heterosexual masculinity while concurrently demonstrating his cosmopolitan benevolence as an open-minded man. Close friendship and kinship with men like Sharif challenged other simplistic interpretations of religion and sexuality. Ambivalence of this sort played out in the differential regulation mechanisms and degrees of exclusions experienced by LGBTQI individuals across South Asian American social spaces. Sharif might not have been welcome or felt comfortable on the basketball court. In fact, he explained to me that gay Muslim South Asian Americans play in gay sporting circuits, where they can be more fully accepted and "loved." While his presence in various social spaces might not trouble heterosexual meanings, the basketball court was not one of those places.

ALI: He [Sharif] is one of the good guys. Sharif is a different breed; he is such a nice guy. What he does, that's not my business, that's his own life. I got my own shit to worry about. Be all you want to be, just don't impose it on me.

Ali's reluctance to practice a homophobia equivalently across social spaces meant that even clearly hermeneutically sealed heterosexual spaces, such as weddings, have openings for gay men. During Ali's nika (Islamic wedding ceremony), Asma auntie and Amin uncle requested Sharif's presence along with that of his brother Salim and his mother, Suad auntie. His queer Muslim masculinity did not jeopardize his belonging in this private religious space where heteronormativity is iterated, reiterated, and institutionalized through marriage. Although marriage is often the site of contentious politics and struggles over heteronormative and homonormative membership,[24] young desi men like Mustafa and Ali welcome Sharif in their private home for the nika ceremony. In a way, Sharif's presence affirmed heterosexual marriage while simultaneously troubling and problematizing heterosexual identity as existing free of gay persons. Sharif played an important role in Mustafa's and Ali's lives. He was an uncle to their children, a respected professional, and revered for his religious piety. However, in the day-to-day experience of basketball that contained such physicality and close proximity of men to other men, several players used anti-gay prejudice and talk of homosexuality as a prevalent tactic to entrench heterosexuality in the homosocial practice of sport.

Engaging with Sharif in private allowed Mustafa and Ali control over the clear boundaries of physical distance, but his presence on the basketball court complicated the presumed heteronormative order of mainstream sport. South Asian American men on the basketball court negotiated heterosexual masculinity through invocation and talk of non-normative, gay, or queer masculinities, but they used Urdu terms to illustrate and set the foundations of this opposition. Mahmoud used "Chakka" and "Gandu" as his ballplayer posture. South Asian American basketball players used the terms to manufacture difference from the non-normative and permanent *insider* to the category of South Asian American–ness and masculinity—the gay desi man. What is more, the gay South Asian American man threatens South Asian American identity on multiple registers of masculinity, ethnicity, and sexuality.[25] The terms "Chakka" and "Gandu" are interwoven into the very structure of identity; they are commonplace terms for young desis with adequate knowledge of Hindi or Urdu languages. Sharif heard these terms before but also understood their polyvalence:

> These terms ["Chakka" and 'Gandu"] in our language can also be used as gender-bending words, and when I use them it does not feel like I

am compromising anything. I can use it to feel empowered through the language used against me. I have heard the Urdu words, and unlike 'fag' or 'faggot,' they are more penetrating. It is sweeter and used in a more painful feeling. It hurts a lot more . . . more offensive . . . kind of sobering. . . . You feel like you get angry when it is in English and feel sober and melancholy when used in Urdu. You feel like anger would be an anger [sic] against your own community and feel individualistic and feel like you are going against the community.

Sharif's reflections indicate that these gendered and sexual terms, like identities, are malleable, dynamic, and multivalent. Whereas Mahmoud used them to affirm binaries of inclusion and exclusion through the categories of gender and sexuality, Sharif readdressed the pleasures that gay Muslims conjure up with such self-identifications through the slurs. As a result, agency and struggle, like homosexuality and heterosexuality, are not two opposite ends of a spectrum; rather, they are a cohabited process of identity. Furthermore, the gender-bending possibilities of these terms give queer subjects a way to take pleasure in the very words that violate them. The use of "Chakka" and "Gandu" is a refusal to be contained within the discursive, symbolic limits of masculinity, femininity, or Western constructions of "homosexuality."

For Sharif, the Western lexicon of sexual exclusion and sexual identification did not have the same power or affect as the Urdu words. The use of "Chakka" and "Gandu" penetrated the safe zone of co-ethnic socialization, making diasporic community formation and ethnic nationalism into hostile spaces for queer subjects. If basketball courts are one key site of South Asian American identity formation, the use of Urdu sexual slurs during play made leisure spaces not equally available to all. Terms like "Chakka" and "Gandu" marked gay men as already failed masculinities. As an ethnic *insider* carrying the penis card, the queer desi complicated the heterosexual terrain of masculinity and troubles the heteropatriarchal demands of sporting, diasporic, and national membership. In the making of masculinity, both the queer and the feminine within the category of South Asian America pose the greatest threat to heterosexual masculinity. Yet both are critical to the social formation of desi masculinity. However, gay black men and Sharif were not present in the brown-out sporting cultures we have examined so far. Without their presence, the coherent boundaries of heterosexual masculinity became ambiguous, thereby making membership and identity into fleeting processes. Finding ways to signal heterosexual masculinity, various players conjured up and offered comedic renditions of queer masculinity. The queer set the parameters for straightening while concurrently queering membership. Players performed heterosexual masculinity through the detailed invocation of gay desires and its respective management and repudiation—this is a strategy of *queerness as intimate irony*.

Queerness as Intimate Irony

March 2009: I got to the parking lot for the Asian Ballers League games and noticed several teams conversing outside on the lot instead of playing indoors. I asked a young Muslim Pakistani American men, "Why aren't you all playing?" Rat Pack player Imran told me, "The guy that opens the gym did not show up. It's closed. Kdol [the Asian Ballers organizer] is calling to get it opened." At this point, Mohammed inquired about my presence. "What are you doing here?" Mustafa had not told them that I was now playing on the Rat Pack. I told those gathered that I had just flown in from Philadelphia, where I had attended my post-engagement ceremonies. As the engagement was news to them, they were surprised and congratulated me. With a smile on his face, Mohammed said, "Damn it, I can't get with Stan now." This statement was not sincere; rather, it was meant to be comic. There were homoerotic undertones coupled with homophobic resonation, but it was socially acceptable for some men to flirt in this comedic way. I told Mohammed, "Hey, I was waiting for you to make a move." Now I was equally guilty of swimming with the current of sexual and gendered regulation by playing along. Mustafa then interjected, "I was trying to get with him, too." The young men joined in a communal laugh.

June 2009: The Atlanta Rat Pack team managed to move deep into the playoffs despite losing Mustafa, their leading scorer, to a severely sprained ankle during the first game in the Asian American tournament in Chattanooga, Tennessee. Around noon, teams were excused to have lunch before the next playoff game. Imran, Amir, Sikh American Ramneet, and Mohammed walked over to Mohammed's beige luxury Toyota Avalon sedan. Mustafa,

Lebanese American Riad, Cambodian American Kdol, and I walked over to Mustafa's red Nissan Altima Sport, with its darkly tinted windows, shiny rims, and a loud exhaust. It was parked across the lot from Mohammed's car. His eyes scrunched in pain, Mustafa slowly got into his car with his buttocks first to ease the swelling on his ankle. As he sat with his legs still dangling on the hot pavement but his behind on the car seat, Imran jokingly shouted across the parking lot, "Hey old man, you need a hand?" Mustafa responded quickly, "Imran, why don't you come over here, I got a lap for you to sit on!" Imran giggled a little uneasily. Although a jokester, Imran did not proceed any further out of deference and respect for Mustafa. Mustafa then pointed at Riad. "Do you want to sit on Riad's lap instead?" Riad played along. "Yeah, come on." He then patted his lap a few times. "I got a lap for you."

Not all men have to clearly perform within straight and narrow lines of heterosexual desire in order to be considered manly. The fluidity of sexuality means that certain men can invoke the mythical norm through contradictory practices of gayness while some men have to perform their straight orientation much more deliberately. As a result of their athletic aptitude, Mustafa, Mohammed, and Riad did not have to worry about their sexuality or their manhood in the same way as other men.

These two vignettes complicate the simple conceptualization of heterosexual masculinity by demonstrating how the *ballplayer posture* involves some desi men performing and invoking desires parallel to heterosexual masculinity. Their appropriation and representation of queer masculinities signals the ways in which non-normativity is always foundational to the construction of normativity.[26] Heterosexual masculinity is a fragile category that is constituted by the very homosexuality that it repudiates. In the case of the vignettes above, even though the invocations of gayness serve to create distance, the young men ironically must know the intimate aspects of queer desire to properly invoke and revoke it.

In reacting to the news of my engagement, both Mohammed and Mustafa targeted me as a site of desire through their symbolic performances of same-sex desire. While black and white bodies stand as ubiquitous exemplars of sporting masculinity in mainstream U.S. culture, Mustafa and Mohammed projected that racialized desire upon a brown body through sexual innuendos. In this sense, they displaced the prominence of black and white racial bodies by using gender and sexuality to inflect South Asian–ness to the sphere of (athletic) desire. Here they narcissistically projected desire upon my brown body as a substitute for their own body. While "get with you" refers to the act of courting a potential partner, it also represents a gaming tactic to test the sexuality of others. Testing of this sort eventually means a loosening of the stringent demands of compulsory heterosexuality. With a simple play on words, they switch fluidly between heterosexual and same-sex desire in a homosocial setting.

As I was already high in this basketball hierarchy as a result of my play, my height, my aggression and my close affiliations with Mustafa, a request to "get with me" was an indirect way to respect, adore, and idolize the brown body. Joking of this sort among these young men served to draw the boundaries of toughness and heterosexuality while signaling insider status. It also demonstrated how fragile identities are, how they are challenged, and how frequently they are recouped using a variety of contradictory strategies, discourses, signs, and symbols. Because Mohammed and Mustafa were seen as exceptional basketball players and commonsensically understood as heterosexual men in these sporting venues, they did not need to engage in strictly bounded acts of hyper-masculinity with their co-ethnic peers to affirm their vaulted status. Their courting gestures to me and the calls by Mustafa and Riad to Imran resembled a sexual game of chicken in which they test the limits of queerness already embedded within masculinity.

The instances above demonstrate how the narrative of heterosexual masculinity is both loosened and perpetuated through homoerotic suggestions. Deconstruction of this sort opened up other possibilities, the possibilities of substantiating alterity at the very moment of repudiating it.[27] Such imitations complicated the homoerotic social interactions already present in sports and point to an unacknowledged desire for the homosexual Other. The cultural theorist E. Patrick Johnson contends, in his examination of the cultural appropriation of blackness and its gendered-sexualized valences, that some men, when involved in queer play, queer heteronormative masculinity by "securing further the dialectic between heterosexuality and homosexuality" (Johnson 2003: 13). In the process of such ironic plays, South Asian American identity is already structured through non-normativity at the moment the young men try to enter aspects of the mythical norm. With this contradictory

and ironic impulse, the young heterosexual men could only add ideological flesh to masculinity by first substantiating the conceptual skeleton
of "gayness." The South Asian American basketball players experienced
queerness as part of the trauma they endure as racialized masculinities
in U.S. society, left on the margins of national belonging.[28] At the same
time, Mohammed, Mustafa, and Riad reconstituted what they deemed
to be normative masculinity by simultaneously engaging in and distancing from this site of trauma—their "queerness." Normative masculinity
was constructed and performed through the very queerness that deconstructs and violates it.

However, trauma is not the only instrumental factor structuring the
performance of gayness as intimate irony. As the young men looked
into and rehashed their pain, there were many moments of pleasure
and delight. Without pleasure, there would not be a reason to continuously play into the very subject position whose racial, gendered, and
sexualized standing causes marginalization. Instead of just sulking in the
pain of non-normative subjectivity, the basketball players rejoice in the
pleasures of these acts that further substantiate the racial, gendered, and
sexual realms of social membership. Mustafa, Riad, and Mohammed
expressed their authority and dominance by subjecting young men like
Imran to inferior social status through their queer play. They could take
pleasure in adopting non-traditional sexualities and put on costumes of
non-normative masculinity as a result of their high social capital. Junior
men in this circuit like Imran and Amir, who had not clearly established
their toughness through sexual conquest and physicality, could not extend this play any further for fear of marginalization. Any extensions
of the play set in motion by Mustafa could, for Imran, constitute a slip
into queerness for which he had little countermaterial other than his
basketball play.

The material absence of the abject subject, in the figure of the black
Other, feminine Other, or gay Other, demands that these men physically
and symbolically create difference within South Asian American masculinity. Here they projected the difference onto younger men like Imran
who bore the brunt of negotiating, managing, and regulating it. Imran
was shorter, slender, and younger than Mustafa, so he was already feminized and emasculated in comparison. He could not take up queer play,
as that would only further cement his distance from normativity. Rather,

Imran had to affirm a very clear heterosexual constitution by walking away and refusing to react in kind. Such an act of walking away emasculated him but did not threaten to dismantle his heterosexual constitution.

Mustafa's response to Imran's jab ("Hey, old man") was to reassert a position of dominance. Calling Mustafa "old" attacks his masculinity and sexual virility—he was not strong enough or stiff enough to play/ penetrate. Mustafa took it upon himself to deflect the trauma back on Imran with homoerotic suggestions. He sought to demonstrate his virility, figuratively, by inviting Imran to sit on his lap (code word for penis). These queered performances allowed Mustafa to slip out of heterosexual masculinity only to staunchly reaffirm an aggressive masculinity through his emasculation of Imran.

While homoerotic actions on the basketball court were dismissed as acts of toughness and aggression, in the parking lot masculinity was carefully performed through queer invocations. It was the sexuality of other men that was compromised when Mustafa, Mohammed, and Riad performed gayness. Both Mustafa and Riad needed Imran's presence and his unease at their playful requests. When they asked him to sit on their respective laps, they were invoking some of the sexual meanings implicit in the strip club scene, with Mustafa substituting an emasculated Imran for the female African American dancer. There are obviously queer readings and possibilities here, but this substitution produces new and old sets of meanings as Mustafa feminized Imran.

When his narrative of a strong heterosexual male was attacked by Imran's description of him as an "old man," Mustafa renarrativized his heterosexuality by *playing gay* as a way to control and test how much of a "Gandu" or "Chakka" Imran was. Even though the exaggerated request contained the possibility of same-sex contact and anal penetration, the ability to penetrate, even the anus, did not dismantle the heterosexual ethos of a sporting space. Mustafa was still in the role of the penetrator. Imran must assert his agency by choosing not to comply with Mustafa's request. It was a dare to see how far he would go with his response. If he were to sit on Mustafa's lap, gyrate his hips, and thrust his backside, these actions would cause this system of carefully tended sexual meanings on the basketball court to implode. The acts of gyrating one's hips and sitting on male laps are gendered feminine. They are reserved for women. As a result, the female subject and respective acts of appropriate femininity are the gendered opposite but *acceptable insiders* to South Asian American identity. Yet, desi women constitute the *outsiders* to masculinity.

South Asian American Femininity: Who Can Play?

Women are present at tournaments. Their presence constitutes part of the pleasure men take in performing athletic masculinity. The men become the main targets of gaze for a wide audience. Additionally, many women play an important role in providing validations of masculinity.[29] They are key players in the game of South Asian American masculinity. South Asian American women played active roles in the maintenance of Indo-Pak Basketball. The type of roles they took on, both on and off the court, complicated the notion of sports as a "male preserve" (Theberge 1985), though women's exclusion from *playing* did ideologically and corporeally legitimate basketball as an activity for men. Young desi men symbolically solidified the acts of playing basketball as masculine while they gendered the other types of work at tournaments (such as bringing in food, caring for players, and maintaining the venue) in ambiguously gendered terms that failed to dismantle the gender binary.

Women's presence at tournaments and their absence from playing on the courts did not mean they were powerless dupes at the mercy of men and the system of patriarchy. Rather, South Asian American women found ways to assert agency and stake a claim to desi identities. Some found that agency through the spaces available to them at Indo-Pak Basketball tournaments and dance clubs, while other women worked outside these leisure spaces to assert agency. Furthermore, there were cases of women not following the rules of South Asian American femininity to be "traditional," "virginal," "fragile," and "chaste." As exceptions, these women confirmed the very mythical norm their presence challenged. Their exceptionality only further substantiated the boundaries of femininity and masculinity as distinct. South Asian American women's inroads into small cracks and crevices of agency showed the limited possibilities of systemic change within one social realm of diasporic and national identity formation.

One particularly interesting case was the South Asian American female athlete Madeleine Venkatesh. As a former collegiate player and current collegiate women's basketball coach, she experienced a problematic connection between basketball, race, masculinity, ability, and heterosexuality. With basketball's symbolic status as a signifier of the heterosexual masculine, she experienced firsthand the paucity of basketball venues, symbolically and materially, for women. As a player and coach, Madeleine confirmed, "I only met two Indian [South Asian American] girls from playing and recruiting for 15 years." She discussed her own anxiety as a young girl about asking her father's permission to play basketball. Madeleine recalled when she was a young woman, "There were no girls' teams. Boys asked me to play in the fifth grade. *I was so scared to ask my dad.*"[30] Not only were there no female desi basketball spaces, there did not even exist a girls' league of any sort for her in Birmingham, Alabama. The taken-for-granted ideology of sport as heterosexual masculine means that young boys are socialized early into sport, but women are not. Madeleine's anxiety about asking her dad affirms the "patriarchal dividend" (Connell 1995) that men have in sport. The assumption, in this case, is that men pass on the knowledge of sport and socialize their children (especially boys) in sport. As a result, men traverse the terrain of sports as normative figures while a woman's presence is questioned, policed, and regulated. Although her parents initially had reservations, "Ultimately my parents said yes and I played with boys for two years."

Her presence on the boys' team did not put in jeopardy the gendered, sexualized identity of the boys. She explained, "I had to wear T-shirts while boys wore tank tops." Although she was in the same league with boys, she was still configured as different in ways that affirm binaries of male-female and masculine-feminine. One key example consisted of the uniform she wore that differed from that of her male teammates. Tank tops are seen as appropriate attire to showcase the male body and its respective muscularity. Madeleine's body could not be shown in the same way, as women are ideologically constructed as bystanders and spectators to this gendered space; she had to wear T-shirts to cover up her arms and chest in order to admit feminine difference. Her body was too naked with the traditional basketball tank tops and would disrupt the taken-for-granted value of sport, especially basketball, as masculine and for boys.

Madeleine's body was a necessary site of difference on a mixed-gender court that had to be protected both visually and morally to protect not only her but also the normative gendered valences that govern basketball and American sport. If not, the very identity of boys would be put in question. The woman's body was asked to differently represent the nation and diaspora. In Madeleine's case, South Asian American women were asked to be representative of (South Asian) nation and diaspora as emblems of unchanging culture, purity, and tradition (Gropinath 2005a). The basketball court and other highly masculinized sporting venues were seen as out of bounds for desi femininity. When Madeleine's body was visible on the court, the other participants read it in a multitude of ways that both allowed and disallowed her from expressing her identity in and out of South Asian American femininity. Madeleine admitted,

> Playing with the guys allowed me to surpass racism because people wanted me on their team. . . . [The university (a Division I collegiate basketball program)] was where I went because of academics and athletics. I got offers from many SEC schools [SEC is the Southeastern Conference, a collegiate athletic association with a superior basketball conference] . . . . Lots of people, like coaches, thought I was black; they made these sharp judgments. . . . People viewed me by my skin color [Her parents are Malayalee and from South India; she has dark skin and is thus part of the population originally referenced as "Kallu"] . . . . Because of my skin color there are perceptions of me as physically and racially black.

Madeleine was an exception to the rule that South Asian American women do not play basketball. Yet her exceptionality did not dismantle the gendered system of inequality; rather, it reinforced it. Madeleine did not play with other South Asian American girls; that opportunity did not present itself in the mid-1980s for Madeleine and is not easily available for young South Asian American women now. By playing with the "guys," she was able to move through the racist and sexist structures of sport as a "tomboy" or as "one of the boys."[31] There were multiple racial meanings that were mapped onto her body, but the blackness ascribed on her female body differed from the ways the young male players took to cultural blackness. Like the young desi men who consumed elements of cultural blackness to navigate sporting realms, Madeleine's misidentification as "black" gave her room to move as a young athlete. This misidentification served her productively as she got a chance to play basketball and to move up the basketball hierarchy. Accordingly, the blackness projected upon her allowed possibilities of athletic excellence, competitiveness, and aggression. The blackness was a point of difference from South Asian American femininity that made her presence on the court acceptable, even normal. She did not wholly reject or dis-identify with blackness regardless of how desi communities understand it.

Desi communities construct South Asian femininity differently from black femininity. South Asian American women are considered traditional, demure, passive, and heterosexual.[32] As a result, women are not seen as having the bodily or cultural toolkit to navigate the competitive realm of the basketball court. Madeleine mainly entered spaces through a misidentified blackness that was not always readily available for other South Asian American men and women. Madeleine used her mother as an example of the dominant reading of South Asian femininity: "My mom was very subservient to my dad. My mom's life revolved around her three kids, no hobbies of her own. Her own desires took back seat to family." Here, Madeleine linked play and hobby as activities for men, positioning women outside the realm of leisure. Her mention of "subservience" is one of the traits that constitute the conservative realm of gender roles, associating South Asian women with tradition, domesticity, and cultural stagnation.[33] Madeleine's description of her mother invoked an essentialist paradigm of South Asian American femininity that erases other possible desires and pleasures outside of domesticity. Even Madeleine's take on the necessary traits for basketball success affirmed this dichotomy: "In order to participate [in basketball] you need to be assertive. . . . [You] cannot be meek or weak. . . . [You] need to take control. . . . [I am] not sure how much of it [feminine subservience and weakness] is culture and how much is my own family." Although women challenge these ideas of passive domesticity every day, social convention indexes women as passive while men are marked as aggressive (see May 2007). Toughness, aggression, and competitiveness were deemed masculine traits that were to be superimposed on male bodies. The notion of female masculinity was an oxymoron for the male players.[34]

When Madeleine and male Indo-Pak Basketball players conjured up a traditional portrait of South Asian femininity, it was a result of prevalent ideologies within South Asian America and not solely those within South Asia. The conservative gender ideologies embodied by my interlocutors erased and hid the complexity of South Asian feminism and queer politics.[35] For example, Madeleine dislocated herself from "Indian-ness" instead of complicating what Indian-ness could mean when she says, "I was not a 'good Indian.' I was not a typical Indian." She conflated "typical" and "good" and saw basketball excellence as a marker of "bad" and "non-typical" Indian-ness. As muscularity, toughness, and competitiveness in sports are often described as corrupting of the female body, leading to loss of femininity (see Farooq Samie 2013; Joseph 2013), the "good" stands in for bodily performances of a sexually attractive but non-athletic femininity.

Despite all these ideological constraints on South Asian American femininity, Madeleine excelled in basketball. She played in a premier Division I collegiate program and set several university records. Such accomplishments should make her a well-known figure within the South Asian American community. But her choice to excel in mainstream sport did not immediately open doors in South Asian American basketball circles: She was neither recognized nor given accolades. Madeleine was in many ways a non-being and an impossibility—she, along with other female basketball players, is rendered outside of femininity. Men in South Asian America and in larger U.S. society get disproportionately more media coverage regardless of the excellence of female athletes.[36] As a result, Parambir, for example, who played for a Vancouver Indo-Pak team, received greater attention. His male body was often the topic of conversation at Indo-Pak tournaments, which perpetuated the celebration of men at the expense of the achievements of women. Earlier we saw the idolization and reverence that players had for Parambir. Madeleine had more significant statistical achievements and records while playing at a Division I collegiate program than Parambir. But these achievements did not translate into challenging the masculine symbolic order of basketball. Femininity, in this instance, served the purpose of masculine opposition, and not affiliation. Young South Asian American women could spectate but did not play on the court aside the young men.

Madeleine expressed sadness about how few South Asian American women play basketball. I asked, "Do you think there are more opportunities for South Asian women?" She thought deeply and replied, "There are more opportunities now to play ball. It is crucial to see older women playing. The cycle needs to be broken since I know only two

Indian women who play basketball." That cycle can only be broken on both symbolic and material grounds. The current cycle of representation is one that legitimates the mythical norm since athletes live up to the dominant dictates of race, religion, gender, sexuality, and class. For one thing, the symbolic legitimacy of the gender binary (masculine vs. feminine) continues to frame certain sports as masculine and some as feminine. The institution of Indo-Pak Basketball simultaneously creates opportunities and forecloses opportunities for women.

Furthermore, the scarcity of female desi players is not a cause for concern in brown-out spaces. Various organizers and team captains at the 2006 and 2008 Chicago IPN worried about the paucity of South Asian American male youth in Indo-Pak Basketball. They reconciled their anxiety through the creation of two tournaments at the 2008 Chicago IPN, an adult Indo-Pak tournament and an under-18 boys' tournament. A girls' tournament did not surface here. There is, however, a women's tournament at the Dallas IPN. In contrast to the men's tourney, there are far fewer women's teams. Dallas IPN has instituted a co-ed tournament,[37] but neither that nor the women's-only tournament draws the prestige afforded to the men's tournament. If the organizers and participants were to recognize and give prestige to the women's tournament, that might jeopardize the fragile boundaries of masculinity. If female basketball players were to be read as "tough" and "aggressive," it would fail to recuperate the queered South Asian American male body as "masculine," "tough," and "heterosexual" when the court space is gender integrated.

Few sporting opportunities have existed for South Asian American women. The prevailing belief has been that one could not be feminine and heterosexual and participate in basketball. However, desi women could participate in a variety of other sports and still maintain many of the symbolic foundations of South Asian American femininity. These other sports were ones that were already gendered and sexualized as heterosexual feminine. Madeleine recognizes the rarity of South Asian Americans in basketball but notices their active participation elsewhere. "Tennis players are Indian at Alabama University [her place of employment as a basketball coach]." Tennis, in opposition to basketball, is infused with elements of middle-class respectability and gender difference.[38] This middle-class respectability in tennis is imagined through heterosexual femininity and the differential structuring of this sport for men and women (such as dress code and duration of matches). Thus, one can still be a "good Indian" and play tennis.

In opposition to the conventional grounding of tennis as heterosexual, in women's basketball the specter of the "butch" is commonplace. By labeling female basketball players "butch," the possibility of athletic achievement and basketball femininity is erased. The butch exists outside the confines of the feminine. By using the label "butch," South Asian Americans expel certain women and locate lesbianism outside the boundaries of South Asian nations and South Asian diasporas.[39] A dislocation of this sort then constitutes culture, diasporic identities, and national identities along lines of "homogeneity, equivalence, normativity, and essence" (Ferguson 2004: 118). Madeleine challenged this singular conception of South Asian femininity by proudly claiming her "bad Indian" status. While "good Indian" categories limit membership and undergo greater regulation, being a "bad Indian" allows her to create multiple affiliations, connections, and performances of self. The association of "bad Indian" with "butch" further expands on the possibilities of identity formation.

The butch figure haunted my informants' conceptualizations of femininity and basketball in ways that demand a regulation of femininity and masculinity simultaneously. When I asked Ali about the WNBA (Women's National Basketball Association) after a long discussion of the NBA season in 2009, he replied, "Basketball is physical. I don't think basketball is a women's sport. I hate the WNBA. I hate it when they act masculine. Chest bumps, tattoos, pounding the chest, and the gear are masculine and childish. They are butch." By labeling the participation of women in basketball as "butch," Ali flattened the possibilities of femininity while marking the "butch" as a failed femininity. His diatribe illuminated the anxiety regarding adult female participation that can invert the gendered meanings of basketball. Gender conservatism of this sort is part of the diasporic engagement with mainstream American culture.[40] Part of the gendered access to basketball stems from the patriarchal, heterosexist structure of major U.S. sports, not simply South Asian cultures (see Messner 2002). The sports scholar Tiffany Muller (2007), in her examination of the ways in which sexuality resurfaces in the WNBA, contends that the WNBA creates media events to explicitly portray women's basketball as appropriately feminine by foregrounding heterosexuality with "family nights." These intentional "family nights" are ways to counter the stigma of "butch" given to female basketball players.

Although players on the South Asian American basketball circuits might share this homophobic sentiment about female basketball players, it is a bit more complicated than that. Ali shared his disdain for women in basketball yet took satisfaction in emphasizing how his toddler daughter will be a great basketball player: "Yes sir! She is going to be a player. She can already play. You got to see how she bounces and holds the [basket]ball." His daughter did not play on the court at the same time as him or his co-ethnic peers. She did not compete against him in pickup basketball or tournament play. Thus, his daughter did not immediately threaten the masculine coherency of basketball, as he was the father passing down sporting expertise to his child. Adult women constituted the outcasts in the realm of basketball play. However, they were present in the basketball venue and found their own ways to assert agency.

Expressions of Agency in Fields of Power

Despite the ideological positioning of basketball as masculine, women were involved in multiple capacities with Indo-Pak Basketball. Women did exist within the sporting milieu, and they challenged the gendered order of basketball and South Asian American–ness, but they did it in ways that could perpetuate the present hierarchies. But to conclude that women were victims and pawns in the games of South Asian American masculinity would be an egregious error that only reifies constructions of femininity as passive and helpless. Radical feminists, queer identities, and everything in-between have always been part of South Asian history.[41] Although male participants of brown outs might construct boundaries of athletic identity and American-ness that limit the articulations of South Asian American femininity, South Asian American women still have been agents. Women have practiced their own forms of resistance and made their own claims to leisure spaces. These forms of resistance expanded upon the possibilities of South Asian American identity, but not always in ways that fundamentally changed the symbolic justification of the categories of masculine and feminine.

At tournaments hosted at a mandir in Atlanta, young South Asian American women worked the scoreboards and managed the clock. At the Chicago IPN, wives and partners of the Chicago Untouchables team helped in the running of the tournament. Rathi articulated the special presence of IPN in her life. "I am one of the directors of the Chicago Indo-Pak National Basketball Tournament (IPNBT), and my husband [Max] is the founder of the IPNBT." She added,

> I actually met so many South Asians outside of my community. I think that I was very limited to my community growing up because I always followed my parents around, and being a girl, my freedom was very limited. I started attending the tournament around the same time I went away to college, so both experiences actually introduced me to many new South Asians. . . . I first heard about and began attending the Chicago tournament in the summer of 1994 just as a social event and a place to meet and mingle with new friends. Since 1998, I have been helping to organize and run the tourney.

Rathi built and expanded upon her experience of South Asian American community through her intimate involvement with Indo-Pak Basketball. As she took pleasures in gazing at desi athletes, she simultaneously played a part in altering the foundations of South Asian American cultural identities that, previously, have not always accommodated mainstream U.S. sporting cultures. These forms of community building celebrate basketball masculinity as metonymic representations of communal identity. Rathi and other spouses took pride in the sporting achievements of their partners. Female participants of the IPN wove their own pleasures into the tournament fabric that incorporated femininity and female bodies in multiple ways. For example, Rathi shared her own reasons for intimate involvement with Indo-Pak Basketball. She reflected, "I was a tomboy. I wanted to date someone athletic and thus was drawn to Max." She met Max at the tournament and they later married. Through prolonged courtship with an athlete, Rathi continues to reside in the sporting realm beyond the "tomboy" years. The queer theorist Judith Halberstam (1998) contends in *Female Masculinity* that the social pressure and gender demarcation of adolescence pressures young girls to follow rigid versions of femininity. As a result, young women who were "tomboys" cannot grow up to be "tom*men*," as adult conceptualizations of masculinity are reserved for adult males. Instead, women encounter social pressure to follow normative feminine identities. By dating and marrying an athlete, Rathi managed the realm of the feminine and her love for sport.

As they did at the dance club, young women also indulge in heterosexual desires in basketball brown outs. At the Indo-Pak Basketball tournament at Georgia State University in 2009, the young men of Atlanta Franchise team played Air Punjab in the finals. Several young, female Punjabi American college students, ages 18 to 22, came to watch. Guneet, one of the fans, glowed in delight at the opportunity to talk to the Indo-Pak Basketball players. A peer-group structured event like this offers more opportunities for flirting and other sexualized activities. When I asked her reasons for attending, she informed me that she was there "to support my brother and see hot Punjabi boys."[42] A certain level of liberation from conservative depictions of South Asian femininity is manifest in Indo-Pak Basketball. However, this form of liberation comes with its own set of limitations. The sport theorist David Brown emphasizes that "new female audiences of male sports and vice versa tend to draw upon and foster very conventional views of sexuality, bodily shape, and comportment" (2006: 179).

Female spectators might not play on the court, but they were involved intimately with the outcome of the game and relevant constructions of identity.[43] Ali and Mustafa's mother, Asma auntie, was a pivotal figure in the basketball life of the Atlanta Outkasts from 1994 till 2000. She was there in the family living room when the team first formed in 1994. She accompanied the team to several intranational tournaments. While popular cultural narrative of sport highlights the sporting cultural transfer from father to son,[44] it was Asma auntie and not Amin uncle who stood in as the key presence at the basketball games. Although Amin uncle played field hockey at the highest levels in Pakistan, Asma auntie asserted herself as the authority figure on the court.[45] In her examination of Caribbean diasporic communities, gender, and cricket, the critical sport studies scholar Janelle Joseph argues that women are always pivotal to diasporic sport cultures.[46] Instead of foregrounding the sporting activities of cricket as sites of masculine play, Joseph deconstructs the leisure space to highlight how women are linked to the predominantly male community through their own forms of gendered performances and caring. Before each game, Asma auntie traversed the court to the

Atlanta Outkasts players' huddle. She offered a prayer and led the play-ers in a recital of a Quranic passage. Once games begin, auntie returned to the stands. From the bleachers, she followed every second of the game with careful attention to detail. Asma auntie would chastise us for bad plays and would scream praises for good plays. While chewing on pan (betel nut), she screeched instructions.

Even though Asma auntie was a central figure for the Outkasts, her presence did not necessarily transform the gendered meanings of bas-ketball. She did disrupt the all-male space with her presence in the hud-dle before games. One must, however, think deeply about her presence. Asma auntie was there as a mother to support her sons. Thus, it was in her role as a mother that she traversed the court and led huddles. She offered caring labor that further affirmed certain bodies as masculine and in need of motherly care, love, and devotion. Her femininity did not challenge the practices of masculinity on the court; rather, it reaf-firmed them as she celebrated the achievements of her sons and their teammates.

Other women at South Asian American basketball venues asserted their own forms of agency. Such agentive acts did not necessarily resem-ble what we might call "resistance" through very visible public assertions of agency; they also did not always dismantle the gendered hierarchy in the sport or challenge the dominant representation of South Asian women as "exotic" and/or "traditional" (Gopinath 2005b). Although the realm of play at the Chicago IPN is dominated by men, Rathi played a pivotal role in its functioning. She additionally provided important basketball suggestions and coaching for her spouse's team. After the second day of the 2008 Chicago IPN, Max, Rathi, and two other Chi-cago Untouchables players and spouses retired to Max and Rathi's home. Two things transpired: first, they watched the videotaped games (taped by the spouses) to review strengths and weaknesses of their team, and second, they discussed the plans for the next day's games and playoff rounds. Speaking in basketball vernacular, Rathi and the spouses pro-vided insightful commentary on the strong athletic deeds, the blunders, the mistakes, and the shortcomings of the Chicago Untouchables at the 2008 Chicago IPN. Coupled with the criticisms, they suggested plans and opportunities for better team play. In front of their TV, Rathi and the other spouses were seen as legitimate conveyers of basketball knowledge. The sheer content and language of the conversations indicated the active role these women take in watching the games, directing players from the stands, and staking a claim to this space.

In addition to offering advice, some women, like Rathi, took a significant role in the running of the tournament. As an organizer, Rathi played an instrumental part in shaping the space and its relevant meanings. Rathi and Jake (a white fellow co-organizer) were the contact persons for all questions players and tournament volunteers might have. Her participation as a key organizer of a highly masculine sporting event bent the gender configurations in significant ways. During our drives from her home to the tournament, Rathi shared stories about past tournaments. Her impressive repertoire of Indo-Pak Basketball history made her a human archive who knew anything and everything about the subject. On game day, Rathi moved between the different courts; talked with scorekeepers and officials; made sure all players she met were enjoying their time at the Chicago IPN; ordered food for officials, volunteers, and players; answered questions concerning the tournament; took on the role as key contact person; and proved to be a reservoir of Indo-Pak Basketball facts. Her active participation was critical to both the smooth functioning of the tournament and the high status the tournament engenders in the North American Indo-Pak Basketball community. She, however, provided a certain type of gendered labor. Her caring labor was a gendered form of work.

Rathi's labor further solidified the symbolic boundaries of femininity and masculinity as distinct and natural. Because she provided some forms of caring labor, she did not necessarily receive appropriate recognition. Rather, players continued to celebrate men for their play and their institutional labor. Max fretted over how his iconicity within Indo-Pak Basketball made invisible the labor of important others.[47] Max said with frustration, "I am getting too much credit when Rathi and Jake are now the main organizers [of Chicago IPN]." He had handed the reins to others, like Rathi and Jake, over a number of years. Rathi and Jake were now the instrumental organizers and had had that role for quite some time. Jake's white racial heritage dislocated him from the symbolic, phenotypic imaginary of Indo-Pak Basketball, although he entered the space much more freely than African American men. Most seasoned players knew Rathi and deferred to her. But first-time teams usually did not recognize Rathi's labor. I made a similar blunder by immediately trying to interview Max first in 2006. He was touted as the "godfather" of Indo-Pak Basketball, and thus I failed early on to recognize Rathi's role. Her invisibility was a key means to celebrate male athletic homosociality.

Just as Rathi's contributions remained somewhat invisible, other women occupied the basketball court in differently visible ways. In between games at the 2008 Chicago IPN, Rathi's nephew and daughter took to the court to take shots. Rathi's daughter's presence on the court signaled a possibility that is not immediate but imminent. Her playing marks an opening for generations to come. Even some South Asian American men in Atlanta, like Sanjeet and Ali, spoke with great pride about their daughters' involvement in basketball. However, they could not reconcile this pride with the simultaneous presence of women on the court as teammates or opponents. Rathi's daughter offered a vision of a different tomorrow.

One of the sponsors, an older South Asian American man, came along with his two teenage daughters to the 2006 Chicago IPN. His daughters were dressed in Chicago Bulls basketball jerseys and athletic warm-up pants. The teenagers' dress differed from that of other women at the basketball venues. The other women at the tournaments often wear body-fitting blouses and jeans to accentuate their curves. In wearing the basketball jersey, which hangs loosely over a T-shirt, the young women were not showcasing their bodily contours in the same way. During the game and post-game awards ceremony, the teenage girls stayed in the stands with their father and watched the game intently. As some women congregated in the bleachers, in the concession stands, and in the hallways, the court represented a male preserve occupied and claimed by men. Once the games ended and the ceremonies were finalized, players and organizers made their way out of the gymnasium. At this point, the two teenagers walked onto the court, not with the intentions of simply walking through it. Rather, they occupied it with their presence and started taking basketball shots. Their smiles and laughter showed their joy in playing basketball. They teased each other and laughed after each shot. These teenagers claimed this space only when the gatekeepers departed and the boundaries of the structured social event were loosened. Unlike other women at the venue, after completion of all of the festivities, the teenagers disrupted the male-dominated physical space of the basketball court with their play. Although they shot when the official time of the games had ended, they still owned the court for a period of time. The young women contested the masculine legitimacy of this space, even in fleeting moments, through their movement and their garb. They drew their own lines and orientations of femininity.

These fleeting moments of women's appropriation of basketball spaces illustrate the powerful symbolic legitimation of male bodies on the basketball court. The heteronormative process validates certain practices, particular desires, and an assortment of bodily comportments as appropriately masculine and appropriately feminine. In order for these young desi men to be read as normative masculinities, they have to simultaneously substantiate who the outsiders are. Although femininity is always present, if bounded, as a way to legitimate heterosexual masculinity, queer masculinity stands as a threat that has to be repudiated. Mahmoud could assure himself that he was a man, that he was properly hanging out with other men, and that he was properly manning up by stigmatizing the black queers at Waffle House. Similarly, players tease out the contours of both heterosexual masculinity and queer masculinity by not simply repudiating the Chakka. Rather, Mohammed and Mustafa ironically played upon "gayness" in order to test the masculine foundations of their peers. By teasing to a certain point, their performances showcase how fragile, shifting, and dynamic the categories of masculinity and heterosexuality are. To conflate heterosexuality and masculinity, players carefully manipulated the contours of queer masculinity and displaced it upon Imran and other co-ethnic peers. In contrast, when the young teenage girls wore basketball jerseys and took shots, they disrupted the masculine ethos of the brown-out court but could only do so once the space had been cleared of men and its respective masculine meanings.

Were the young women a threat to the strategy of browning out and manning up? The young women offered different ways of seeing the possibilities of basketball as identity formation. However, there are two threats that could dismantle the structure of making desi masculinity. The very process of browning out to man up is spatially and temporally constrained. The conclusion explores the content of those threats while imagining what the future might hold for the institution of Indo-Pak Basketball and the making of desi masculinity.

Conclusion

South Asian American men use sporting cultures as one way to negotiate, challenge, and reconfigure their racialized masculinity. Within
exclusive basketball spaces, through acts of browning out, the young
men are able to man up in ways that invert dominant stereotypes of
them. Basketball provides an interesting and accessible venue in which
to perform masculinity while claiming belonging in both the diasporic
and national fabric. The interplay of people, symbols, and institutions in
the strategy of browning out to man up unpacks meanings and engagement with power that are pertinent to understanding South Asian
American life and the contours of belonging implicated in American-
ness. Their gestures are conversant with a mainstream discourse of
sporting masculinity—a certain type of American-ness. Thus, desi basketball players' attempts at inclusion into this sporting masculinity mean
active participation in perpetuating the exclusions that govern U.S.
sporting cultures. These sporting arenas provide important information
on how American-ness is raced, gendered, classed, and sexualized.

Sport is often imagined as the one place where the vile racist, sexist,
and homophobic bile of society is discarded. However, as evident in the
social interactions and organizing structure of desi basketball, racialized
men perform sporting masculinity with the same categories that originally dislocated them from American-ness. When the young desi men
we have met in this book took to basketball—be it pickup ball, Indo-Pak
tournaments, or in the Asian Ballers League, they were utilizing it as a
stage on which to perform, make, and fashion cultural citizenship at the
intersections of masculinity, race, middle-class respectability, and heterosexuality. For young desi men, the dominant heterosexual and tough
masculine claims in a sport like basketball provide a backdrop to work
through their "racial castration" (Eng 2001), but only by manufacturing
other exclusions. As South Asian Americans experience a multitude of
alienations stemming from their stereotype as effeminate, nerdy, or ter-

roristic, they are compelled to take up acts of excluding others to substantiate their own normative masculinity. Part of this substantiation requires conjuring up and repudiating various communities that have already endured differential levels of marginalization in U.S. society, such as African Americans, LGBTQI communities, women, and the working poor. Therefore studying racialized masculinities in sports requires attention to the contours of inclusion as well as to the exclusions that give substance to membership in and out of national categories. In this case, by studying South Asian American engagement with sport, we can decipher how racialized communities in the United States understand the larger contours of membership and normative masculinity.

By incorporating conservative ideas of masculinity, race, and sexuality to combat their racialization, the participants of brown-out basketball failed to take part in acts of resistance that dismantle the very racial, gender, and sexual binaries that marginalize them. Rather, players legitimated the same binaries in order to be read as sporting men. These binaries are critical to the functioning of American sport and corresponding masculinities. The players found ways to represent themselves as men, but that meant that they also had to give substance to those persons who did not, or could not, *man up* through the acceptable channels—such as women, African American men, and gay men.

With this strategy of browning out to man up, there are limitations. Brown-out spaces are safe spaces for co-ethnic sporting interactions, possibilities to perform basketball moves without racialized judgments, and a venue to expand the contours of South Asian American identity. It is the co-ethnic peer group and their structuring of space that legitimates and validates a sense of a sporting identity for the participants. However, the very structure of the exclusionary racial, gendered, and sexualized space is one that could lead to its demise. By making this an exclusive space, the manhood created and valued in brown-out basketball is not transportable outside of this exclusive basketball arena. It cannot be diffused into the larger South Asian American community or into multiracial basketball contexts. Limitations in its reach pose threats to its very existence. Each threat could possibly undo the process of browning out to man up. The first threat is that desi players express anxiety about how their bodies are still read in stereotypical ways outside of the Indo-Pak community and frustration that within the greater

South Asian American community there is a lack of investment in integrating these sporting practices into the cultural fabric of South Asian American–ness. As a result, some desi basketball players fear that in time the threat of containment may devalue the meanings of masculinity they carefully make in brown-out spaces. The second threat pertains to the process of browning out: the very nature of "brown" is being reworked in different frameworks from the foundational heterogeneity in Indo-Pak Basketball. The increasing ethnic insularity threatens to dismantle the institution, or brown out, of Indo-Pak Ball. Without this variety of brown-out basketball, corresponding performances of sporting masculinity would not be possible. As a result, Indo-Pak Basketball, as already created by certain cohorts of young desi men and their peers, is already temporally and spatially limited.

Threat 1: Why Aren't There More Uncles and Aunties in the Stands?

Players and organizers have anxieties about the possible implications of brown-out basketball and corresponding practices of sporting masculinity. They worry about the reach of their negotiations, challenges, and reconfigurations of South Asian American masculinity. One particular worry that surfaces again and again is the dissonance between conceptions of manhood among players and the larger desi community. The current state of Indo-Pak Basketball does not successfully translate the athletic masculinities made on the basketball court into other social spaces. The time, money, and energy invested in the game guarantees enjoyment for the players but does not guarantee recognition for them in other public spaces. For example, at the 2006 Chicago IPN, other than a few desi sponsors and Indo-Pak alumni, very few members of Chicago's large South Asian American community attended the tournament. In contrast, there are large, well-attended gatherings for Indian and Pakistani Independence Day Parades, Eid Mubarek, Diwali, Christmas, Holi, and other ethno-religious festivals, both in Chicago and Atlanta.

At the dinner table in a local Italian restaurant after the 2006 Chicago IPN, Max, Charles, Rathi, Jake, and the volunteers (mostly Malayalee Christian Americans) met to reflect on the highpoints and low points and possible strategies for future tournaments. The aroma of herbs, meatballs, and spaghetti, along with the smell of soda, infiltrated the air. Max and his co-organizers discussed many topics, including the gym space, evaluations of referees, and the effective use of volunteers. With frustration in his voice, Max asked, "Why can't we get the community out there? I know a few uncles and aunties came. But, why aren't there more uncles and aunties in the stands? You [young volunteers and young players] should be getting your parents out here."

The presence of talented basketball players at Chicago IPN was not enough for Max. His worry about the lack of parental involvement diminished the many highlights of the tournament. For him, there were things to celebrate, but these come with limitations. The high level of competition brought great pleasures in the structured, coordinated rituals of male bonding. Out of the seventeen teams that received an invitation to the 2006 Chicago IPN, Maryland Five Pillars emerged as the dominant team. Players' passions spread across the court during the championship game. Chicago IPN is a space where desi men can concurrently perform a sense of self and a sense of community. This community of Indo-Pak players opens up possibilities for athletic legibility by performing South Asian American identity at the crux of masculinity and basketball. The joys of competitive play left many of these young men desiring to return for next year's tournament.

Yet Max's anxiety centered on other aspects of the Chicago IPN experience as metonymic of larger concerns about this strategy of making desi masculinity. He worried that, with the lack of "aunties and uncles" at the event, basketball identities were imagined in South Asian America as passing, whimsical, and temporary. For him, only the members of this immediate sporting community seemed to view basketball masculinity positively and as something to perform through a life course. Although basketball brown outs offer a safe space where South Asian American men can man up to their renditions of American-ness, the exclusive nature of the brown outs mean that these performances were not translated and diffused to other realms of social life. The men had created an identity for themselves that allowed them to bridge two worlds, South Asian-ness and American-ness, entering into an American masculinity that was safe for them. But it was safe only in a limited understanding of time and space. The embodiment of sporting masculinity did not fit perfectly, and the men could not necessarily transport it with the same value/worth to other social arenas. Members of the larger South Asian American community, even players' families, did not collaborate with the players to diffuse the cultural ethos of basketball masculinity into the larger South Asian American cultural fabric.

For the parents of players, basketball passions are seen as appropriate for a certain time and space—during adolescence and youth. Sport participation, for community elders, represents the transition of a boy to a man, but they do not envision it as more. For the elders, sporting cultures are to be temporally contained within adolescence. Khan, of the Atlanta Rat Pack, and Kashif, of the Sand Brothaz, alluded to their parents' ambivalence regarding the status of basketball in their children's lives.

> KHAN: They like when I play ball, except when I get injured. Thats [sic] when they tell me to stop playing.
> KASHIF: They say "do not play" because it wastes time.

Dr. Said, the father of Sultan and Imran, as well as a respected Muslim community member in Atlanta, bragged about some of the sporting accomplishments of his sons. He asked me, "Did you see all the trophies in our basement?" Dr. Said expounded, "Imran has won a lot of trophies. The entire basement [he smiles] is covered with them. He [Imran] has gone to different states and brought home championships, trophies." He then started listing off the various states in the southeast United States where Imran and his team, the Atlanta Rat Pack, have won. When Dr. Said shared this story, Imran was in college. Such athletic endeavors for a college student are seen as acceptable. Dr. Said did not talk with pride about Sultan's athletic achievements. These were minuscule in comparison to younger sibling Imran, but this silence was part of a pattern I noticed among the players' parents of older children. Sultan was in his late twenties and beyond a stage seen as appropriate for systematic basketball playing. The men's parents, as representatives of larger South Asian American communities, had reservations about continued basketball passions. Mustafa's and Ali's parents echoed similar sentiments. They no longer came to watch their sons, who are in their thirties, play games. Asma auntie thought it time for Mustafa to give up playing bas-ketball. She wanted him to focus on his fraught relationship with his wife, take care of his children, maintain his home, and have job stability. She had been a vehement supporter during Mustafa's and Ali's younger days. But she—and the community of uncles and aunties—did not see basket-ball as a central component to being a grown man, nor did they see it as critical to maintaining manhood. As a result, very few parents came out to support their adult children at tournaments. The players became their own supporters and voyeurs; they endorsed the valuations of manliness without their bodies being read equivalently in other settings.

By contrast, when Max organized the early Chicago IPN tournaments in the late 1980s and early 1990s, parents attended in greater numbers. He intimated that they came to support the young adults. Max spoke with pride and joy about the old days: "The old tournament was in a small gym and with uncles and aunties banging pots and pans [in a tra-ditional South Asian way to cheer for their teams]." Max's recollection evoked nostalgia for a time past that he hoped would continue through generations. He had hoped that the support during the earlier days would grow into community-wide endorsement of basketball. Rather, the opposite seemed to be happening. As the cohort of Indo-Pak play-ers became adult men, their configurations of masculinity did not fit neatly within the larger community expectations. Other than spouses, the majority of the people in the stands were other players. There were few other South Asian American community members to "bang pots" and affirm these activities as part of the desi cultural fabric. The very brown out they had created could not guarantee manning up across all social spaces.

Worry about the absence of uncles and aunties at the tournament existed alongside a desire for greater recognition. If uncles and aunties did not validate such masculine practices, then the assumption is that the larger U.S. society would not do so, either. The desire for visibil-ity was evident in two sets of dreams expounded by players: The first was a dream of a South Asian American community with much more deliberate and active basketball cultures, and the second was a long-ing for a mainstream desi basketball hero. In the first case, South Asian American players tended to deflect and transplant their desires upon Vancouver's South Asian Canadian community. They imagined that the desi communities in Vancouver embodied the necessary cultural attributes to institutionalize sporting masculinity into the cultural fabric of everyday lives. Desi basketball players in the United States assumed that Vancouver's South Asian community had intentionally and successfully woven basketball practices into the cultural constitution of South Asian identity. In the second case, as noted earlier, many players spoke of a desire to find an "Indian Yao Ming" who would be seen as a remedy to the failed attempts to spread the brand of brown-out basketball masculinity. There was hope that an Indian Yao Ming would garner greater mainstream appreciation for the brown sporting body. The emergence of a global superstar was imagined to be the cure for the limited appeal of the local brown sporting body.

Vancouver: "Everybody's There"

United States–based Indo-Pak players referenced the South Asian cultural ethos of Vancouver as an important counterpoint to South Asian American life. Vancouver's South Asian community is seen as a vision of what South Asian America can (and shall) be. The future, through a reference to Vancouver, is always part of the Indo-Pak experience. Krush, a member of the Maryland Five Pillars team, along with Atlanta Rat Pack player Mohammed, elaborated upon the greatness of the Vancouver players and attributed it to generational difference institutionalized within the cityscape.

Players imagined Vancouver as an ideal city where modernity, cosmopolitanism, and sporting identity are interwoven.[1] The choice of Vancouver is complex and interesting, but also contradictory. It is not a city with a celebrated basketball history; it is not a site of global fantasies of basketball excellence. Vancouver's defunct NBA franchise, the Grizzlies, lost traction and was moved to Memphis. Why, then, did the players not identify with teams in their own cites in the United States where a cosmopolitan identity and urban sporting practices are much more accessible? Part of the answer lies in the South Asian American players' perceptions of South Asian Canadian sporting cultures in Vancouver through the figure of Parambir. They use Vancouver as a site of relational opposition to desire the contours of desi America. In particular, Parambir stands as a both a hero and a critique of South Asian America.

As a result of his playing days in the U.S. collegiate basketball Atlantic Coast Conference and his excellence in the Canadian Junior Olympic national team, Parambir is idolized by the participants of the North American Indo-Pak Basketball circuit. His home is Vancouver. Indo-Pak players assumed that something about the cultural makeup of the Vancouver community allowed for the basketball brilliance of Parambir. With this assumption, they desired their U.S. communities to resemble Vancouver. Indo-Pak players could not rely on their local communities to incorporate basketball masculinity into the cultural constitution of South Asian American–ness. But they saw Vancouver as offering a hope for the development of this kind of conceptualization in the near future. They wanted their own localized desi hero.

My interlocutors made their fascination with Vancouver abundantly clear. It stemmed from the fact that Vancouver is the only city that has a player who even comes close to being a possible "Indian Yao Ming," a large-scale desi basketball hero. They connected Parambir's excellence with his local environment by believing that it was something about the local desi community that made his iconicity possible. Parambir is recognized across racial, ethnic, and class communities in Vancouver. As a result of his prominence outside of (as well as within) brown-out spaces, desi players projected their dreams and aspirations onto Parambir in their desires for their local cities to resemble Vancouver. There was a widespread belief that basketball masculinity is the norm for South Asian Canadians in Vancouver. In reference to Vancouver IPN, Krush, of the Maryland Five Pillars team, emphasized that "they [the fans in Vancouver] *pack* the stands, the *community* comes out to watch. It's loud. You got to go and check it out. *Everybody's* there."[2] His teammate, Anil, added, "Vancouver is seen as the place with the best competition *period*. They run summer camps there, and there are people who get paid to run the summer camp."[3] In particular, Anil referred to Parambir, who worked with various institutions to run basketball camps and conduct leadership programs for young people, including South Asian youth but not limited to just them.

Parambir's recognition, within and outside of the desi community in Vancouver, was a source of envy. South Asian American players did not feel familial or community-wide support for playing basketball as adults, never mind staking a career to it in the way Parambir has. Rather, they experienced resistance from their localized communities who envisioned basketball as just a "rite of passage" (Turner 1969)from adolescence to adulthood. Accordingly, parents and the local communities supported basketball participation as a liminal activity but not a lifelong activity/ identity. As most participants of Indo-Pak Basketball were the first generation of South Asian Americans born on U.S. soil, many of them hoped that perhaps their grandchildren would grow up in a South Asian community similar to Vancouver where basketball is part of one's identity.

Many, including Krush, Mohammed, and Charles (a 2006 Chicago IPN organizer) assumed the difference between Vancouver and U.S. desi communities to be generational. Charles demonstrated his extensive historical knowledge of South Asians in North America through his reference to Vancouver as fourth generation. He foregrounded this generational divide: "In Vancouver, it is generational. They've been here since the 1850s. They are huge." He used the supposed generational gap to talk about corporeal difference, an assumption that Vancouver's desi bodies are more masculine and bigger than those of South Asians in the United States. Unlike the U.S. players whose parents arrived after 1965, South Asians arrived on Vancouver's shores in the late 1800s and early 1900s,[4] but we cannot assume that this generational difference has such clear-cut physical implications.

Several U.S. players assumed that in a few generations their community will resemble Vancouver's South Asian community. They idolized South Asian Canadian masculinity, as imprinted on Parambir's body and spatalized across Vancouver, and aspired for their own community to attain similar achievements. But such idolization tended to elide the problems that Vancouver teams experience with localized racism and inequality. It also projects a monolithic view of South Asian Canada, failing to account for the complex histories that shape the Canadian communities differently from U.S. communities. Moreover, this type of aspiration did not account for the move of the 7-foot-tall Sikh Bhullar brothers, Sim and Tanveer, from Toronto, Canada, to Saltsburg, Pennsylvania to play basketball.[5] In order to attain widespread recognition, experience a different quality of training, and have access to basketball networks, these rising star players enrolled at the Kiski School in Saltsburg. They did not go from Toronto to Vancouver. Vancouver could not have offered them the same exposure and the possibility of playing in a premier Division I collegiate basketball program as an elite high school in the United States. Thus, the aspiration for a Vancouver-esque desi community might be more of a psychological strategy than a material reality. The Bhullar brothers' strategy for basketball visibility involved a move to the United States as a way to be seen as tough basketball players. Their move stood in counterpoint to the aspirations of Indo-Pak Basketball players. To return to Max's longing for aunties and uncles to bang pots, the possible solution to this threat and anxiety would be for this generation of Indo-Pak Ballers to become the *pot bangers*, the supporters and coaches for the next generation of South Asian American youth. Through that avenue, they could once again reinstitute IPN as part of the journey through and into manhood.

"I Want to Find the Yao Ming of India"

While players celebrate and idolize Parambir, they still long for a South Asian basketball hero with greater appeal. Parambir is only a short-term remedy, one whose reach is confined to Vancouver and the North American Indo-Pak Basketball circuit. He is a national hero, but those national feats do not translate into the prestige one is guaranteed by playing in the NBA. Indo-Pak players long for a South Asian (American) who plays and dominates in the NBA through masculine virtues of toughness, physicality, aggression, and athletic creativity.[6] Charles, one of the 2006 Chicago IPN organizers and a member of the Chicago Domenators team,[7] talked about the present and possible future of Indo-Pak Basketball (IPB): "We are giving it [a great basketball experience] to you right now. Next year we are trying to get a webcam. . . . Our goal is to make this a better tournament every year; our goal is to get new people here." He followed up, "I want to get involved with a PR [public relations] firm, maybe do an Indo-Pak magazine." There was a pause and some hesitation: "That is a lot of work; it is too much work. But people need to know that we [South Asian America] have guys that play Division I basketball. We got 6'10", 6'11" guys that can play basketball." Charles then listed three Division I South Asian American basketball players. Many of the Indo-Pak players paid attention to the Bhullar brothers, hoping that Sim Bhullar, who, in 2014, played for New Mexico State University, would be drafted someday into the NBA. Charles followed this list with his desire for greater social appeal for brown men and brown-out basketball: "I would love to see what's happening outside the U.S. I hear the basketball is strong in the UK; I would love to bring one of the UK teams here." Sanjay, of the California Shockwaves, emphasized the levels of skill in Indo-Pak Basketball with the possibility of crossing U.S. borders: "Our best player is getting offers to play overseas . . . places like Finland and the Philippines." Finland is not a hotbed for professional basketball, and most everyday practitioners of sport do not recognize that the Philippines has one of the oldest professional basketball leagues in the world.[8] Yet mention of these two places highlights how players immediately incorporate the global scene in offering a solution to this first threat to manning up.

Some players expressed a desire for brown bodies outside of U.S. borders. This desire showcased the limited success that Division I basketball players, overseas players, and Parambir have had in changing the stereotype of desis in the United States. Andrew, of the New York Ballaholics, sought a remedy for this threat through his hope of finding an "Indian Yao Ming." He explained, "I feel like going to India and going through the jungles, finding that Indian Yao Ming. Man, that 7-foot Indian dude is out there. I want to sign him and bring him over [to the NBA and the United States]. That is my dream [he laughs and then sighs]. That will be the day, man, when we put ourselves, South Indian people, on the map." Players like Andrew envisioned greater public visibility and public acceptance of brown athletic bodies, both within South Asian America and in larger U.S. society, with a South Asian player in the NBA. Parambir did not play in the NBA, which is considered the epitome of professional basketball. Not many basketball enthusiasts outside of Indo-Pak Basketball know him. Since no South Asians play in the NBA, Indo-Pak players have no other pan-ethnic reference other than the Chinese player Yao Ming. Yao has become a metaphorical representation of possible desi basketball excellence. His Asian-ness is refracted as a template of the South Asian hero who can, players hope, undo racializing discourses in the United States in ways desi players perceive that he has done for the Asian American community. The figure of Yao Ming presents different gendered and racial meanings from African American basketball icons. The rhetoric around Yao Ming's iconicity situates him as a controlled, team-oriented, selfless player in a mold that desi players, at least in theory, tried to imitate and embody.[9] His body is seen as a long-term remedy to the limitations of manning up in brown outs. An Indian Yao Ming, regardless of how problematic this vision may be, presents a way to counter the first threat.

While the first threat undermining the strategy of browning out thus relates to players' inability to completely subvert stereotypical readings of their South Asian bodies by others, the second threat is related to the proliferation of highly insular ethno-religious basketball formats. While the original Indo-Pak Basketball was constituted through heterogeneity, increased South Asian immigration to the United States has multiplied the population in such a way that the next generation of South Asian American basketball players no longer needs Indo-Pak Basketball as their brown-out basketball venue to make desi masculinity. Rather, they create exclusive ethno-religious brown-out basketball as a means to man up.

Threat 2: Heterogeneity and "Less Inflow of New Blood"

The scheme with which to create safe spaces for manning up faces a threat to which there is no easy solution. The presence of an Indian Yao Ming would not provide a counter to this particular threat. Although Indo-Pak Basketball in the United States was institutionalized in 1989, it is both a contemporary and temporary phenomenon. It is limited by time and space. Even with the careful institutionalization of the Chicago IPN and its continued partnership with the Boys and Girls Club, the occupants of the gyms during the tournaments consist of mostly volunteers, a few spouses supporting their partners, and players watching their opponents play. Max, Rathi, Charles, and John, organizer of the Dallas Indo-Pak tournament, recognized and worried that "the youth" do not come anymore. Charles's own experiences are not translated across to the newest cohort of South Asian American ballers: "I'm 27; I have known IPB since I was nine. It was basically through my older brother. I used to just come, tag along with him; the games were the most exciting thing for me. That's how I got into basketball, through my older brother. . . . I started playing in the national tournament [Chicago IPN] at age 14." This kind of intimate involvement for the next generation was not evident to the organizers of Chicago IPN. With such concerns in mind, Chicago IPN organizers send out notices to incorporate an under-18 division for young South Asian American men at the 2008 tournament. However, other than a team from North Carolina headed by a former Indo-Pak Basketball player, all the under-18 teams were from Chicago. In 1989, a heterogeneous South Asian community assembled on some outdoor basketball courts to play in the first Chicago IPN. Max described this experience: "What started off as more a Punjabi and Malayalee thing [the tournament], Gujaratis wanted to play." This led to the incorporation of various ethnic and religious communities that have directly affected the production of competitive basketball. Fast-forward 20 years, and a diverse desi community was present at the 2008 tournament. Whereas young South Asian American men in the 1990s would travel to multiple cities to play, the same did not prove true at the 2008 under-18 tournament. Rather than seeking out Indo-Pak Basketball as the brown out of choice in which to man up, a growing number of young South Asian American people are turning to other ethnically insular spaces to play basketball. The heterogeneity that constituted the IPN tournaments is now a threat to the very structure of this brown-out space.

The fear of a disappearing tradition, such as the brown out of Indo-Pak Basketball, points to a phenomenon that anthropologist Madhulika Khandelwal (2002) addresses in her work, *Becoming American, Being Indian*.[10] Her research illustrates how increased immigration from South Asia changed the contours of South Asian America. Khandelwal narrates how a smaller community of desis in New York City had originally congregated under an umbrella category as South Asian Americans. However, with increased South Asian migration to the United States, South Asian communities splintered and formed ethnic enclaves around much more specific ethnic and religious characteristics. They no longer congregate as South Asian Americans but instead through their ethnic or religious origins as Gujaratis, Punjabis, Sikhs, or Malayalees. Though increased population has led to multiethnic interactions in Indo-Pak Basketball and other brown-out basketball spaces, this increased population has also led to divergent patterns of community formation through stricter ethno-religious lines. The very institution of Indo-Pak Basketball and other brown-out basketball spaces like the pickup games in Atlanta are in danger of disappearing or, worse, of becoming irrelevant. With the ability of South Asian American communities to form their own ethnic enclaves that provide an escape from the politics of the other basketball leagues, these brown-out spaces now do not always attract young people who value increased ethnic and religious specificity. Here we can see how the goal of intense inter-ethnic competition that is critical to performances of sporting masculinity has not necessarily transcended time. Charles alluded to this situation: "All the same teams were playing each other. We were not getting better. We did not compete well at the Indo-Pak tournaments. We allowed Asians [Asian Americans] to play, [and] this brought in new blood."

In Atlanta, the local Indo-Pak Basketball tournaments are few and infrequent. The participants in Atlanta's Indo-Pak tournaments are often young men with a limited basketball lexicon. They have had little exposure to basketball circuits outside of their brown-out spaces at religious institutions and cultural centers; therefore their skill level is quite diminished compared to that of the players on Indo-Pak Basketball teams in the North American circuit or even those teams, such as the Rat Pack, Sand Brothaz, and Hit Squad teams, that play in the Asian Ballers League. In fact, Suleiman, who coordinated a few Indo-Pak Basketball tournaments, chose to set up and orchestrate the April 4 Asian American Tournament. Is there a specific process taking place in Atlanta like that of Chicago? In ways similar to Charles's account of the changing parameters of local Chicago Indo-Pak Basketball leagues to incorporate Asian Americans, Atlanta's South Asian American basketball community also shifts from Indo-Pak to the Asian Baller's League. The established teams of higher caliber in Atlanta play in the Asian Ballers League locally and in the Asian Baller's Tournament nationally. However, in Fall 2009, Kdol decided to shut down the Asian Baller's League, thus removing one key venue of exhilarating basketball play for South Asian American men. Kdol shared, "I want to expand Asian Ballers across the country, I want to host the tournament in Chicago and Cali [California]. I want to start a semi-pro Asian American league, but I need money and sponsorship for that. . . . The Asian Americans with money don't provide the funding." Mustafa and Kdol agreed on the popularity of Asian American basketball across the United States[11] but also recognized the shifting patterns of social organization and funding among these ethnic American communities. Accordingly, South Asian American migration and concentration in other cities such as Orlando, Miami, and Tampa affected the formation of brown-out spaces in Atlanta. Whereas the 1996 Atlanta Olympics positioned Atlanta as an emerging economic and political power experiencing increased South Asian migration,[12] heightened immigration control has changed the subsequent demographic.[13]

Dr. Said highlighted the pervasive negative effects of racial profiling following September 11, 2001. He stated unequivocally, "The growth of Muslims in Atlanta is proportionally low in relation to other communities because of immigration barriers, and there is less inflow of new blood. This will have an impact in ten to fifteen years." That impact has already been felt. A survey of the Atlanta brown-out basketball scene illuminates the ways in which both the pickup scene and organized tournaments have changed shape. The pickup circuit presently incorporates white and African Americans players more so than during the core period of my research. However, the low level of basketball skills in co-ethnic and pickup ball has led committed basketball players to seek competition elsewhere. The Atlanta Rat Pack travels to North Carolina and Florida for their South Asian American, Asian American tournaments, and Muslim tournaments. Indo-Pak Basketball is diminishing in its reach and quality in Atlanta.

With the disbanding of various leagues and teams, another phenomenon has continued to take shape. New leagues have formed with strict adherence to ethnic or national ties. This is becoming the new pattern for performing South Asian American masculinity. For example, as the Asian Baller's League struggles to produce players and teams for the second half of the 2009 summer session, the 3-on-3 Muslim tournament has had a large turnout of young men.[14] At the request of the local South Asian American and Asian American communities, Kdol resumed the league after a brief hiatus. Similarly, there is an active Ismaili-only Muslim league in the United States. Mustafa bragged about how he, as a Sunni Muslim, is able to religiously pass and play in the Ismaili league. He specifically mentioned how he dominates that league but then provides his critique of Ismailis: "I play with the Ismailis but don't hang out with them too much. They are not real Muslims." Language and belief systems like this can create exclusionary forces within South Asian America's Muslim communities through the production of the "normal" (Sunni) versus "abject" (Ismaili). Just the talk of dominating in Ismaili tournaments positions Mustafa as a strong masculinity in relation to a weak Ismaili man. This kind of "intraethnic Othering" (Abelmann 2009) can only lead to a sense of marginalization within co-ethnic spaces, thus leading the marginalized subject to bear the pain, engage in greater insularity, or enter mainstream public forums of play. With increased insularity, brown-out basketball could cease to exist in its current form. There is no real solution for how to survive this threat.

It is not clear how desi men will re-invent the contours of masculinity without the particularity of the brown-out basketball space. I imagine that my informants may ponder whether these masculine norms in Indo-Pak Basketball will break down with the loss of intentional playing spaces. With the changing demography of gender practices and identities in U.S. society in general, the racial, gender, sexual, and class binaries that held together the strategy of the brown out may not be relevant moving forward. If the dismantling of gender bifurcations elsewhere spill over into Indo-Pak Basketball, there could be an overt attempt at community building that incorporates all South Asian Americans regardless of gender identification and sexual orientation. A movement to change the gender dynamics within brown-out basketball could also disrupt racial hierarchies and lead to radical coalition building strategies. There could be real possibilities, as the cultural theorist Erica Rand proposes in *Red Nails, Black Skates*, to realize the potential for liberation in sport and its accompanying pleasures while staying attuned to the power dynamics prevalent in it.[15] The safe space of brown-out basketball, if it is malleable and open to different memberships and politics, could lend itself to greater social appeal, thus providing a venue for the systematic transformation of gender, racial, sexual, and class hierarchies. Only with such openness, flexibility, and queer possibilities can a version of American-ness and South Asian American-ness emerge that allows livability within the nation and in the diaspora, instead of solely at the margins.

NOTES

INTRODUCTION

1 See Madan (2000).

2 See Lowe (1996).

3 I understand the problematic conceptualization of "American" as it is also used throughout the Americas, North and South, to talk about inhabitants. In other South American and North American countries other than the United States, it is also a point of self-reference that challenges the hegemony of the United States. In this book, I use the term "American" as it was commonly used by my informants and used in mainstream sports media discourse.

4 Popular culture presents one venue for minority communities to engage with mainstream communities and challenge the parameters of "belonging." See Lipsitz (1990, 1994); Maira and Soep (2005); Espana-Maram (2006); and Nguyen and Tu (2007).

5 See Puar and Rai (2002, 2004) for a discussion of the particular constellation of the stereotypes of the "model minority" and "terrorist" that creates a certain kind of national subject that is always seen as non-normative. As a result, we can see the racial flexibility and fluctuation among various racial categories and their material implications for South Asian Americans (Visweswaran 1997).

6 For the relationship of race, masculinity, sport, and nation, see Burdsey (2011); and Sugden and Tomlinson (2012).

7 See Davé (2013) for critical work on Apu. See Volpp (2003); and Ahmad (2004) for discussion of the "terrorist."

8 See Butler (1990, 1993); Boris (1995); and Archetti (1999).

9 See Birell and MacDonald (2000); Moore (2004); and Bolin (2005).

10 See James (2003); Farred (2006); Hylton (2009); and Carrington (2010).

11 This category of gender is never separate of race, sexuality, class, and ability (see Collins 2006, 2009).

12 See Enloe (1990); Bruce et al. (1998); Mumford (2001); Dworkin (2005); Tomlinson and Young (2005); Burdsey (2007, 2011); Bruce and Wensing (2009); and Adair (2011).

13 See Thangaraj, Burdsey, and Dudrah (2014).

14 See Burdsey (2004, 2007, 2011); Farooq Samie (2011, 2013); Pandya (2013); and Walle (2013).

15 See Chin (2011); Joo (2012); and Regalado (2012).

16 See Bachin (2005); and Espana-Maram (2006).

17 See MacAloon (1984); and Carter (2008).

18 I completely understand that sex is not determined in advance and is not neutral ground for performing gender identities. Sex is itself the key site for regulating gender, and it is shifting and dynamic (see Butler 1993; Fausto-Sterling 2000; Halberstam 2005; Rubin 2012).

19 Players use their bodies as sites of pleasure that appropriate various aspects of the larger social world and are in turn appropriated by it. See Bourdieu (1977); and Camaroff and Camaroff (1992). See also Sahlins (1981, 1987); and Connerton (1989).

20 See Farnell (1994); and Taylor (1994).

21 See Chan (1991) and Prashad (2000) for details on South Asian migration to Canada and the U.S. West Coast in the late 1700s and 1800s. Bald (2013) looks at the movement of Bengali merchants in the U.S. South and in Harlem, New York. My informants are not directly connected to any of these early waves, although they know some of these histories.

22 See Mazumdar (1989); Garcha (1992); and Leonard (1992).

23 See Shah (2005).

24 See Leonard (1992); Shah (2005); Koshy (2007); and Puar (2007).

25 See Hing (2001); Guglielmo (2004); and Ngai (2005).

26 For studies of second-generation South Asian immigrants in the United States, see Agarwal (1991); Maira (2002); Purkayansta (2005); Shankar (2008); Sharma (2010); and Dhingra (2007).

27 See Prashad (2000).

28 See Joshi (2006); and Dhingra (2007, 2013). See also Prashad and Mathew (1999/2000); and Mathew (2005).

29 See Khandelwal (2002).

30 The performances of masculinity also illustrate how citizenship is similarly a fluctuating category (Castles and Davidson 2005).

31 See Nelson (1998); Thangaraj (2010a, 2010b); and Belkin (2012).

32 See Reddy (1997, 2011); and Ferguson (2004).

33 On the politics of counteridentification, see Medina (2003, 2013).

34 See Hall (2003).

35 See Butler (1990, 1993); and Ramirez (2004).

36 See also Butler (1993).

37 See Butler (1990); Foucault (1990, 2010); and Pringle (2007).

38 See Reid-Pharr (2001); Johnson (2003); Ferguson (2004); Kim (2005); and Wray (2006).

39 See Bolin and Granskog (2005a).

40 See Agarwal (1991); Chan (1991); and Louie (2003).

41 See Shankar and Srikanth (1998); and Davé et al. (2000).

42 The terms of hyper-masculinity used to represent African American and Latino communities stood in the same space with their effeminization that accompanied

their demand for state resources. Thus, politicians and journalists painted black and Latino communities as failed men who needed the support of the state as they could not support themselves in any appreciable social realm other than entertainment and incarceration.

43 Here, as the theorist Jacques Derrida (1978) emphasizes, difference works to institute a hierarchy and deference, but not equivalence. See also Lorde (1984); and Andrews (2000).

44 See Messner (2002); Kimmel (2005); and Nylund (2006).

45 The cover photo is itself problematic, as it affirms various types of gender, sexual, and racial orders through the representation of white heterosexual men on the cover.

46 *Nirali Magazine* provides a forum for South Asian Americans to express their issues. It is also a site where advertisers appeal to the South Asian American community. The magazine is run by South Asian Americans.

47 See *Nirali Magazine* (2005a). "Desi" is a South Asian term used to refer to "native," "countryman," or those "of the country," and it is a common reference to South Asian diasporic subjects. See Agarwal (1991); Prashad (2000); Maira (2002); Shankar (2008); and Sharma (2010) for more details.

48 See *Nirali Magazine* (2005b).

49 See Miller (2001).

50 See Bourdieu (2001); and Brown (2006).

51 See also Visweswaran (1997); Morning (2001); and Dhingra (2003a, 2003b) in regard to the complex and shifting racial classifications and identifications of South Asian Americans.

52 See Goode (2002).

53 See Visweswaran (1997) and Bald (2013).

54 See also Jamal and Naber (2008); Alsultany (2012); Cacho (2012); and Naber (2012).

55 I agree with the anthropologist John L. Jackson, Jr., who contends, "By co-constructing our social spaces, we co-construct our social selves" (2001: 15).

56 See Kalaf (2014).

57 "Desi" is itself a dynamic, fluctuating, contradictory, and shifting term. By using "desi," Mustafa marks himself, as a Muslim Pakistani American, as different athletically from desis, whom he commonly categorizes as Indian Americans. Ironically, he also at various times identifies or is identified by others as desi. As a result, "desi" is used in the book in many ways to emphasize the complexity of the identity term. I also use the term "South Asian American," although my informants rarely used it in their everyday activities and discourse. My choice of the term "South Asian American" stems from an intentional choice to involve a discussion of subjects who fall outside of the simple binary of Hindu-India and Muslim-Pakistan. The players we meet in this book come from various national and diasporic sites that refuse to be contained in a simple binary, and I hope the term "South Asian American," with all its limitations, serves a useful purpose for complicating the analysis.

58 See Moallem (2002); Maira (2009); Rana (2011); and Afzal (2014).

59 See Baylor (1996); and Keating (2001).

60 See Kruse (2007).

61 See U.S. Census Bureau (2012).

62 All these figures are part of the designation on the census forms that includes individuals who identify solely with these categories as well as in combination with other categories. These numbers do not accurately represent the entire South Asian American community as it attends to only those who responded to the survey. As a result, the real population numbers are higher.

63 See Dhingra (2013).

64 See Marcus (1999).

65 See Roy (1998); Gopinath (2005a, 2005b); and Dasgupta (2007).

66 See Shah (2001); and Kim (2005).

67 See Clifford and Marcus (1986); Abu-Lughod (1991); Behar and Gordon (1996); Clifford (1997); and Marcus (1999).

CHAPTER 1. EVERYDAY PLAY

1 See Davis (1985); Ferguson (2004); and Gopinath (2005a).

2 See Thangaraj (2010b).

3 Alexander (2004); Keaton (2006); Bayoumi (2009b, 2010); Kumar (2012); Apuzzo and Goldman (2013).

4 This information came from an activist organization in Atlanta called "Movement to End Israeli Apartheid–Georgia"; they organized to support this local mosque.

5 These quotes come from Movement to End Israeli Apartheid–Georgia and their archiving of quotes from TV news from the local CBS station as well as the *Gwinnett Daily Post* newspaper. These quotes were sent out in an e-mail to MEIA members, and that is how I received them in 2009.

6 See Balibar and Wallerstein (1991); Goldberg (1993); Rana (2007, 2011); and Naber (2012).

7 Various mosques in Atlanta have been very active players in the interfaith coalition. Al-Farooq Masjid holds an annual symposium on Islam and other religions of the world where practitioners of other religions serve on panels.

8 This was Dr. Said's emphasis.

9 See George (1992); Farred (2006); and Yep (2009, 2012).

10 See Baylor (1996).

11 See Kearns and Philo (1993); Bainer (2006); and Carter (2006) for a study of the role of sport in constructing a particular image of cities.

12 See also Gibson (1988); Dhingra (2007); and Manohar (2008) for scholarship on desi communities in the U.S. South.

13 Thangaraj (2010b, 2013).

14 See Theberge (1985); Dunning (1986); and Bryson (1987).

15 See Butler (1993); Halberstam (1998, 2005); and Rubin (2012).

16 This gender segregation and its respective symbolic justification is part of the South Asian American Muslim experience and did not pertain to all Muslim communities in the United States (see Karim 2009). For a discussion of Muslims in Europe, see Keaton (2006).

17 See Gopinath (1995, 2005a); Appadurai (1996); Maira (2002); and Shankar (2008). Desai (2004, 2005) argues that we look "beyond Bollywood" to see how various other popular cultural forms emerge as sites of representation.

18 For greater detail on black cultural forms, cultural blackness, and the politics of cool, see Boyd (1997); Kelley (1997); Cole and King (1998); and Vargas (2007).

19 See also Prashad (2001); and Kim (2005).

20 See Davis (1985).

21 See Cheng and Yang (2000); and Osajima (2000).

22 Thomas Sugrue (2005) shows the shifting contours of Detroit and the intersections of race, union labor, and industrial shifts in post-Fordist towns where small towns and rural areas became the host sites for U.S. industry. See also Sassen (1999); and Fink (2004).

23 See Prashad and Mathew (1999/2000); and Mathew (2005).

24 Alongside doctors, engineers, and scientists, nurses, mostly Malayalee women like Daniel's mom, were also recruited by the U.S. State Department to fill the voids in the hospitals (see George 2005).

25 Sultan's emphasis.

26 See Prashad (2000).

27 Reuters (2004).

28 Brooks does bring in the example of Jayvin, a Native American athlete who travels to play in Philly. See George (1992) for a greater examination and history of schoolyard ball versus playground ball.

29 Kathleen Yep (2009) provides a wonderful historical entrée into the world of Chinese American basketball. See Farred's (2006) take on Yao Ming. See also the work on Native Americans and basketball as well as Guam and basketball (Diaz 2002).

30 See Joshi (2006); and Bald (2013).

31 See Bruner (2002).

32 The poor public transportation system in Metro Atlanta, known as MARTA (Metropolitan Atlanta Rapid Transit Authority), is aligned with a north-south and east-west route that limits the mobility of poor and communities of color, preventing them from going through white residential areas (see Kruse 2007).

33 See the discussion of "Kallu" later in the chapter.

34 See Kruse and Sugrue (2007) for an examination of the politics of suburbia in relation to city life. For an in-depth study of white flight in Atlanta, see Kruse (2007).

35 See O'Mara (2007).

36 Desi players and their peers drive from their places of residence while poor black home owners are being pushed to areas without any public transportation. For

those African American communities with middle-class status, they move to the black suburbs in College Park (south of Atlanta in Fulton County and Clayton County) and Lithonia (east of Atlanta in DeKalb County).

37 See Sassen (2002).

38 See Jones-Correa (2007).

39 For more information on the underground economy, refer to Venkatesh (2009).

40 Kelley (1997) contends that African Americans use the remaining resources, such as public gyms, for social mobility and economic advancement.

41 In his description of Atlanta's public services, Kruse (2007: 124) states that, "unwilling to share public spaces with blacks, white Atlantans once again looked for a private altnerative."

42 See Kruse (2007).

43 Frug (2007) argues convincingly about the manner in which exclusion and erosion of public services took place through the legal system and the discourse of law.

44 See Sassen (1999, 2002).

45 See Manalansan (2003); Ramirez (2004).

46 For more information on the Internet and community formation, see Rai (1995).

47 Daniel's emphasis.

48 See Malone (1996).

49 Masculinity is practiced, expressed, and evaluated by men in the presence of other men (see Chauncey 1994; Espana-Maram 2006).

50 For a discussion of racial displacement, see Andrews (2000). For a study of mimesis, see Taussig (1993).

51 See Depro and Hartmann (2006); May (2007); Hartmann (2012).

52 See also Brooks (2009).

53 See Nayak (2006); Patillo (2007); and Pierre (2012) for an extensive discussion of the ways to conduct ethnographies of race that attest to the multiplicity of blackness and underscore difference within the category of "black."

54 See Carrington (1998, 2002, 2010); Hoberman (1997); and King and Springwood (2001).

CHAPTER 2. "WHO IS DESI?"

1 Malayalees are an ethnic group in India located in the state of Kerala. They speak Malayalam. George (2005) details their diasporic history in the United States.

2 His emphasis.

3 See Balibar and Wallerstein (1991).

4 See Visweswaran (1997).

5 See Lorde (1984); Lowe (1996); Nelson (1998); Eng (2001, 2010); Castles and Davidson (2005); Gopinath (2005a, 2005b); Nguyen (2012); Burdsey, Thangaraj, and Dudrah (2013).

6 I use the term "arsenal" intentionally as metaphorically there is tremendous overlap between sport and war. See Nylund (2006).

7 For work on difference as a critical unit of women of color critique, see Women of South Asian Descent Collective (1993); Hong (2006); and Hong and Ferguson (2011).

8 See Hartmann (2003).

9 See Shaheen (2009); and Alsultany (2012).

10 See Jamal and Naber (2008).

11 See Rana (2007, 2011); and Naber (2012).

12 The racial slur, with its use of "sand," homogenizes and conflates various places in the Middle East and Asia. It stands as an adjective of foreignness that is put in front of "nigger" as the quintessential non-normative subject.

13 See Omi and Winant (1994); Hartmann (2003); Burdsey (2007); and Carrington (2010, 2012).

14 His emphasis.

15 See Cole and King (1998); LeFeber (1999); Page (1999); and Andrews (2000).

16 For more detail about FOKANA, see Maira (2002); and George (2005).

17 See Islam (1993); Prashad (2000); Shukla (2003); Khan (2004); and Kibria (2011).

18 For a critical exploration of space and Asian America, see Bonus (2000) and Shukla (2001, 2003). See also Pile and Keith (1993).

19 This is a pseudonym.

20 See Nylund (2006) for a detailed study of discourse and masculinity.

21 See De (2013) for a fuller description of the term "bauji."

22 Dhingra (2007) addresses how linguistic commonalities reassure a sense of community and intimacy in Indian American communities.

23 Panjabi MC (1998).

24 See Khandelwal (2002); Ray (2004); and Ku, Manalansan, and Mannur (2013).

25 See Ray (2004) for scholarship on South Asian American identity formation through culinary spaces, food, and respective meanings.

26 These cultural practices resist singular location while underscoring cultures as always dynamic and situated in interconnected spaces (Gupta and Ferguson 1997).

27 See De Palma (1987).

28 In present-day Indian politics, "untouchable" is seen as a derogatory word, and therefore members of the lowest caste have created their own identity as "Dalits." See Gorringe (2005) for a study of the Dalit movement in South India.

29 See George (2005).

30 For an examination of how sport play is voluntary (in most cases) and not conscripted, see James (2003).

31 Khandelwal (2002) argues that the types of heterogeneous socializing found across religious and ethnic lines in South Asian America differ from the segregation one notices in South Asia.

32 See Islam (1993); Visweswaran and Mir (1999); and Radhakrishnan (2003) for the hegemony of India and Hindu in the construction of South Asia and South Asian America. This hegemony is challenged with the daily practices of self of various members of the expansive South Asian America category.

33 See Portes (1996); and Portes and Rumbaut (2001a, 2001b).

34 See Hendrickson (1995); Berdahl (1999); and Shukla (2003).

35 See Roediger (1991, 2005); and Wray (2006).

36 The masculinity studies scholar Robert Connell argues that "gender is not fixed in advance of social interaction, but is constructed in interaction" (1995: 35).

37 His emphasis.

38 See Arnaldo (in press), who describes the ways in which the cross-over holds such status that when a Filipina American "crosses over" a Filipino American, the young man feels emasculated.

39 See Trujillo (2000).

40 For more about the politics of piety, see Mahmood (2005).

41 See Steward (1990); DeMello (2000); Pitts (2003); and Sanders and Vail (2008).

42 See Burdsey (2007); and Rana (2011).

43 See Afzal (2006, 2010).

44 See Afzal (2014).

45 See Prashad and Mathew (1999/2000); Abraham (2000); Prashad (2000, 2001); and Mathew (2005).

46 See Bayoumi (2009a); and Rana (2011: 41).

47 See Chakravartty and Ferreira da Silva (2012).

48 I do not provide any information about the website or the resource from which I gained this information as that would compromise the confidentiality and anonymity of Parambir and others.

49 Collins (2009) defines class as not just a symbolic marker but as a clear dictum of political economy and access to resources. Class, as a result, is an indication of power and inequality.

50 Whannel (2007) stresses the link between masculinity and morality determined, in this case, through ideas of middle-class respectability. This is a disciplining regime limiting the participation of certain others.

51 Lorde (1984); and Thangaraj (2012).

52 Mustafa uses "ghetto" as a way to talk about a tough masculinity and to label a certain subject who is seen as prone to fighting. For more on ghetto, see Jones (2010).

53 See Keating (1998); and Johnson (2003).

54 See Roediger (1991, 2005, 2008); and Ortiz (2006).

55 George (1992); Farred (2006, 2007); and Brooks (2009).

56 For information on South Asian American communities in New York, see Fisher (1980); and Khandelwal (2002).

57 See Thangaraj (2010a, 2012).

58 See hooks (1994) for a treatise on the contradiction of mimicking and desiring the black body but only as a commodity confined to a racialized marketplace.

59 For information on the one-drop rule and hypo-descent, see Roediger (2008).

60 In addition to black bodies, sometimes players objected to the presence of racial and cultural Others. Anil of the Maryland Five Pillars team spoke about

experiences of exclusion of the Persian American on their team: "One of the years, we did not come because Chicago [tournament organizers] would not let Tehrani play because he is Persian. With the Vancouver team, they have Michael Smith who is not South Asian, but he is not questioned. We [DC IPN] are lax about who could play, and thus Afghans can play. John [Dallas IPN] questioned letting Tehrani play."

61 See Thangaraj (2012).

62 My emphasis.

63 See also Radhakrishan (2011), who looks at how the contours of the "good" Indian is manufactured, challenged, and contested in various diasporic sites.

CHAPTER 3. RACIAL AMBIGUITY

1 Pascoe (2007) discusses how sexuality and gender are constructed through the realms of the excelling academic person and the premier athlete.

2 See Kanew (1984).

3 See Shankar and Srikanth (1998); and Davé et al. (2000).

4 See Alter (1992) for an examination of wrestling in India and how the body is a signifier of larger social processes in and out of sport. See also Burdsey (2005).

5 See Kibria (1996, 1998). As a side note, most Asian American teams included more mixed race white-Asian and black-Asian players than South Asian American teams.

6 See Kim (1999); and Bow (2010).

7 See King and Springwood (2001); and Ortiz (2006).

8 See Bow (2010); Thangaraj (2012); and Yep (2012a).

9 See Tarasawa (2009); and Thangaraj (2010b).

10 For more on the Muslim tournaments in Atlanta, see Thangaraj (2010b).

11 For more information on the various refugee populations from post–Vietnam War, see Fadiman (1999); Ong (2003); Vang (2010); and Nguyen (2012).

12 See Lowe (1996); Ong (2003); Vo (2004); and Schein (2009). See Bascara (2006) for the ways in which the "model minority" moniker hides the heterogeneity within Asian America.

13 See Shankar and Srikanth (1998); and Davé et al. (2000) for a description of South Asian American affinity and distance from Asian America.

14 Shankar and Srikanth (1998); and Davé et al. (2000).

15 See Chan (1991); Leonard (1992); and Luibheid and Cantu (2005).

16 See Haney-Lopez (1994); and Hong (2006).

17 See Ono and Pham (2008); and Lee (2011).

18 See Visweswaran (1997); Mazumdar (1989), and Koshy (1998, 2007).

19 See Yep (2009); Chin (2011); Regalado (2012); and Reft (2014a, 2014b).

20 See Puar (2007).

21 See Chauncey (1994).

22 See Lowe (1996).

23 Persuad, a South Asian player, vehemently claimed a Caribbean identity outside the physical and ideological parameters of South Asian America. However, Persuad could play in this league since his phenotype and players' genotypic evaluations afforded him status as Asian American.

24 See Dasgupta (2007); and Visweswaran (2011) for an examination of the ways in which Nepalese and Bhutanese are situated both in South Asia and in South Asian America.

25 See an exploration of "cultural citizenship" by Rosaldo (1994); Maira (2002, 2009); and Miller (2006).

26 See Diaz (2002) for an exploration of how Pacific Islanders understood and challenged U.S. imperialism while performing indigeneity through football.

27 For a systematic examination of these early racializations, see Chan (1991); Eng (2001); and Shah (2001, 2005).

28 See Halberstam (1998); and Fausto-Sterling (2000).

29 See Andrews (2006).

30 Sethi (2010).

31 See Lelyveld (1993); and Cohn (1998).

32 See Kingston (1989); Chan (1991); and Shah (2001).

33 See Hefner (2000); Gladney (2004); and O'Connor (2012).

34 The Asian Ballers National Tournament is held just once a year. The Asian Ballers League takes place throughout the year.

35 See Andrews (1996); and Farred (2006).

36 See Espana-Maram (2006).

37 See Farred (2006).

38 See Wang (2012a).

39 See Hsu (2012); Ng (2012); Pan (2012); Wang (2012b, 2012c); and Yep (2012b).

40 Vecsey (2009).

41 See Wertheim (2012).

42 See Roediger (2008).

43 See Oscar Lewis's (1959) thesis on the "culture of poverty," which posits culture as a hereditary trait with pathological consequences in communities of color. See Vargas (2007); Jones (2010); and Rios (2011) for a critique of this thesis.

44 For a nuanced reading of failure and whiteness, see Halberstam (2011).

45 See Keating (2001); McDermott (2006); and Tarasawa (2009).

46 Unlike Asian Ballers, there is also an active women's circuit as well.

47 See Newton (2008); and Cacho (2012).

48 See Rana (2007, 2011).

49 See Jamal and Naber (2008); and Naber (2008, 2012).

50 See Goode (2002) for an explanation for how one's racial identity is critical to one's belonging as a citizen. Without a race-based identity, she argues, one is at threat of not having citizenship.

51 See Rios (2011) for details on the racialization of Latinos as tough, thuggish, and criminal.

52 I want to make clear that I am not conflating race and culture; rather, I am stating that both are used in interesting ways—ways that sometimes overlap—to determine membership. For more on this distinction, see Visweswaran (1998).

CHAPTER 4. GETTING "DIGITS"

1 For a general introduction to Southern hip hop, see *Wikipedia* (2014).

2 See Dyson (1993); Rose (1994).

3 See Kim (2005); and Pitt and Sanders (2009).

4 Daniel Kim (2005) offers a sharp analysis of how Asian American men and scholars have demanded a particular hypermasculinity as the means to enter normative masculinity. Thus, in order to fight off effeminate stereotypes, Asian American men call for black styles as a way to regain masculinity.

5 For information on trash talking and discourses of masculinity, see Nylund (2006).

6 The term "player" constitutes part of the foundations of a normative American masculinity, which is itself ambiguous and continuously shifting, but the men perform as "normative" the opposite of the racializations they endure in mainstream society.

7 There is an interpellation of Latinas as already heterosexual and part of the performance of heterosexual masculinity at the intersections of race, gender, and sexuality. In the process, there is problematic essentialization and commodification of their bodies. See Garcia (2009).

8 See Mumford (2001); and Ngo (2014).

9 For politics of decency at the intersections of sexuality and race, see Findlay's (2000) take on rape in Puerto Rico.

10 See España-Maram (2006).

11 By aspiring to a heterosexual masculinity, practices of masculinity in leisure spaces re-affirm the gender binary and "its perpetuation of heteronormativity of leisure" (Johnson and Kivel 2007: 94). See also Bogle (2008).

12 The historian Linda España-Maram (2006) demonstrates the importance of peer-group structured leisure activities in identity formation.

13 For information on "straightening" and the ways in which persons are oriented toward heterosexuality, see Ahmed (2006).

14 In his ethnographic project, May (2007) illustrates the link between an athletic, aggressive masculinity and a propensity to covet sexual favors from young women.

15 See Baez (2007).

16 See Gopinath (2005b).

17 Black women's bodies have not been treated as equivalent to white women's bodies in U.S. history. Rather, at the intersection of race, gender, sexuality, and violence, black women's bodies and bodies of women of color have been seen as justifiably rapeable. See Davis (1985); Collins (1998); Pierce-Baker (1998); and Smith (2005).

18 See Abraham (2000); Rudrappa (2004); and Dasgupta (2007).

19 His emphasis.

20 See Kugle (2010).

21 See Ronen (2010).

22 See Brown (2006).

23 For a reading of the South Asian body as transgressive in the realm of dance, see Chatterjea (2004).

24 The actual bodies in play, their movements, and their social context are key sites for the workings of discourse of masculinity and its relevant power structures (Pringle 2005).

25 For more information on strip clubs, see Frank (2002).

26 See Belkin (2012) to see how masculinity and sexuality are critical to affirming a binary between masculine and feminine as well as straight and queer.

27 The Gold Club shut down in 2001 after a major financial scandal.

28 See Eagen, Frank, and Johnson (2006); and Price (2008).

29 See Zelizer (2005).

CHAPTER 5. BREAKING THE CYCLE

1 Mahmoud's emphasis.

2 See Shah (2001, 2005); Gopinath (2005a); and Canaday (2011).

3 See Messner (2002); and Anderson (2005).

4 The cultural studies scholar Toby Miller (2001) challenges the hierarchical order of masculinities theorized by the foundational masculinities scholar Robert Connell (1995) with his reference to various gay athletes, including gay Australian rugby player Ian Roberts.

5 See Featherstone (2013).

6 See James (2003: xii); see also Wynter (1992).

7 See Cheng (1999) for an elaboration of the relationship of racialized masculinities to dominant forms of normative masculinity.

8 His emphasis.

9 Lorde (1984: 112).

10 See Johnson (2003); Ferguson (2004); and Kim (2005).

11 See Dayal (1998).

12 See Johnson (2003).

13 See also Reid-Pharr (2001) for an explanation of how black masculinity is firmly situated within heterosexuality and naturalized as such through the negation of the gay black subject.

14 See Anderson (2005); Nylund (2006); and Aitchison (2007).

15 Bay (2007).

16 See Rubin (2012) for a beautiful elaboration of intersex bodies as a place that complicates the commonsensical neutrality afforded to sex and provides a different history of the concept of gender.

17 See Sedgwick (1986).

18 See Amaechi (2007).

19 For more information on the relationship of sexuality and sport, see Anderson (2005); and Caudwell (2006).

20 For a detailed definition of heteronormativity, see Rubin (1984); Schilt and Westbrook (2009); Ward and Schneider (2009).

21 In fact, the current global climate—the "global war on terror"—already relies on an interpellation of Muslims as homophobic and sexist in order to justify U.S. imperial maneuvers (see Puar 2007; Nguyen 2011, 2012; Rana 2011).

22 See Kulick (2009); Manalansan (2009); and Murray (2009).

23 See Kugle (2010) for an exploration of homosexuality and queer readings of the Quran.

24 See Duggan (2003); Ferguson (2004); Manalansan (2005); Reddy (2011).

25 See Roy (1998).

26 See Johnson (2003); and Pascoe (2007).

27 See Bersani (1986). Bersani contends that heterosexual narratives are put in place by denarrativizing moments in which the abject becomes the subject. It is a form of mimesis that emphasizes alterity.

28 The American literary theorist Leo Bersani (1986) offers a way of seeing this simultaneous invocation and repudiation of queer masculinity. Thus, the pain stems from the simultaneous recognition and repression of the non-normative subjectivity (see also Edelman 2004).

29 See Grasmuck (2005).

30 Her emphasis.

31 For a discussion of "tomboy" and the particular masculine attributes associated with girls, see Halberstam (1998).

32 The demands of representing culture and tradition are put upon South Asian women. This demand also requires that they also be heterosexual and middle class. See Abraham (2000); Durham (2001); Maira (2002); Rudrappa (2004); Gopinath (2005a, 2005b); Gupta (2006); and Dasgupta (2007).

33 See Dudrah (2002); Rudrappa (2004); Gopinath (2005a); and Dasgupta (2007) about the symbolic associations and constructions of South Asian femininity as static, demure, and traditional. These associations are then metonymic of diaspora and nation.

34 See Halberstam (1998).

35 For work on Global Feminism and South Asian Queer politics, see Mohanty (2003); Gopinath (2005a); and Puar (2007).

36 See Bolin (2005); Bolin and Granskog (2005a, 2005b); and Brown (2006).

37 In addition, there are co-ed tournaments being hosted in Dallas. However, the very structuring of the co-ed game limits what kind of plays can take place, who can guard whom, and the how one can score points. As such, there is still a clear distinction made in co-ed tournaments about the masculine and feminine player.

38 See Brake (2010).

39 See Gopinath (2005a). For the relationships between sexuality, lesbianism, and sport, see Griffin (1998); and Brackenridge, Rivers, Gough, and Llewellyn (2007).

40 See Gopinath (2005a) for an elaborate discussion and salvage ethnography in which she challenges the linear projection of sexual orientations whereby the West is seen as the site of liberation and the East is seen as sexually stunted. Gopinath complicates such a configuration and demonstrates how queer the East already is.

41 See Kumar (2000); and Gopinath (2005a).

42 Guneet added the emphasis.

43 See Kennedy (2007).

44 See Messner (1992, 2002); and May (2007).

45 Even the global golf icon Tiger Woods, before the 2009 "incident"—when his infidelity and extra-marital affairs came to be known—was narratively held together by showing the link between him and his father (see Cole and Andrews 2001; and Andrews 2006).

46 See Joseph (2014).

47 A women's labor does not carry the same value as that of men (see Kingfisher 2002).

CONCLUSION

1 Lozada (2006) demonstrates how Shanghai cosmopolitan identity is negotiated through consumptive practices of global sports and not necessarily by local teams. In the case of South Asian Americans, there is a consumption of Vancouver sporting symbols as a means to negotiate one's place in the United States.

2 My emphasis.

3 His reference.

4 See Chadney (1984); and Axel (2001).

5 There is talk of the 7-foot tall Bhullar brothers, who have received greater recognition within collegiate recruiting circles as a result of their size and basketball capabilities. However, this recognition is only in the recruiting circles and not widespread throughout the basketball cultures in the United States. For more information on the brothers Sim and Tanveer Bhullar, see Fedotin (2010). See also Thangaraj, Burdsey, and Dudrah (2014).

6 In 2014, Sim Bhullar was picked up by the NBA Sacramento Kings, but the verdict is not in on his basketball ability as the season had not started when I was writing this book. The Kings are owned by an Indian American, and there is speculation that the signing was a move to increase the appeal of the NBA brand in India, not necessarily about the talents of Sim Bhullar.

7 This is a team of young men from Christian, Muslim, and Sikh backgrounds whose places of worship have domes, and they play upon that word by substituting it into "dominators."

8 See Reft (2014a, 2014b).

9 See Farred (2006).

10 See also Afzal (2006, 2010).

11 See Yep (2009, 2012b); and Chin (2011).

12 See Baylor (1996); and Keating (2001).

13 See Joshi (2006); and Karim (2009).

14 Teams in a 3-on-3 tournament consist of only three players who go against other teams made up of three players, instead of the standard format of five players on each team. For more information about this 3-on-3 Muslim tournament, see Thangaraj (2010b).

15 See Rand (2011).

BIBLIOGRAPHY

Abelmann, Nancy. 2009. *The Intimate University: Korean American Students and the Problems of Segregation.* Durham, NC: Duke University Press.

Abraham, Margaret. 2000. *Speaking the Unspeakable: Marital Violence among South Asian Immigrants in the United States.* New Brunswick, NJ: Rutgers University Press.

Abu-Lughod, Lila. 1991. "Writing against Culture." In *Recapturing Anthropology: Working in the Present,* ed. Richard G. Fox. Santa Fe, NM: School of American Research Press.

Adair, Daryl. 2011. *Sport, Race, and Ethnicity: Narratives of Difference and Diversity.* Morgantown, WV: Fitness Info Tech.

Afzal, Ahmed. 2014. *Lone Star Muslims: Transnational Lives and the South Asian American Experience in Texas.* New York: New York University Press.

———. 2010. "From an Informal to a Transnational Muslim Heritage Economy: Transformations in the Pakistani Ethnic Economy in Houston, Texas." *Urban Anthropology* 39(4): 397–424.

———. 2006. "From South Asian to a Muslim Heritage Economy: Religious Transnationalism and Transformations in the Pakistani Ethnic Economy in Houston, Texas." Presented at "South Asian Religious Transnationalism: Regional Dynamics, Global Passages" conference, August, Chicago.

Agarwal, Priya. 1991. *Passage from India: Post 1965 Indian Immigrants and Their Children.* Palos Verdes, CA: Yuvait Publications.

Ahmad, Muneer. 2004. "A Rage Shared by Law: Post September 11th Racial Violence as Crimes of Passion." *California Law Review* 92(5): 1259–1330.

Ahmed, Sara. 2006. *Queer Phenomenology: Orientations, Objects, Others.* Durham, NC: Duke University Press.

Aitchison, Cara Carmichael. 2007. "Gender, Sport, and Identity: Introducing Discourses of Masculinities, Femininities, and Sexualities." In *Sport and Gender Identities: Masculinities, Femininities and Sexualities,* ed. Cara Michael Aitchison. Abingdon: Routledge.

Alexander, Claire. 2004. "Embodying Violence: 'Riots', Dis/order and the Private Lives of the 'Asian Gang.'" In *Making Race Matter: Bodies, Space and Identity,* ed. Clair Alexander and Caroline Knowles. Basingstoke: Palgrave Macmillan.

Alsultany, Evelyn. 2012. *Arabs and Muslims in the Media: Race and Representation after 9/11.* New York: New York University Press.

Alter, Joseph. 1992. *The Wrestler's Body: Identity and Ideology in North India*. Berkeley: University of California Press.

Amaechi, John. 2007. *Man in the Middle*. New York: ESPN.

Anderson, Benedict. 1991. *Imagined Communities: Reflections on the Origin and Spread of Nationalism*. New York: Verso.

Anderson, Eric. 2005. *In the Game: Gay Athletes and the Cult of Masculinity*. Albany: State University of New York Press.

Andrews, David L. 2006. *Sport-Commerce-Culture: Essays on Sport in Late Capitalist America*. New York: Peter Lang.

———. 2000. "Excavating Michael Jordan's Blackness." Pp. 166–205 in *Reading Sport: Critical Essays on Power and Representation*, ed. Susan Birrell and Mary G. McDonald. Boston: Northeastern University Press.

Andrews, Vernon. 1996. "Black Bodies—White Control: The Contested Terrain of Sportsmanlike Conduct." *Journal of African American Men* 2(1): 33–59.

Appadurai, Arjun. 1996. *Modernity at Large: Cultural Dimensions of Globalization*. Minneapolis: University of Minnesota Press.

Apuzzo, Matt, and Adam Goldman. 2013. *Enemies Within: Inside the NYPD's Secret Spying Unit and Bin Laden's Final Plot against America*. New York: Touchstone.

Archetti, Eduardo P. 1999. *Masculinities: Football, Polo, and the Tango in Argentina*. London: Berg Publishers.

Arnaldo, Constancio, Jr. In press. "Embodying Scales of Filipina/o American Sporting Life: Transnational Sporting Cultures and Practices in the Filipina/o Diaspora." In *Asian American Crossroads*, ed. Shilpa Davé et al. New York: New York University Press.

Axel, Brian. 2001. *The Nation's Tortured Body: The Sikh Diaspora*. Durham, NC: Duke University Press.

Bachin, Robin. 2003. *Building the South Side*. Chicago: University of Chicago Press.

Baez, Jillian M. 2007. "Towards a *Latinidad Feminista*: The Multiplicities of Latinidad and Feminism in Contemporary Cinema." *Popular Communication* 5(2): 109–128.

Bahri, Deepika, and Mary Vasudeva. 1998. *Between the Lines: South Asians and Postcoloniality*. Philadelphia: Temple University Press.

Bairner, Alan. 2006. "Titanic Town: Sport, Space, and the Re-imag(in)ing of Belfast." In "Special Issue: The Sport of Cities." *City and Society* 18(2): 159–179.

Bald, Vivek. 2013. *Bengali Harlem: And the Lost Histories of South Asian America*. Cambridge, MA: Harvard University Press.

Balibar, Etienne, and Emmanuel Wallerstein. 1991. *Race, Class, Nation: Ambiguous Identities*. New York: Verso.

Bascara, Victor. 2006. *Model Minority Imperialism*. Minneapolis: University of Minnesota Press.

Bay, Michael, dir. 2007. *Transformers*. DreamWorks Productions.

Baylor, Ronald H. 1996. *Race and the Shaping of Twentieth-Century Atlanta*. Chapel Hill: University of North Carolina Press.

Bayoumi, Moustafa. 2010. "Being Young, Muslim and American in Brooklyn." Pp. 161–174 in *Being Young and Muslim: New Cultural Politics in the Global North and South*, ed. Linda Herrera and Asef Bayat. Oxford: Oxford University Press.

———. 2009a. "East of the Sun (West of the Moon): Islam, the Ahmadis, and African America." Pp. 69–78 in *Black Routes to Islam*, ed. Manning Marable and Hisham Aidi. New York: Palgrave Macmillan.

———. 2009b. "Racing Religion." Pp. 99–108 in *American Studies*, ed. Janice Radway, Kevin Gaines, Barry Shank, and Penny Von Eschen. Malden, MA: Blackwell.

Behar, Ruth, and Deborah A. Gordon. 1996. *Women Writing Culture*. Berkeley: University of California Press.

Belkin, Aaron. 2012. *Bring Me Men: Military Masculinity and the Benign Façade of American Empire, 1898–2001*. New York: Columbia University Press.

Beltran, Mary, and Fojas, Camilla. 2008. *Mixed Race Hollywood*. New York: New York University Press.

Berdahl, Daphne. 1999. *Where the World Ended: Re-unification and Identity in the German Borderland*. Berkeley: University of California Press.

Bersani, Leo. 1986. *The Freudian Body*. New York: Columbia University Press.

Bhatia, Sunil. 2007. *American Karma: Race, Culture and Identity in the Indian Diaspora*. New York: New York University Press.

Birrell, Susan, and Mary G. McDonald. 2000. "Reading Sport, Articulating Power Lines." Pp. 3–13 in *Reading Sport: Critical Essays on Power and Representation*, ed. Susan Birrell and Mary G. McDonald. Boston: Northeastern University Press.

Bogle, Kathleen. 2008. *Hooking Up: Sex, Dating, and Relationships on Campus*. New York: New York University Press.

Bolin, Anne. 2005. "Beauty or the Beast: The Subversive Soma." In *Athletic Intruders: Ethnographic Research on Women, Culture, and Exercise*, ed. Anne Bolin and Jane Granskog. Albany: State University of New York Press.

Bolin, Anne, and Jane Granskog. 2005a. "Introduction." In *Athletic Intruders: Ethnographic Research on Women, Culture, and Exercise*, ed. Anne Bolin and Jane Granskog. Albany: State University of New York Press.

———. 2005b. "Afterword: Pastimes and Presentimes: Theoretical Issues in Research on Women in Action." In *Athletic Intruders: Ethnographic Research on Women, Culture, and Exercise*, ed. Anne Bolin and Jane Granskog. Albany: State University of New York Press.

Bonilla-Silva, Eduardo. 2007. *Racism without Racists: Color-Blind Racism and the Persistence of Racial Inequality in America*. New York: Rowman & Littlefield.

Bonus, Rick. 2000. *Locating Filipino Americans*. Philadelphia: Temple University Press.

Boris, Eileen. 1995. "The Racialized Gendered State: Constructions of Citizenship in the United States." *Social Politics* 2(2): 160–180.

Bourdieu, Pierre. 2001. *Masculine Domination*. Stanford, CA: Stanford University Press.

———. 1984. *Distinction: A Social Critique of the Judgment of Taste*. Cambridge, MA: Harvard University Press.

———. 1977. *Outline of a Theory of Practice.* Cambridge: Cambridge University Press.

Bow, Leslie. 2010. *Partly Colored: Asian Americans and Racial Anomaly in the Segregated South.* New York: New York University Press.

Boyd, Todd. 1997. ". . . The Day the Niggaz Took Over: Basketball, Commodity Culture, and Black Masculinity." In *Out of Bounds: Sports, Media, and the Politics of Identity*, ed. Aaron Baker and Todd Boyd. Bloomington: Indiana University Press.

Brackenridge, Celia, Ian Rivers, Brendan Gough, and Karen Llewellyn. 2007. "Driving Down Participation: Homophobic Bullying as a Deterrent to Doing Sport." In *Sport and Gender Identities: Masculinities, Femininities and Sexualities*, ed. Cara Michael Aitchison. New York: Routledge.

Brake, Deborah. 2010. *Getting in the Game: Title IX and the Women's Sports Revolution.* New York: New York University Press.

Brooks, Scott. 2009. *Black Men Can't Shoot.* Chicago: University of Chicago Press.

Brown, David. 2006. " Pierre Bourdieu's 'Masculine Domination' Thesis and the Gendered Body in Sport and Physical Culture." *Sociology of Sport Journal* 23(2): 162–188.

Brown, Wendy. 2008. "The Impossibility of Women's Studies." In *Women's Studies on the Edge*, ed. Joan Scott. Durham, NC: Duke University Press.

Brownell, Susan. 1995. *Training the Body for China: Sports in the Moral Order of the People's Republic.* Chicago: University of Chicago Press.

Bruce, Toni, et al. 1998. *Sport and Post-modern Times.* Albany: State University of New York Press.

Bruce, Toni, and E. Wensing. 2009. "'She's not one of us': Cathy Freeman and the Place of Aboriginal People in Australian National Culture." *Australian Aboriginal Studies* 2: 90–100.

Bruner, Tasgola Karla. 2002. "Georgia Ranks 12th in Job Bias Cases by Muslims, Others." *Atlanta Journal Constitution*, May 24.

Bryson, Lois. 1987. "Sport and the Maintenance of Masculine Hegemony." *Women's Studies International Forum* 10(4): 349–360.

Burdsey, Daniel, ed. 2011. *Race, Ethnicity and Football.* Abingdon: Routledge.

———. 2007. *British Asians and Football: Culture, Identity, Exclusion.* London: Routledge.

———. 2005. "Role with the Punches: The Construction and Representation of Amir Khan as a Role Model for Multiethnic Britain." *Sociological Review* 55(3): 611–631.

———. 2004. "'One of the lads'? Dual Ethnicity and Assimilated Ethnicities in the Careers of British Asian Professional Footballers." *Ethnic and Racial Studies* 27(5): 757–779.

Burdsey, Daniel, Stanley Thangaraj, and Rajinder Dudrah. 2013. "Playing through Time and Space: Sport and South Asian Diasporas." *South Asian Popular Culture* 11(3): 211–218.

Burns, T. F. 1980. "Getting Rowdy with the Boys." *Journal of Drug Issues* 10: 273–286.

Butler, Judith. 1993. *Bodies That Matter: On the Discursive Limits of "Sex."* New York: Routledge.

————. 1990. *Gender Trouble: Feminism and the Subversion of Identity.* New York: Routledge.

Cacho, Lisa. 2012. *Social Death: Racialized Rightlessness and the Criminalization of the Undocumented.* New York: New York University Press.

Camaroff, John, and Jean Camaroff. 1992. *Ethnography and the Historical Imagination.* Boulder, CO: Westview Press.

Canaday, Margot. 2011. *The Straight State: Sexuality and Citizenship in Twentieth Century America.* Princeton, NJ: Princeton University Press.

Carrington, Ben. 2012. "Sport Matters: Politics, Identity and Culture." *Ethnic and Racial Studies* 35(6): 961–971.

————. 2010. *Race, Sport, and Politics: The Sporting Black Diaspora.* London: Sage.

————. 2002. "Race, Representation, and the Sporting Body." CUCR Occasional Paper Series. London: Centre for Urban and Community Research, University of London.

————. 1998. "Sport, Masculinity and Black Cultural Resistance." *Journal of Sport and Social Issues* 22(3): 275–298.

Carter, Thomas. 2008. *The Quality of Home Runs: The Passion, Politics, and Language of Cuban Baseball.* Durham, NC: Duke University Press.

————. 2006. "Introduction: The Sport of Cities." In "Special Issue: The Sport of Cities." *City and Society* 18(2): 151–158.

Castles, Stephen, and Alastair Davidson. 2005. *Citizenship and Migration: Globalization and the Polticis of Belonging.* Abingdon: Routledge.

Caudwell, Jayne, ed. 2006. *Sport, Sexualities and Queer/Theory.* Abingdon: Routledge.

Chadney, James S. 1984. *The Sikhs of Vancouver.* New York: AMS Press.

Chakravartty, Paula, and Denise Ferreira da Silva. 2012. "Accumulation, Dispossession, and Debt: The Racial Logic of Global Capitalism—An Introduction." *American Quarterly* 64(3): 361–385.

Chan, Sucheng. 1991. *Asian Americans.* London: Twayne Publishers.

Chatterjea, Ananya. 2004. *Butting Out: Reading Resistive Choreographies through Works by Jawole Willa Jo Zollar and Chandralekha.* Middletown, CT: Wesleyan University Press.

Chauncey, George. 1994. *Gay New York: Gender, Urban Culture, and the Making of the Gay Male World, 1890–1940.* New York: Basic.

Cheng, Cliff. 1999. "Marginalized Masculinities and Hegemonic Masculinity: An Introduction." *Journal of Men's Studies* 7(3): 295.

Cheng, Lucie, and Philip Q. Yang. 2000. "The 'Model Minority' Deconstructed." Pp. 459–482 in *Contemporary Asian America: A Multidisciplinary Reader*, ed. Min Zhou and James V. Gatewood. New York: New York University Press.

Chin, Christine. 2011. "Hoops, History, and Crossing Over: Boundary Making and Community Building in Japanese American Youth Basketball Leagues." Dissertation, University of California, Los Angeles.

Clifford, James. 1997. *Routes: Travel and Translation in the Late Twentieth Century.* Cambridge, MA: Harvard University Press.

Clifford, James, and George E. Marcus, eds. 1986. *Writing Culture: The Poetics and Politics of Ethnography*. Berkeley: University of California Press.

Cohn, Bernard. 1998. *An Anthropologist among the Historians*. Delhi: Oxford University Press.

Cole, C. L., and David L. Andrews. 2000. "Tiger Woods: America's New Son." Cultural Studies: A Research Annual 5: 107–122.

Cole, C. L., and Samantha King. 1998. "Representing Black Masculinity and Urban Possibilities: Racism, Realism, and Hoop Dreams." Pp. 49–86 in *Sport and Postmodern Times*, ed. G. Rail. Albany: State University of New York Press.

Collins, Patricia Hill. 2009. *Black Feminist Thought: Knowledge, Consciousness, and the Politics of Empowerment*. New York: Routledge.

———. 2006. *Black Sexual Politics: African Americans, Gender, and the New Racism*. New York: Routledge.

———. 1998. *Fighting Words*. Minneapolis: University of Minnesota Press.

Connell, Robert. W. 1995. *Masculinities*. Cambridge: Polity Press.

———. 1987. *Gender and Power: Society, the Person, and Sexual Politics*. Palo Alto, CA: Stanford University Press.

Connerton, Paul. 1989. *How Societies Remember*. Cambridge: Cambridge University Press.

Dasgupta, Shamita Das. 2007. *Body Evidence: Intimate Violence against South Asian Women in America*. New Brunswick, NJ: Rutgers University Press.

Davé, Shilpa. 2013. *Indian Accents: Brown Voice and Racial Performance in American Television and Film*. Champaign: University of Illinois Press.

Davé, Shilpa, Pawan Dhingra, Sunaina Maira, Partha Mazumdar, Lavina Dhingra Shankar, Jaideep Singh, and Rajini Srikanth. 2000. "De-privileging Positions: Indian Americans, South Asian Americans, and the Politics of Asian American Studies." Journal of Asian American Studies 3(1): 67–100.

Davé, Shilpa, LeiLani Nishime, and Tasha G. Oren, eds. 2005. *East Main Street: Asian American Popular Culture*. New York: New York University Press.

Davis, Angela. 1985. *Women, Culture, and Politics*. New York: Vintage.

Dayal, Samir. 1998. "Min(d)ing the Gap: South Asian Americans and Diaspora." In *A Part, yet Apart: South Asians in Asian America*, ed. Lavina D. Shankar and Rajini Srikanth. Philadelphia: Temple University Press.

De, Aparajita. 2013. "Sporting with Gender: Examining Sport and Belonging at Home and in the Diaspora through *Patiala House* and *Chak De! India*." South Asian Popular Culture 11(3): 287–300.

De Garis, Laurence. 2000. "'Be a Buddy to Your Buddy': Male Identity, Aggression, and Intimacy in a Boxing Gym." In *Masculinities, Gender Relations, and Sport*, ed. Jim McKay, Michael Messner, and Don Sabo. London: Sage.

———. 1999. "Experiments in Pro Wrestling." *Sociology of Sport Journal* 16(1): 65–77.

DeMello, Margo. 2000. *Bodies of Inscription: A Cultural History of the Modern Tattoo Community*. Durham, NC: Duke University Press.

De Palma, Brian, dir. 1987. *The Untouchables*. Film. Paramount Pictures.

Depro, Brooks, and Douglas Hartmann. 2006. "Rethinking Sports-Based Community Crime Prevention: A Preliminary Analysis of the Relationship between Midnight Basketball and Urban Crime Rates." *Journal of Sport and Social Issues* 30: 180–196.

Derrida, Jacques. 1978. *Writing and Difference*. New York: Routledge.

Desai, Jigna. 2005. "Planet Bollywood: Indian Cinema Abroad." In *East Main Street: Asian American Popular Culture*, eds. Shilpa Davé, LeiLani Nishime, and Tasha G. Oren. New York: New York University Press.

———. 2004. *Beyond Bollywood: The Cultural Politics of South Asian Diasporic Film*. New York: Routledge, 2004.

Dhingra, Pawan. 2013. *Life behind the Lobby*. Palo Alto, CA: Stanford University Press.

———. 2007. *Managing Multicultural Lives: Asian American Professionals and the Challenge of Multiple Identities*. Palo Alto, CA: Stanford University Press.

———. 2003a. "Becoming American between Black and White: Second Generation Asian American Professionals' Racial Identities." *Journal of Asian American Studies* 6(2): 117–148.

———. 2003b. "The Second Generation in 'Big D': Korean American and Indian American Organizations in Dallas, Texas. Sociological Spectrum 23(2): 247–278.

Diaz, Vicente M. 2002. "'Fight Boys till the Last': Football and the Remasculinization of Indigeneity in Guam." In *Pacific Diaspora: Island Peoples in the United States and the Pacific*, ed. Paul Spickard, Joanne Rondilla, and Deborah Hippolite-Wright. Manoa: University of Hawai'i Press.

Douglas, Mary. 1978. *Purity and Danger: An Analysis of the Concepts of Pollution and Taboo*. New York: Routledge.

Dudrah, Rajinder. 2002. "Drum 'n' Dhol: British Bhangra Music and Diasporic South Asian Identity Formation. *European Journal of Cultural Studies* 5(3): 363–383.

Duggan, Lisa. 2003. *The Twilight of Equality? Neoliberalism, Cultural Politics, and the Attack on Democracy*. Boston: Beacon.

Dunning, Eric. 1986. "Sport as a Male Preserve: Notes on the Social Sources of Masculine Identity and Its Transformations." *Theory, Culture, and Society* 3(1): 79–90.

Dupri, Jermaine. 2002. *Instructions*. Compact disc. So So Def Productions.

Durham, Meenakshi Gigi. May 2001. "Displaced Persons: Symbols of South Asian Femininity and the Returned Gaze in U.S. Media Culture." *Communication Theory* 11(2): 201–217.

Dworkin, Shari L. 2005. "A Woman's Place is in the . . . Cardiovascular Room? Gender Relations, the Body, and the Gym." In *Athletic Intruders: Ethnographic Research on Women, Culture, and Exercise*, ed. Anne Bolin and Jane Granskog. Albany: State University of New York Press.

Dyson, Michael Eric. 1993. *Reflecting Black: African-American Cultural Criticism*. Minneapolis: University of Minnesota Press.

Eagen, Danielle, Katherine Frank, and Merri Lisa Johnson, eds. 2006. *Flesh for Fantasy: Producing and Consuming Exotic Dance*. New York: Thunder's Mouth Press.

Edelman, Lee. 2004. *No Future: Queer Theory and the Death Drive*. Durham, NC: Duke University Press.

Eng, David L. 2010. *The Feeling of Kinship: Queer Liberalism and the Racialization of Intimacy*. Durham, NC: Duke University Press.

———. 2001. *Racial Castration: Managing Masculinity in Asian America*. Durham, NC: Duke University Press.

Enloe, Cynthia 1990. "Nationalism and Masculinity." Pp. 42–64 in *Bananas, Beaches, and Bases: Making Feminist Sense of International Politics*. Berkeley: University of California Press.

España-Maram, Linda. 2006. *Creating Masculinity in Los Angeles's Little Manila*. Berkeley: University of California Press.

Fadiman, Anne. 1999. *The Spirit Catches You and You Fall Down*. New York: Farrar, Straus & Giroux.

Fajardo, Kale. 2011. *Filipino Crosscurrents: Oceanographies of Seafaring, Masculinities, and Globalization*. Minneapolis: University of Minnesota Press.

Farnell, Brenda. December 1994. "Ethno-graphics and the Moving Body." *MAN: The Journal of the Royal Anthropological Institute* 29(4): 929–974.

Farooq Samie, Samaya. 2013. "Hetero-Sexy Self/Body Work and Basketball: The Invisible Sporting Women of British Pakistani Muslim Heritage." *South Asian Popular Culture* 11(3): 257–270.

———. 2011. "'Tough Talk,' Muscular Islam and Football: Young British Pakistani Muslim Masculinities." In *Race, Ethnicity and Football*, ed. Daniel Burdsey. Abingdon: Routledge.

Farred, Grant. 2007. "The Event of the Black Body at Rest: Melee in Motown." *Cultural Critique* 66: 58–77.

———. 2006. *Phantom Calls: Race and the Globalization of the NBA*. Chicago: Prickly Paradigm Press.

Fausto-Sterling, Anne. 2000. *Sexing the Body: Gender Politics and the Construction of Sexuality*. New York: Basic.

Featherstone, Simon. 2013. "Sport and the Performative Body in the Early work of C.L.R. James." *Identities: Global Studies in Culture and Power*. Doi: 10.1080/1070289X.2013.866559.

Fedotin, Jeff. 2010. "7-Foot Brothers Stand Out in a Crowd." *Highschool.rivals.com*. https://basketballrecruiting.rivals.com/content.asp?CID=1087336.

Ferguson, James. 2006. *Global Shadows: Africa in the Neoliberal World Order*. Durham, NC: Duke University Press.

Ferguson, Roderick. 2012. *The Reorder of Things: The University and Its Pedagogies of Difference*. Minneapolis: University of Minnesota Press.

———. 2004. *Aberrations in Black: Toward a Queer of Color Critique*. Minneapolis: University of Minnesota Press.

Findlay, Eileen Saurez. 2000. *Imposing Decency: The Politics of Sexuality and Race in Puerto Rico, 1870–1920*. Durham, NC: Duke University Press.

Fink, Leon. 2004. *The Maya of Morgantown: Work and Community in the Nuevo New South*. Chapel Hill: University of North Carolina Press.

Fisher, Maxine P. 1980. *The Indians in New York City*. New Delhi: Heritage Publishers.

Foucault, Michel. 2010. *The Birth of Bio-politics: Lectures at the College de France, 1978–1979*. New York: Picador.

———. 1990. *The History of Sexuality*. Vol. 1: *An Introduction*. New York: Vintage.

Frank, Katherine. 2002. *G-Strings and Sympathy: Strip Club Regulars and Male Desire*. Durham, NC: Duke University Press.

Fracher, J., and M. Kimmel. 1998. "Hard Issues and Soft Spots: Counseling Men about Sexuality." In *Men's Lives*, ed. Michael Kimmel and Michael Messner. Boston: Allyn & Bacon.

Frug, Gerald. 2007. "The Legal Technology of Exclusion in Metropolitan America." In *The New Suburban History*, ed. Kevin Kruse and Thomas Sugrue. Chicago: University of Chicago Press.

Gaffney, C., and Bale, J. 2004. "Sensing the Stadium." In *Sites of Sport*, ed. P. Vertinsky and J. Bale. Abingdon: Routledge.

Garcha, Rajinder. 1992. "The Sikhs in North America: History and Culture." *Ethnic Forum* 12(2): 80–93.

Garcia, Lorena. 2009. "'Now Why Do You Want to Know about That?': Heteronormativity, Sexism, and Racism in the Sexual (Mis)education of Latina Youth." *Gender and Society* 23(4): 520–541.

Geertz, Clifford. 1973. *The Interpretation of Cultures*. New York: Basic.

George, Nelson. 1992. *Elevating the Game: Black Men and Basketball*. New York: HarperCollins.

George, Sheba Marian. 2005. *When Women Come First: Gender and Class in Transnational Migration*. Berkeley: University of California Press.

Gibson, M. A. 1988. *Accommodation without Assimilation: Sikh Immigrants in an American High School*. Ithaca, NY: Cornell University Press.

Gilbert, Matthew Sakiestewa. 2010. "Hopi Footraces and American Marathons, 1912–1930." *American Quarterly* 62(1): 77–101.

Gladney, Dru C. 2004. *Dislocating China: Muslims, Minorities, and Other Subaltern Subjects*. Chicago: University of Chicago Press.

Goldberg, Theo. 1993. *Racist Culture: Philosophy and the Politics of Meaning*. New York: Blackwell.

Goode, Judith. 2002. "From New Deal to Bad Deal: Racial and Political Implications of U.S. Welfare Reform." In *Western Welfare in Decline: Globalization and Women's Poverty*, ed. Catherine Kingfisher. Philadelphia: University of Pennsylvania Press.

Gopinath, Gayatri. 2005a. *Impossible Desires: Queer Diasporas and South Asian Public Cultures*. Durham, NC: Duke University Press.

———. 2005b. "Bollywood Spectacles: QUEER DIASPORIC CRITIQUE IN THE AFTERMATH OF 9/11." *Social Text* 23 (3–4 84–85): 157–169.

———. 1995. "Bombay, UK, Yuba City: Bhangra Music and the Engendering of Diaspora." *Diaspora* 4(3): 303–330.

Gorringe, Hugo. 2005. *Untouchable Citizens: Dalit Movements and Democratization in Tamil Nadu*. London: Sage.

Grasmuck, Sherri. 2005. *Protecting Home: Class, Race, and Masculinity in Boys' Baseball*. New Brunswick, NJ: Rutgers University Press.

Greaves, Stanley. 2002. *Horizons: Selected Poems, 1969–1998*. Leeds: Peepal Tree Press.

Griffin, P. 1998. *Strong Women, Deep Closets: Lesbians and Homophobia in Sport*. Champaign: Human Kinetics.

Guglielmo, Thomas. 2004. *White on Arrival*. New York: Oxford University Press.

Gupta, Akhil, and James Ferguson. 1997. *Culture, Power, Place: Explorations in Critical Anthropology*. Durham, NC: Duke University Press.

Gupta, Monisha Das. 2006. *Unruly Immigrants: Rights, Activism, and Transnational South Asian Politics in the United States*. Durham, NC: Duke University Press.

Halberstam, Judith. 2011. *The Queer Art of Failure*. Durham, NC: Duke University Press.

———. 2005. *In a Queer Time and Place: Transgender Bodies, Subcultural Lives*. New York: New York University Press.

———. 1998. *Female Masculinity*. Durham,NC: Duke University press.

Hall, Stuart. 2003. "Cultural Identity and Diaspora." In *Theorizing Diaspora*, ed. Jana Evans Braziel and Anita Mannur. Malden, MA: Blackwell.

Haney-Lopez, Ian. 1994. *White by Law: The Legal Construction of Race*. New York: New York University Press.

Hartmann, Douglas. 2012. "Beyond the Sporting Boundary: The Racial Significance of Sport through Midnight Basketball." *Ethnic and Racial Studies* 35(6): 1107–1123.

———. 2003. *Race, Culture, and the Revolt of the Black Athlete*. Chicago: University of Chicago Press.

Hefner, Robert. W. 2000. *Civil Islam: Muslims and Democratization in Indonesia*. Princeton, NJ: Princeton University Press.

Hendrickson, Carol. 1995. *Weaving Identities: Construction of Dress and Self in a Highland Guatemala Town*. Austin: University of Texas Press.

Hing, Bill. 2001. *To Be an American: Cultural Pluralism and the Rhetoric of Assimilation*. New York: New York University Press.

Hoang, Kimberly. 2015. *Dealing in Desire: Asian Ascendency, Western Decline, and the Hidden Currencies of Global Sex Work*. Berkeley: University of California Press.

———. 2011. "'She's not a low-class dirty girl': Sex Work in Ho Chi Minh City, Vietnam." *Journal of Contemporary Ethnography* 40(4): 367–396.

———. 2010. "Economies of Emotion, Familiarity, Fantasy, and Desire: Emotional Labor in Ho Chi Minh City's Sex Industry." *Sexualities* 13(2): 255–272.

Hoberman, John. 1997. *Darwin's Athletes: How Sport Has Damaged Black America and Preserved the Myth of Race*. Boston: Mariner Books.

hooks, bell. 1994. "Feminism Inside: Toward a Black Body Politic." In *Black Male: Representations of Masculinity in Contemporary American Art*, ed. Thelma Golden and Henry Louis Gates. New York: Whitney Museum of Art.

Hong, Grace Kyungwon. 2006. *The Ruptures of American Capital*. Minneapolis: University of Minnesota Press.

Hong, Grace Kyungwon, and Roderick Ferguson, eds. 2011. *Strange Affinities: The Gender and Sexual Politics of Comparative Racializations*. Durham, NC: Duke University Press.

Hsu, Hua. 2012. "Everyone Else's Jeremy Lin." *Amerasia Journal* 38(3): 126–128.

Hylton, Kevin. 2009. *"Race" and Sport*. Abingdon: Routledge.

Ifekwunigwe, Jayne. 2004. *"Mixed Race" Studies: A Reader*. Abingdon: Routledge.

Islam, Naheed. 1993. "In the Belly of the Multicultural Beast, I am Named South Asian." Pp. 242–245 in *Our Feet Walk the Sky: Women of the South Asian Diaspora*, ed. Women of the South Asian Descent Collective. San Francisco: Aunt Lute Books.

Jackson, John L., Jr. 2001. *HarlemWorld*. Chicago: University of Chicago Press.

Jamal, Amaney, and Nadine Naber. 2008. *Race and Arab Americans Before and After 9/11: From Invisible Citizens to Visible Subjects*. Syracuse, NY: Syracuse University Press.

James, C. L. R. 2003. *Beyond a Boundary*. Durham, NC: Duke University Press.

Johnson, Corey W., and Beth Kivel. 2007. "Gender, Sexuality, and Queer Theory in Sport." In *Sport and Gender Identities: Masculinities, Femininities, and Sexualities*, ed. Cara Aitchison. Abingdon: Routledge.

Johnson, E. Patrick. 2003. *Appropriating Blackness: Performance and the Politics of Authenticity*. Durham, NC: Duke University Press.

Jones, Nikki. 2010. *Between Good and Ghetto*. New Brunswick, NJ: Rutgers University Press.

Jones-Correa, Michael. 2007. "Reshaping the American Dream: Immigrants, Ethnic Minorities, and the Politics of the New Suburbs." In *The New Suburban History*, ed. Kevin Kruse and Thomas Sugrue. Chicago: University of Chicago Press.

Joo, Rachael. 2012. *Transnational Sport*. Durham, NC: Duke University Press.

Joseph, Janelle. 2014. "A Narrative Exploration of Gender Performances and Gender Relations in the Caribbean Diaspora." *Identities*: 1–15.

Joshi, Khyati. 2006. *New Roots in America's Sacred Ground: Religion, Race, and Ethnicity in Indian America*. New Brunswick, NJ: Rutgers University Press.

Kalaf, Samer. 2014. "High School Students Chant 'We Want Slurpees' at Indian Basketball Player." *Deadspin*. January 28. http://deadspin.com/high-school-students-chant-we-want-slurpees-at-indian-1511159652.

Kanew, Jeff, dir. 1984. *The Revenge of the Nerds*. Film. Twentieth Century-Fox Corp.

Karim, Jamillah. 2009. *American Muslim Women: Negotiating Race, Class, and Gender within the Ummah*. New York: New York University Press.

Kearns, Gerry, and Chris Philo, eds. 1993. *Selling Places: The City as Cultural Capital, Past and Present*. Oxford: Pergamon.

Keating, Ann Louise. 1998. "Interrogating 'Whiteness,' (De)Constructing 'Race.'" Pp. 186–209 in *Teaching African American Literature: Theory and Practice*, ed. Maryemma Graham, Sharon Pineault-Burke, and Marianna White Davis. New York: Routledge.

Keating, Michael. 2001. *Atlanta*. Philadelphia: Temple University Press.

Keaton, Trica. 2006. *Muslim Girls and the Other France: Race, Identity Politics, and Social Exclusion*. Bloomington: Indiana University Press.

Kelley, Robin D. G. 1997. *Yo Mama's Disfunktional!* Fighting the Culture Wars in Urban America. Boston: Beacon.

Kennedy, Eileen. 2007. "Watching the Game." In *Sport and Gender Identities*, ed. Cara Aitchison. Abingdon: Routledge.

Khan, Aisha. 2004. *Callaloo Nation: Metaphors of Race and Religious Identity among South Asians in Trinidad*. Durham, NC: Duke University Press.

Khandelwal, Madhulika. 2002. *Becoming American, Being Indian: An Immigrant Community in New York City*. Ithaca, NY: Cornell University Press.

Kibria, Nazli. 2011. *Muslims in Motion: Islam and the National Identity in the Bangladeshi Diaspora*. Brunswick, NJ: Rutgers University Press.

———. 1998. "The Racial Gap: South Asian American Racial Identity and the Asian American Movement." In *A Part, yet Apart: South Asians in Asian America*, ed. Lavina D. Shankar and Rajini Srikanth. Philadelphia: Temple University Press.

———. 1996. "Not Asian, Black or White? Reflections on South Asian American Racial Identity." *Ameriasia Journal* 22(2): 77–86.

Kim, Claire Jean. 1999. "The Racial Triangulation of Asian Americans." *Politics and Society* 27: 105–138.

Kim, Daniel. 2005. *Writing Manhood in Black and Yellow*. Stanford, CA: Stanford University Press.

Kimmel, Michael. 2005. *Manhood in America: A Cultural History*. London: Oxford University Press.

King, Richard C., and Charles Fruehling Springwood. 2001. *Beyond the Cheers: Race as Spectacle in College Sport*. Albany: SUNY Press.

Kingfisher, Catherine. 2002. "Neoliberalism I: Discourses of Personhood and Welfare Reform." In *Western Welfare in Decline: Globalization and Women's Poverty*, ed. Catherine Kingfisher. Philadelphia: University of Pennsylvania Press.

Kingston, Maxine Hong. 1989. *China Men*. New York: Vintage.

Klein, Alan. 1993. *Little Big Men: Bodybuilding Subculture and Gender Construction*. Binghamton, NY: SUNY Press.

Koshy, Susan. 2007. *Sexual Naturalization*. Stanford, CA: Stanford University Press.

———. 1998. "Crisis Category: South Asian Americans and the Questions of Race and Ethnicity." *Diaspora* 7(3): 285–320.

Kruse, Kevin. 2007. *White Flight: Atlanta and the Making of Modern Conservatism*. Princeton, NJ: Princeton University Press.

Kruse, Kevin, and Thomas Sugrue, eds. 2007. *The New Suburban History*. Chicago: University of Chicago Press.

Ku, Robert Ji-Song, Martin Manalansan, and Anita Mannur, eds. 2013. *Eating Asian America: A Food Studies Reader*. New York: New York University Press.

Kugle, Scott. 2010. *Homosexuality in Islam*. Oxford: One World.

Kulick, Don. 2009. "Can There Be an Anthropology of Homophobia?" In *Homophobias: Lust and Loathing across Time and Space*, ed. David Murray. Durham, NC: Duke University Press.

Kumar, Amitva. 2000. *Passport Photos*. Berkeley: University of California Press.

Kumar, Deepa. 2012. *Islamophobia and the Politics of Empire*. New York: Haymarket Books.

LaFeber, W. 1999. *Michael Jordan and the New Global Capitalism*. New York: Norton.

Lee, Julia. 2011. *Interracial Encounters: Reciprocal Representations in African and Asian American Literatures, 1896–1937*. New York: New York University Press.

Lelyveld, David. 1993. "The Fate of Hindustani: Colonial Knowledge and the Project of National Language." In *Orientalism and the Post-colonial Predicament: Perspectives on South Asia*, ed. Carol Breckenridge and Peter van der Veer. Philadelphia: University of Pennsylvania Press.

Leonard, Karen. 1992. *Making Ethnic Choices: California's Punjabi Mexican Americans*. Philadelphia: Temple University Press.

Lewis, Oscar. 1959. *Five Families: Mexican Case Studies in the Culture of Poverty*. New York: Mentor.

Lipsitz, George. 1994. "Who'll Stop the Rain? Youth Culture, Rock'n'Roll, and Social Crisis." In *The Sixties*, ed. David Barber. Chapel Hill: University of North Carolina Press.

———. 1990. *Time Passages: Collective Memory and American Popular Culture*. Minneapolis: University of Minnesota Press.

Lorde, Audre. 1984. *Sister Outsider*. Trumansburg, NY: Crossing Press.

Louie, Andrea. 2003. *Chineseness across Borders*. Durham, NC: Duke University Press.

Lowe, Lisa. 1996. *Immigrant Acts*. Durham, NC: Duke University Press.

Lozada, Eriberto. 2006. "Cosmopolitanism and Nationalism in Shanghai Sports." In "Special Issue: The Sport of Cities." *City and Society* 18(2): 207–231.

Luibhéid, Eithne, and Lionel Cantu, Jr., eds. 2005. *Queer Migrations: Sexuality, U.S. Citizenship, and Border Crossings*. Minneapolis: University of Minnesota Press.

MacAloon, John. 1984. "Olympic Games and the Theory of Spectacle in Modern Societies." In *Rite, Drama, Festival, Spectacle: Rehearsals toward a Theory of Cultural Performance*, ed. John MacAloon. Philadelphia: Institute for the Study of Human Issues.

Madan, Manu. 2000. "It's Not Just Cricket!' World Series Cricket: Race, Nation, and Diasporic Indian Identity." *Journal of Sport and Social Issues* 24(1): 24–35.

Mahmood, Saba. 2005. *Politics of Piety: The Islamic Revival and the Feminist Subject*. Princeton, NJ: Princeton University Press.

Maira, Sunaina. 2009. *Missing: Youth, Citizenship, and Empire after 9/11*. Durham, NC: Duke University Press.

———. 2002. *Desis in the House*. Philadelphia: Temple University Press.

Maira, Sunaina, and Elizabeth Soep, eds. 2005. *Youthscapes: The Popular, the National, the Global*. Philadelphia: University of Pennsylvania Press.

Majors, Richard. 2001. "Cool Pose: Black Masculinity and Sports." Pp. 208–217 in *The Masculinities Readers*, ed. Stephen Whitehead and Frank Barrett. Cambridge: Polity Press.

Malone, Jacqui. 1996. *Steppin' on the Blues: The Visible Rhythms of African American Dance*. Urbana: University of Illinois Press.

Manalansan, Martin. 2009. "Homophobia at Gay Central." Pp. 34–47 in *Homophobias: Lust and Loathing across Time and Space*, ed. David Murray. Durham, NC: Duke University Press: 34–47.

———. 2005. "Race, Violence and Neoliberal Spatial Politics in the Global City." *Social Text* 23(3–4 84–85): 141–155.

———. 2003. *Global Divas*. Durham, NC: Duke University Press.

Manohar, Namita. 2008. "'Sshh . . . !!! Don't Tell My Parents': Dating among Second-Generation Patels in Florida." *Journal of Comparative Family Studies* 39(4): 571–588.

Marcus, George. 1999. *Through Thick and Thin*. Princeton, NJ: Princeton University Press.

Mathew, Biju. 2005. *Taxi! Cabs and Capitalism in New York City*. New York: New Press.

May, Reuben. 2007. *Living Through the Hoop: High School Basketball, Race, and the American Dream*. New York: New York University Press.

Mazumdar, Sucheta. 1989. "Race and Racism: South Asians in the United States." Pp. 24–38 in *Frontiers of Asian American Studies*, ed. Gail M. Nomura, Russell Endo, Stephen H. Sumida, and Russell C. Leong. Pullman: Washington State University Press.

McDermott, Monica. 2006. *Working-Class White: The Making and Unmaking of Race Relations*. Berkeley: University of California Press.

Medina, Jose. 2013. *The Epistemology of Resistance: Gender and Racial Oppression, Epistemic Injustice, and Resistant Imaginations*. New York: Oxford University Press.

———. 2003. "Identity Trouble: Disidentification and the Problem of Difference." *Philosophy and Social Criticism* 29(6): 655–680.

Messner, Michael. 2002. *Taking the Field: Women, Men, and Sports*. Minneapolis: University of Minnesota Press.

———. 1992. *Power at Play: Sports and the Problem of Masculinity*. Boston: Beacon.

Miller, Toby. 2006. *Cultural Citizenship: Cosmopolitanism, Consumerism, and Television in a Neoliberal Age*. Philadelphia: Temple University Press.

———. 2001. *Sportsex*. Philadelphia: Temple University Press.

Mitchell, Jonathan, and Gary Armstrong. 2006. "Six Trophies and a Funeral: Performance and Football in the City of Valletta." *City and Society* 18(2): 180–206.

Moallem, Minoo. 2002. "Whose Fundamentalism?" *Meridians: Feminisms, Race, Transnationalism* 2(2): 298–301.

Mohanty, Chandra. 2003. *Feminism without Borders: Decolonizing Theory, Practicing Solidarity*. Durham, NC: Duke University Press.

Moore, Robert. 2004. "Scouting an Anthropology of Sport." *Anthropologica* 46(1): 37-46.

Morning, Ann. 2001. "The Racial Self-Identification of South Asians in the United States." *Journal of Ethnic and Migration Studies* 27(1): 61–79.

Muller, Tiffany K. 2007. "The Contested Terrain of the Women's National Basketball Association Arena." In *Sport and Gender Identities: Masculinities, Femininities and Sexualities*, ed. Cara Michael Aitchison. Abingdon: Routledge.

Mumford, Kevin. 2001. *Interzones*. New York: Columbia University Press.

Murray, David, ed. 2009. *Homophobias: Lust and Loathing across Time and Space*. Durham, NC: Duke University Press.

Naber, Nadine. 2012. *Arab America: Gender, Cultural Politics, and Activism*. New York: New York University Press.

———. 2008. "Arab Americans and U.S. Racial Formation." In *Race and Arab Americans Before and After 9/11: From Invisible Citizens to Visible Subjects*, ed. Amaney Jamal and Nadine Naber. Syracuse, NY: Syracuse University Press.

Nayak, Anoop. 2006. "After Race: Ethnography, Race, and Post-race Theory." *Ethnic and Racial Studies* 29(3): 411–430.

Nelson, Dana. 1998. *National Manhood: Capitalist Citizenship and the Imagined Fraternity of White Men*. Durham, NC: Duke University Press.

Newton, Lina. 2008. *Illegal, Alien, or Immigrant: The Politics of Immigration Reform*. New York: New York University Press.

Ng, Konrad. 2012. "#Linsanity." *Amerasia Journal* 38(3): 129–132.

Ngai, Mae. 2005. *Impossible Subjects: Illegal Aliens and the Making of Modern America*. Princeton, NJ: Princeton University Press.

Ngo, Fiona. 2014. *Imperial Blues: Geographies of Race and Sex in Jazz Age New York*. Durham, NC: Duke University Press.

Nguyen, Mimi. 2012. *The Gift of Freedom: War, Debt, and Other Refugee Passages*. Durham, NC: Duke University Press.

———. 2011. "The Biopower of Beauty: Humanitarian Imperialisms and Global Feminisms in the War on Terror." *Signs: Journal of Women in Culture and Society* 26(2): 359–383.

Nguyen, Mimi, and Thuy Nguyen Tu, eds. 2007. *Alien Encounters: Asian American Pop Culture*. Durham, NC: Duke University Press.

Nirali Magazine. 2005a. "The (D)Evolution of the Desi Dude." February 7. http://niralimagazine.com/2005/02/the-devolution-of-the-desi-dude/.

———. 2005b. "Finding a Thoroughly Modern Male." April 4. http://niralimagazine.com/2005/04/finding-a-thoroughly-modern-male/.

Nylund, David. 2006. *Beer, Babes, and Balls: Masculinity and Sports Talk Radio*. Albany, NY: SUNY Press.

O'Connor, Paul. 2012. *Islam in Hong Kong: Muslims and the Everyday Life in China's World City*. Hong Kong: Hong Kong University Press.

O'Mara, Margaret. 2007. "Uncovering the City in the Suburb: Cold War Politics, Scientific Elites, and High-Tech Spaces." In *The New Suburban History*, ed. Kevin Kruse and Thomas Sugrue. Chicago: University of Chicago Press.

Omi, Michael, and Winant, Howard. 1994. *Racial Formation in the United States: From the 1960s to the 1990s*. New York: Routledge.

Ong, Aihwa. 2003. *Buddha Is Hiding: Refugees, Citizenship, the New America*. Berkeley: University of California Press.

Ono, Kent, and Vincent Pham. 2008. *Asian Americans and the Media*. Malden, MA: Polity Press.

Ortiz, Paul. 2006. *Emancipation Betrayed: The Hidden History of Black Organizing and White Violence in Florida from Reconstruction to the Bloody Election of 1920*. Berkeley: University of California Press.

Osajima, Keith. 2000. "Asian Americans as the Model Minority: An Analysis of the Popular Press Image in the 1960s and 1980s." Pp. 449–458 in *Contemporary Asian*

America: A Multidisciplinary Reader, ed. Min Zhou and James V. Gatewood. New York: New York University Press.

Page, Helen. 1999. "'Black Male' Imagery and Media Containment of African American Men." *American Anthropologist* 99(1): 99–111.

Pan, Arnold. 2012. "Asian American Studies after Linsanity." *Amerasia Journal* 38(3): 124–125.

Pandya, Sameer. 2013. "Situating Vijay Singh in (Asian) America." *South Asian Popular Culture* 11(3): 219–230.

Panjabi MC [Raj Singh Rai]. 1998. "Mundian To Bach Ke" (Beware of the boys). Single. Compact disc.

Pascoe, C. J. 2007. *Dude You're a Fag: Masculinity and Sexuality in High School*. Berkeley: University of California Press.

Patillo, Mary. 2007. *Black on the Block: The Politics of Race and Class in the City*. Chicago: University of Chicago Press.

Pierce-Baker, Charlotte. 1998. *Surviving the Silence*. New York: Norton.

Pierre, Jemima. 2012. *The Predicament of Blackness: Postcolonial Ghana and the Politics of Race*. Chicago: University of Chicago Press.

Pile, Steve, and Michael Keith, eds. 1993. *Place and the Politics of Identity*. Abingdon: Routledge.

Pitt, Richard, and George Sanders. 2009. "Revisiting Hypermasculinity: Shorthand for Marginalized Masculinities?" Pp. 33–51 in *What's Up with the Brothers?* ed. Whitney Harris and Ronald Ferguson. Harriman, TN: Men's Studies Press.

Pitts, Victoria. 2003. *In the Flesh: The Cultural Politics of Body Modification*. London: Palgrave Macmillan.

Portes, Alejandro, ed. 1996. *The New Second Generation*. New York: Russell Sage Foundation.

Portes, Alejandro, and Ruben Rumbaut. 2001a. *Legacies: The Story of the Immigrant Second Generation*. Berkeley: University of California Press.

———, eds. 2001b. *Ethnicities: Children of Immigrants in America*. Berkeley: University of California Press.

Prashad, Vijay. 2001. *Everybody Was Kung Fu Fighting: Afro-Asian Connections and the Myth of Cultural Purity*. Boston: Beacon.

———. 2000. *The Karma of Brown Folk*. Minneapolis: University of Minnesota Press.

Prashad, Vijay, and Biju Mathew, eds. 1999/2000. "Satyagraha in America: The Political Culture of South Asian Americans." *Amerasia Journal* 25(3): ix–xv.

Price, Kim. 2008. "Keeping the Dancers in Check": The Gendered Organization of Stripping Work in the Lion's Den." *Gender and Society* 22(3): 367–389.

Pringle, Richard. 2007. "Sport, Males and Masculinities." Pp. 355–380 in *Sport in Aotearoa/New Zealand Society*, 2nd ed., ed. C. Collins and S. Jackson. Palmerston North: Dunmore Press.

———. 2005. "Masculinities, Sport, and Power: A Critical Comparison of Gramscian and Foucauldian Inspired Theoretical Tools." *Journal of Sport and Social Issues* 29(3): 256–278.

Puar, Jasbir K. 2007. *Terrorist Assemblages*. Durham, NC: Duke University Press.

Puar, Jasbir K., and Amit Rai. 2004. "The Remaking of a Model Minority." *Social Text* 22(3): 75–104.

———. 2002. "Monster, Terrorist, Fag: The War on Terrorism and the Production of Docile Patriots." *Social Text* 20(3): 117–148.

Purkayastha, Bandana. 2005. *Negotiating Ethnicity: Second-Generation South Asian Americans Traverse a Transnational World*. New Brunswick, NJ: Rutgers University Press.

Quinn, Beth. 2002. "Sexual Harassment and Masculinity: The Power and Meaning of 'Girl Watching.'" *Gender and Society* 16(3): 309–326.

Radhakrishnan, R. 2003. "Ethnicity in the Age of Diaspora." In *Theorizing Diaspora*, ed. Jana Evans Braziel and Anita Mannur. Malden, MA: Blackwell.

Radhakrishnan, Smitha. 2011. *Appropriately Indian: Gender and Culture in a New Transnational Class*. Durham, NC: Duke University Press.

Rai, Amit S. 1995. "India On-line: Electronic Bulletin Boards and the Construction of a Diasporic Hindu Identity." *Diaspora* 4(1): 31–57.

Ramirez, Horacio Roque. 2004. "A Living Archive of Desire." In *Archive Stories*, ed. Antoinette Burton. Durham, NC: Duke University Press.

Rana, Junaid. 2011. *Terrifying Muslims: Race and Labor in the South Asian Diaspora*. Durham, NC: Duke University Press.

———. 2007. "The Story of Islamophobia." *Souls: A Critical Journal of Black Politics, Culture, and Society* 9(2): 148–161.

Rand, Erica. 2011. *Red Nails, Black Skates: Gender, Cash, and Pleasure On and Off the Ice*. Durham, NC: Duke University Press.

Ray, Krishnendu. 2004. *The Migrant's Table: Meals and Memories in Bengali-American Households*. Philadelphia: Temple University Press.

Reddy, Chandan. 2011. *Freedom with Violence*. Durham, NC: Duke University Press.

———. 1997. "Home, Houses, Nonidentity: 'Paris Is Burning.'" In *Burning Down the House: Recycling Domesticity*, ed. Rosemary Marangoly George. Boulder, CO: Westview Press.

Reft, Ryan. 2014a. "Filing the Lane, Here and Abroad: Filipino American Identity and Basketball." Television station KCET. February 13. https://tropicsofmeta.wordpress.com/2014/05/15/filing-the-lane-here-and-abroad-filipino-american-identity-and-basketball.

———. 2014b. "Masculinity, Femininity, and Asian American Basketball in 20th Century California." Television station KCET. January 30. www.kcet.org/socal/departures/columns/intersections/masculinity-femininity-and-asian-american-basketball-in-20th-century-california.html.

Regalado, Samuel O. 2012. *Nikkei Baseball*. Urbana: University of Illinois Press.

Reid-Pharr, Robert. 2001. *Black Gay Men*. New York: New York University Press.

Reuters. 2004. "Indiana Boy Wins U.S. Spelling Bee, Runner-Up Faints." *Free Republic*, June 3. www.freerepublic.com/focus/f-news/1147198/posts.

Rich, Adrienne. 1994. *Blood, Bread, and Poetry: Selected Prose, 1979–1985*. New York: Norton.

Rios, Victor. 2011. *Punished*. New York: New York University Press.

Roediger, David. 2008. *How Race Survived U.S. History*. New York: Verso.

———. 2005. *Working towards Whiteness: How America's Immigrants Became White*. New York: Basic.

———. 1991. *Wages of Whiteness*. New York: Verso.

Romano, Andrew, and Tony Dokoupil. 2010. "Man Up." *Newsweek*, September 23.

Ronen, Shelly. 2010. "Grinding on the Dance Floor: Gendered Scripts and Sexualized Dancing at College Parties." *Gender and Society* 24(3): 355–377.

Rosaldo, Renato. 1994. "Cultural Citizenship and Educational Democracy." *Cultural Anthropology* 9(3): 402–411.

Rose, Tricia. 1994. *Black Noise: Rap Music and Black Culture in Contemporary America*. Middletown, CT: Wesleyan University Press.

Roy, Sandip. 1998. "The Call of Rice: (South) Asian American Queer Communities." In *A Part, yet Apart*, ed. Lavina D. Shankar and Rajini Srikanth. Philadelphia: Temple University Press.

Rubin, David. 2012. "'An Unnamed Blank That Craved a Name': A Genealogy of Intersex as Gender." *Signs* 37(4): 883–908.

Rubin, Gayle. 1984. "Thinking Sex: Notes for a Radical Theory of the Politics of Sexuality." Reprinted in *The Lesbian and Gay Studies Reader*, ed. Henry Abelove, Michele Aina Barale, and David M. Halperin. New York: Routledge, 1993.

Rudrappa, Sharmila. 2004. *Ethnic Routes to Becoming American: Indian Immigrants and the Cultures of Citizenship*. New Brunswick, NJ: Rutgers University Press.

Sahlins, Marshall. 1987. *Islands of History*. Chicago: University of Chicago Press.

———. 1981. *Historical Metaphors and Mythical Realities: Structure in the Early History of the Sandwich Islands Kingdom*. Ann Arbor: University of Michigan Press.

Sanders, Clinton, and D. Angus Vail. 2008. *Customizing the Body: The Art and Culture of Tattooing*. Philadelphia: Temple University Press.

Sands, Robert. 2002. *Sport Ethnography*. Champaign, IL: Human Kinetics.

Sassen, Saskia. 2002. *The Global City: New York, London, Tokyo*. Princeton, NJ: Princeton University Press.

———. 1999. *Globalization and Its Discontents: Essays on the New Mobility of People and Money*. New York: New Press.

Schein, Louisa. 2009. "Gran Torino's Boys and Men with Guns: Hmong Perspectives." *Hmong Studies Journal* 10: 1–52.

Schilt, Kristen, and Laurel Westbrook. 2009. "Doing Gender, Doing Heternormativity: 'Gender Normals,' Transgender People, and the Social Maintenance of Heterosexuality." *Gender and Society* 23(4): 440–464.

Sedgwick, Eve. 1986. *Between Men: English Literature and Male Homosocial Desire*. New York: Columbia University Press.

Sethi, Parmeet. 2010. *Badmaash Company*. Yash Raj Films.

Shah, Nayan. 2005. "Between 'Oriental Depravity' and 'Natural Degenerates': Spatial Borderlands and the Making of Ordinary Americans." *American Quarterly* 57(3): 703–725.

———. 2001. *Contagious Divides: Epidemics and Race in San Francisco's Chinatown.* Berkeley: University of California Press.

Shaheen, Jack. 2009. *Reel Bad Arabs: How Hollywood Vilifies a People.* Northhampton, MA: Olive Branch Press.

Shankar, Lavina Dhingra, and Rajini Srikanth. 1998. "Introduction: Closing the Gap? South Asians Challenge Asian American Studies." In *A Part, yet Apart: South Asians in Asian America*, ed. Lavina D. Shankar and Rajini Srikanth. Philadelphia: Temple University Press.

Shankar, Shalini. 2008. *Desi Land: Teen Culture, Class, and Success in Silicon Valley.* Durham, NC: Duke University Press.

Sharma, Nitasha. 2010. *Hip Hop Desis.* Durham, NC: Duke University Press.

Shukla, Sandhya. 2003. *India Abroad: Diasporic Cultures in Postwar America and England.* Princeton, NJ: Princeton University Press.

———. 2001. "Locations for South Asian Diasporas," in *Annual Review of Anthropology* (30): 551–572.

Singh, Amritjit. 1998. "African Americans and the New Immigrants." In *Between the Lines: South Asians and Postcoloniality*, ed. Deepika Bahri and Mary Vasudeva. Philadelphia: Temple University Press.

Smith, Andrea. 2005. *Conquest: Sexual Violence and American Indian Genocide.* Boston: South End Press.

Steward, Samuel. 1990. *Bad Boys and Tough Tattoos: A Social History of the Tattoo with Gangs, Sailors and Street-Corner Punks, 1950–1965.* New York: Routledge.

Sugden, John, and Alan Tomlinson, eds. 2012. *Watching the Olympics: Politics, Power, and Representation.* Abingdon: Routledge.

Sugrue, Thomas. 2005. *The Origins of the Urban Crisis: Race and Inequality in Postwar Detroit.* Princeton, NJ: Princeton University Press.

Tarasawa, Beth. 2009. "New Patterns of Segregation: Latino and African American Students in Metro Atlanta High Schools." *Southern Spaces*, January 19. www.southernspaces.org/2009/new-patterns-segregation-latino-and-african-american-students-metro-atlanta-high-schools.

Taussig, Michael. 1993. *Mimesis and Alterity: A Particular History of the Senses.* New York: Routledge.

Taylor, Julie. 1994. *Paper Tangos.* Durham, NC: Duke University Press.

Thangaraj, Stanley I. 2013. "Competing Masculinities: South Asian American Identity Formation in Asian American Basketball Leagues." *South Asian Popular Culture* 11(3): 243–255.

———. 2012. "Playing through Difference: The Black-White Racial Logic and Interrogating South Asian American Identity." *Ethnic and Racial Studies* 35(6): 988–1006.

———. 2010a. "Ballin' Indo-Pak Style: Pleasures, Desires, and Expressive Practices of 'South Asian American' Masculinity." *International Review for the Sociology of Sport* 45(3): 372–389.

———. 2010b. "Liting It Up: Popular Culture, Indo-Pak Basketball, and South Asian American Institutions." *Cosmopolitan Civil Societies: An Interdisciplinary Journal* 2(2): 71–91.

Thangaraj, Stanley, Daniel Burdsey, and Rajinder Dudrah. 2014. *Sport and South Asian Diasporas: Playing through Space and Time.* Abingdon: Routledge.

Theberge, Nancy. 1985. "Toward a Feminist Alternative to Sport as a Male Preserve." *Quest* 37(2): 193–202.

Tomlinson, Alan, and Christopher Young, eds. 2005. *National Identity and Global Sports Events.* Albany: State University of New York Press.

Trujillo, Nick. 2000. "Hegemonic Masculinity on the Mound: Media Representations of Nolan Ryan and American Sports Culture." Pp. 14–39 in *Reading Sport: Critical Essays on Power and Representation*, ed. Susan Birrell and Mary G. McDonald. Boston: Northeastern University Press.

Turner, Victor. 1969. *The Forest of Symbols: Aspects of Ndembu Ritual.* Ithaca, NY: Cornell University Press.

U.S. Census Bureau. 2012. *2010 Census Summary File 1 (United States): 2010 Census of Population and Housing.* Washington, DC: U.S. Census Bureau. www.census.gov/prod/cen2010/doc/sf1.pdf.

Vang, Chia Youvee. 2010. *Hmong America: Reconstructing Community in Diaspora.* Champaign: University of Illinois Press.

Vargas, Joao. 2007. *Catching Hell in the City of Angels.* Minneapolis: University of Minnesota Press.

Vecsey, George. 2009. "Pioneering Knick Returns to the Garden." *New York Times,* August 10.

Venkatesh, Sudhir. 2009. *Off the Books: The Underground Economy of the Urban Poor.* Cambridge, MA: Harvard University Press.

Visweswaran, Kamala, ed. 2011. *Perspectives on Modern South Asia.* Boston: Wiley-Blackwell.

———. 1998. "Race and the Culture of Anthropology." *American Anthropologist* 100 (1): 70–83.

———. 1997. "Diaspora by Design: Flexible Citizenship and the South Asian Diaspora in U.S. Racial Formations." *Diaspora* 6(1): 5–29.

Visweswaran, Kamala, and Ali Mir. 1999. "On the Politics of Community in South Asian American Studies." *Amerasia Journal* 25(3): 97–110.

Vo, Linda. 2004. *Mobilizing an Asian American Community.* Philadelphia: Temple University Press.

Volpp, Leti. 2003. "The Citizen and the Terrorist." In *September 11 in History: A Watershed Moment?* ed. Mary L. Dudziak. Durham, NC: Duke University Press.

Wacquant, Loïc. 2006. *Body and Soul: Notebooks of an Apprentice Boxer.* New York: Oxford University Press.

Walle, Thomas. 2013. "Cricket as 'Utopian Homeland' in the Pakistani Diasporic Imagination." *South Asian Popular Culture* 11(3): 301–312.

Wang, Oliver. 2012a. "Jeremy Lin Puts the Ball in Asian American's Court." *Los Angeles Times*, February 21. http://articles.latimes.com/2012/feb/21/entertainment/la-et-jeremy-lin-20120221.

———. 2012b. "Lin Takes the Weight." *Atlantic*, March 1. www.theatlantic.com/entertainment/archive/2012/03/lin-takes-the-weight/253833/.

———. 2012c. "Living with Linsanity." *Los Angeles Review of Books*, March 6. http://lareviewofbooks.org/essay/living-with-linsanity.

Ward, Jane, and Beth Schneider. 2009. "The Reaches of Heteronormativity." *Gender and Society* 23(4): 433–439.

Wenner, Lawrence A. 1998. "In Search of the Sports Bar: Masculinity, Alcohol, Sports, and the Mediation of Public Space." In *Sport and Postmodern Times*, ed. Genevieve Rail. Albany, NY: SUNY Press.

Wertheim, Jon. 2012. "Decades before Lin's Rise, Misaka made history for Asian Americans." *Sports Illustrated* (February 11). www.si.com/more-sports/2012/02/11/jeremy-linwatarumisaka.

Whannel, Garry. 2007. "Representing Masculinities: The Production of Media Representations in Sport." In *Sport and Gender Identities: Masculinities, Femininities and Sexualities,* ed. Cara Michael Aitchison. New York: Routledge.

Wikipedia. 2014. "Southern Hip Hop." August 31. http://en.wikipedia.org/wiki/Southern_hip_hop.

Wolf, Eric. 1962. *Sons of the Shaking Earth*. Chicago: University of Chicago Press.

Women of South Asian Descent Collective. 1993. *Our Feet Walk the Sky: Women of the South Asian Diaspora*. 1st ed. San Francisco: Aunt Lute Books.

Wray, Matt. 2006. *Not Quite White: White Trash and the Boundaries of Whiteness*. Durham, NC: Duke University Press.

Wynter, Sylvia. 1992. "Beyond the Categories of the Master Conception: The Counterdoctrine of the Jamesian Poiesis." In *CLR James's Caribbean*, ed. Paget Henry and Paul Buhle. Durham, NC: Duke University Press.

Yep, Kathleen. June 2012a. "Peddling Sport: Liberal Multiculturalism and the Racial Triangulation of Blackness, Chineseness and Native American-ness in Professional Basketball." *Ethnic and Racial Studies* 35(6): 971–987.

———. 2012b. "Linsanity and Centering Sport in Asian American Studies and Pacific Islander Studies." *Amerasia Journal* 38(3): 133–138.

———. 2009. *Outside the Paint: When Basketball Ruled at the Chinese Playground*. Philadelphia: Temple University Press.

Zelizer, Viviana. 2005. *The Purchase of Intimacy*. Princeton, NJ: Princeton University Press.

INDEX

Abdul-Rahim, Sharif, 33
Abdul-Rauf, Mahmoud, 33
Abraham, Margaret, 157
African Americans: and American-ness,
38, 88; Asian American exclusion of,
136–37, 143–44; bodies of, 13; desi appropriation of culture of, 25, 38–39,
62–64, 77, 83, 85–88, 103–4, 110, 146,
172, 175–76; desi attitudes toward
female, 156, 169; desi exclusion of,
25, 39, 64–66, 77, 103–10, 143–44,
163; gentrification affecting, 46–48,
65; in Indo-Pak Basketball, 105–6;
masculinity of, 7, 9, 86–88, 105–10,
115, 146–47, 172, 174–76; one-drop
rule for, 137; and playground/pickup
basketball, 53–54, 62; settlement
patterns of, 46–48, 65, 224n36; stereotypes of, 137
Afzal, Ahmed, 99–100
agency: of gays, 181–82; of women, 188,
195–201
Ahmadiyya Islam, 100–101
Air Punjab/Hit Squad, 114, 124, 197, 216
Amaechi, John, 178
Amateur Athletic Union (AAU), 96
ambiguity, racial, 17, 25, 114–15, 136, 138–43
American culture and American-ness:
Asian Americans' relationship to, 122;
black cultural forms and, 38, 88; desi
consumption of, 85; emulation or
assimilation of, 87; Islam and, 30–33,
35–36; racism and, 74; South Asian
Americans' relationship to, 3, 7–8, 23,

26, 72, 74, 77, 87–88, 122, 173; sports
and, 203
"and 1" play, 93
Arnaldo, Jr., Constancio, 226n38
Asian Americans: "Chapte" as idiom for,
127–28; as effeminate, 128, 131; ethnic
leagues of, 112–13 (*see also* Asian
Ballers League); as foreign, 119–20;
heterogeneity/diversity of, 120; identities of, 117–18; as model minority, 13,
114; Muslims in relation to, 129–30;
nerd stereotype of, 111–13; South Asian
Americans in relation to, 110, 113–14,
117–22, 127–29, 133; sports participation
of, 2
Asian American Tournament, 141
Asian Ballers League, 1, 3–4, 6, 9, 19,
24–25, 113–18, 120, 123–39, 143–44, 183,
216–17, 228n34
Asian Ballers National Tournament, 129–
31, 133–34, 228n34
Atlanta, Georgia: counties of metropolitan, 21, 33–34; Latinos/as in, 139; settlement patterns in, 21–22, 46–48, 223n36;
South Asian Americans in and around,
21–22, 34–35, 116, 145, 217; Southern
hip-hop in, 145; Summer Olympics in,
34–35, 48
Atlanta Franchise, 32, 109, 116, 139, 197
Atlanta Latino League, 112, 115–17, 139–
44
Atlanta Outkasts, 19, 20, 30, 32, 37–43,
86–87, 90, 104, 114, 124, 129, 132, 141,
145–46, 177, 197–98

ABOUT THE AUTHOR

Stanley I. Thangaraj is Assistant Professor of Anthropology at the City College of New York. He is a former player and coach at the high school and collegiate level with a passion for working with young people. His anthropological work looks at the intersections of ethnic studies, gender studies, sexuality studies, and citizenship in diaspora formations.

CPSIA information can be obtained
at www.ICGtesting.com
Printed in the USA
LVOW12s1543170717

541644LV00001B/72/P